International Indigenous Rights in Aotearoa New Zealand

International Indigenous Rights in Aotearoa New Zealand

Edited by Andrew Erueti

Victoria University Press

VICTORIA UNIVERSITY PRESS
Victoria University of Wellington
PO Box 600 Wellington
vup.victoria.ac.nz

Copyright © Andrew Erueti and contributors

First published 2017

ISBN 9781776560486

This book is copyright. Apart from
any fair dealing for the purpose of private study,
research, criticism or review, as permitted under the
Copyright Act, no part may be reproduced by any
process without the permission of
the publishers.

A catalogue record for this book is available from the
National Library of New Zealand.

Published with the assistance of a grant from

Printed by YourBooks, Wellington

Contents

Foreword   7
Professor Megan Davis

Contributors   9

Introduction   13
Andrew Erueti

Part I: Setting the Scene: The Declaration and Human Rights

1. A Mixed-Model Interpretative Approach to the Declaration   23
    Andrew Erueti

2. The Treaty and Human Rights in New Zealand Law: 41
    Can We Add the Declaration and Stir?
    Kirsty Gover

Part II: The Declaration's Application

3. The Status and Effect in New Zealand Law of the UN Declaration   78
    on the Rights of Indigenous Peoples
    Matthew S R Palmer and Matthew S Smith

4. The Declaration and the Implementation of the Rights   86
    of the Indigenous Child in Aotearoa
    Claire Breen

5. The "False Generosity" of Treaty Settlements: Innovation   99
    and Contortion
    Linda Te Aho

6. International Indigenous Rights and Mining in Aotearoa New Zealand   118
    Sarah Down & Andrew Erueti

Part III: The Declaration and Indigenous Rights Advocacy in New Zealand

7. Use It or Lose It: The Value of Using the Declaration on the Rights   137
    of Indigenous Peoples in Maori Legal and Political Claims
    Claire Charters

8. The UN Special Procedures and Indigenous Peoples' Rights 152
   Fleur Te Aho

9. The World Conference on Indigenous Peoples 2014 175
   Tracey Whare

10. The Declaration in the Universal Periodic Review:
    Current Status and Future Prospects 191
    Natalie Baird

    Appendix: The United Nations Declaration on the
       Rights of Indigenous Peoples 211

    Index 227

Foreword

There is very little doubt that over the last few decades, culminating in the adoption of the UN Declaration on the Rights of Indigenous Peoples in 2007, international law has been transformative for indigenous peoples.

Indigenous peoples are in the international sphere, not just as a manifestation of our external self-determination, but because international law has mattered. International law has made substantive and concrete changes in the lives of indigenous peoples. In Australia in the 1970s it led to the abolition of the protection legislation and permit system so my grandfather and his brother had freedom of movement and freedom of speech. It has led to substantial gains in rights – especially land rights – for indigenous peoples in Australia: in particular, the *Racial Discrimination Act 1975* (Cth) and the *Aboriginal Land Rights Act (Northern Territory) 1975* (Cth). In the absence of entrenched rights and protections in Australia, international standards, whether binding or non-binding, have been vital in the development of indigenous rights in the Australian legal and political system.

Much the same can be said for another liberal democratic just across the ditch from my own. In New Zealand, while there have been many notable gains made in a new era of indigenous rights reforms, there are still many challenges faced by Māori, as noted in the chapters set out in this book.

The UN Declaration on the Rights of Indigenous Peoples has played and will continue to play an authoritative role in the lives of Indigenous peoples globally, whether binding or not. This month, on the tenth anniversary of the UN General Assembly's adoption – a birthday we were never certain we would be celebrating – it is timely to consider comprehensively what have been and are likely to be the effects of the UN Declaration on the Rights of Indigenous Peoples for Aotearoa New Zealand's legal system.

Megan Davis
Professor of Law, Pro Vice-Chancellor Indigenous University of New South Wales
August 2017

Contributors

Natalie Baird is a Senior Lecturer at the School of Law, University of Canterbury. Before joining academia, Natalie worked in the public service for ten years. This included four years at the Crown Law Office working on Treaty of Waitangi claims; and 18 months at the New Zealand Law Commission with Commissioners Sir Edward Taihakurei Durie and Helen Aikman, exploring the tensions between customary law and human rights, resulting in the report *Converging Currents: Custom and Human Rights in the Pacific* (NZLC, Wellington, 2006). Natalie's current research interests lie in the areas of international human rights, refugee law and Pacific legal studies. She has a particular interest in the impact of international human rights monitoring mechanisms at the domestic level, and this is her fourth publication exploring aspects of the UN Human Rights Council's universal periodic review mechanism.

Dr Claire Breen is an Associate Professor in Law at Te Piringa Faculty of Law at the University of Waikato. She holds a BCL from the National University of Ireland (University College Cork). She also holds an LLM (International Law) and a PhD from the University of Nottingham. Claire Breen's research interests focus on the confluence of international human rights law and international humanitarian law, with a particular interest in states' legal obligations arising from post-conflict reconstruction. She has published numerous journal articles in this area, as well as the book *Economic and Social Rights and the Maintenance of International Peace and Security* (Routledge, 2017). Dr Breen has been the recipient of two New Zealand Law Foundation grants in support of her research into the various challenges to maintaining international peace and security. Dr Breen also publishes extensively in the area of children's rights.

Claire Charters from Ngāti Whakaue, Ngāti Tūwharetoa, Tainui and Ngāpuhi. She is an Associate Professor in the Faculty of Law, University of Auckland, and is working on the establishment of the Aotearoa/New Zealand Centre for Indigenous Peoples and the Law. Claire has long worked with the indigenous peoples' movement on the rights of indigenous peoples, including during the negotiations on the Declaration on the Rights of Indigenous Peoples, and she was the secretary of the UN Expert Mechanism on the Rights of Indigenous Peoples between 2010 and 2013. Claire's publications examine international and comparative constitutional law and indigenous peoples and include *Making the Declaration Work: The United Nations Declaration on the Rights of Indigenous Peoples* (IWGIA, 2009), co-edited with Rodolfo Stavenhagen.

Professor **Megan Davis** is a Professor of Law and Pro Vice Chancellor Indigenous UNSW. Megan is an expert member of the United Nations Expert Mechanism on the rights of Indigenous peoples, a subsidiary body of the UN Human Rights Council in Geneva. Davis is formerly Chair and expert member of the United Nations Permanent Forum on Indigenous Issues (2011–2016). As UNPFII expert she held portfolios including Administration of Justice, Gender and Women, and was the focal point for UN Women and UN AIDS. Megan was the Rapporteur of the UN EGM on an Optional Protocol to the UNDRIP in 2015, the UN EGM on Combating violence against indigenous women and girls and the UN Rapporteur for the International EGM on Indigenous Youth. Professor Davis researches in public law and public international law. Her current research focuses on constitutional design, democratic theory and indigenous peoples. Megan is one of the CIs in an ARC project on the impact of extra-legal factors on the sentencing of indigenous offenders of sexual abuse of Aboriginal women in the Northern Territory.

Sarah Down is a PhD candidate at the Australian National University, Australia, where she is undertaking research on Māori mineral rights. Sarah holds an LLB (First Class Honours) and a BA from the University of Canterbury, New Zealand. She has researched and written for a number of indigenous organisations including the Ngāi Tahu Research Centre, University of Canterbury and the National Aboriginal and Torres Strait Islander Legal Services (NATSILS), Australia.

Andrew Erueti lectures in indigenous rights and human rights at the Law Faculty of the University of Auckland. His PhD thesis examines the politics behind the drafting of the UN Declaration on the Rights of Indigenous Peoples and its implications for domestic application. From 2009–2013 Andrew was Amnesty International's adviser on indigenous rights in its head office London and then the UN-office in Geneva. He has also taught at Te Piringa Faculty of Law, Waikato University and Victoria University. He is from Ngā Ruahinerangi and Ngāti Ruanui (Taranaki) and Āti Hau (Whanganui).

Kirsty Gover, LLB (Canterbury), LLM (Columbia), JSD (New York University), Associate Professor, Melbourne Law School. Kirsty Gover's research addresses the law, policy and political theory of indigenous rights, institutions and jurisdiction, and the role played by "indigeneity" in settler state political theory and international law. Dr. Gover is the author of *Tribal Constitutionalism: States, Tribes and the Governance of Membership* (Oxford University Press, 2010). She is currently working on a book entitled *When Tribalism meets Liberalism: Political Theory and International Law* (Oxford University Press, 2018).

Matthew S R Palmer's first association with the Draft Declaration on the Rights of Indigenous Peoples was as Deputy Secretary for Justice between 1995–2000. In that role he was responsible for providing advice to the Minister of Justice and other Ministers on the position New Zealand should take in relation to the Draft Declaration. This involved liaising with other "CANZUS" governments – Canada, Australia, New Zealand and the United States. During his tenure at Justice, New Zealand did not oppose the Draft Declaration. He was present at the United Nations' adoption of the Declaration in September 2007, along with the class in Comparative Indigenous Peoples' Rights he was teaching at Yale Law School. Formerly the Dean of Law at Victoria University of Wellington and the author of *The Treaty of Waitangi in New Zealand's Law and Constitution* (VUP, 2008), Matthew was appointed a Judge of the High Court of New Zealand in 2015.

Matthew S Smith is a barrister at Thorndon Chambers in Wellington. He has a broad public and commercial law practice, encompassing regulatory, Māori, human rights and environmental law, and with a special expertise in judicial review and the use of public law tools to achieve meaningful outcomes for clients. Matthew works across the entire range of public law and has acted for public sector bodies (including Crown entities and commissions of inquiry), individuals, entities of many kinds (including companies, incorporated societies, trusts and Māori incorporations), industry groups and NGOs. He has appeared in all of the higher Courts, and in a number of specialist courts and tribunals – including the Waitangi Tribunal and the Māori Land Court. Matthew's non-litigation work tends to involve the provision of legal and strategic advice and support in a range of settings, including public inquiries, regulatory investigations, consultation processes and parliamentary/law reform processes. Matthew is the sole author of the *New Zealand Judicial Review Handbook* – a comprehensive text on judicial review in New Zealand that is now in its second edition.

Fleur Te Aho (Ngāti Mutunga ki Taranaki) lectures on indigenous peoples' rights and criminal law in the Law Faculty at the University of Auckland. Fleur is also an Honorary Research Fellow at the Australian National University's (ANU) National Centre for Indigenous Studies. Prior to joining the University of Auckland, Fleur taught and researched at the ANU College of Law and National Centre for Indigenous Studies. Fleur has a PhD from ANU and an LLM (Distinction) from Victoria University of Wellington. Fleur has several years' experience practicing as a solicitor in Wellington, including assisting iwi in the negotiation of historical Treaty of Waitangi settlements with the Crown, and working as in-house legal counsel in the United Kingdom. Fleur's publications include 'Diluted Control: A Critical Analysis of the Wai262 Report on Māori Traditional Knowledge and Culture' in Matthew Rimmer (ed) *Indigenous Intellectual Property: A Handbook of Contemporary Research* (Edward Elgar, Cheltenham and Northampton, 2015); 'Māori and the Bill of Rights Act: A Case of Missed Opportunities?' *NZJPIL* (2013); and 'The UN Special Rapporteur on the Rights of Indigenous Peoples and New Zealand: A Study in Compliance Ritualism' *NZYIL* (2012).

Linda Te Aho is the Associate Dean Māori and an Associate Professor at Te Piringa Faculty of Law, University of Waikato, and is co-editor of *The Waikato Law Review*. Linda provides expert advice on Treaty of Waitangi claims and post-settlement governance issues to iwi and hapū organisations, and technical advice on Māori legal issues in relation to lands and freshwater to iwi leaders, Crown agencies and government departments.

Tracey Whare (Raukawa and Te Whānau ā Apanui) graduated with an LLB from Victoria University of Wellington. She is currently completing her LLM by thesis at the University of Auckland while working as a kaiwhakaako at the law school. Upon graduating she worked for the Ngāi Tahu Māori Law Centre, focusing on Māori land and resource management before taking up a position with the Greater Wellington Regional Council as a policy adviser on iwi issues. She then moved into general private practice before specialising in property and trusts. In 1998 Tracey was an indigenous fellow at the UN Office of the High Commissioner for Human Rights in Geneva, a role which sparked her interest in indigenous peoples' rights. Tracey helped establish the Aotearoa Indigenous Rights Trust, a charitable trust that focuses on Māori advocacy of indigenous peoples' rights in international fora. She is also a member of the Monitoring Mechanism, a working group created by the national Iwi Chairs Forum to monitor New Zealand's implementation of the UN Declaration on the Rights of Indigenous Peoples. Prior to commencing her LLM thesis, Tracey served as the Secretariat of the GCG, the indigenous working group established to coordinate indigenous participation in the General Assembly special session known as the World Conference on Indigenous Peoples 2014.

Introduction

Andrew Erueti

The United Nations Declaration on the Rights of Indigenous Peoples (the Declaration)[1] has been heralded as a "landmark" achievement for indigenous peoples.[2] With the Declaration's adoption by the UN General Assembly in 2007 by 143 states, international indigenous rights have become a significant field in international law. Although other international treaties, standards and policies on indigenous rights exist, notably International Labour Organization Convention No 169,[3] no other international instrument provides such robust protections for groups within states. This includes Article 3 of the Declaration, which provides: "Indigenous peoples have the right to self-determination. By virtue of that right they freely determine their political status and freely pursue their economic, social and cultural development."[4] This restates the language in Article 1 of the International Covenant on Civil and Political Rights (ICCPR) and International Covenant on Economic, Social, and Cultural Rights (ICESCR), but with reference to *indigenous* peoples. Despite the continuing controversy over the meaning of self-determination and whether it can apply to "peoples" outside of the colonial context, indigenous peoples succeeded in having it included in the Declaration, albeit conditioned by states' rights to territorial integrity.[5] Not only that, the Declaration also includes the right to self-government;[6] historical

---

1 *United Nations Declaration on the Rights of Indigenous Peoples* GA Res 61/295, UNGAOR, 61st Sess, Supp No 49, UN Doc A/RES/61/295 (2007) [The Declaration].
2 Claire Charters "The Road to the Adoption of the Declaration on the Rights of Indigenous Peoples" (2007) 4 NZYBIL 121; Claire Charters and Rodolfo Stavenhagen *Making the Declaration Work* (IWGIA, Copenhagen, 2009).
3 Convention (No. 169) Concerning Indigenous and Tribal Peoples in Independent Countries, 27 June 1989, 28 ILM 1382 (entered into force 5 September 1991). See also, Convention (No. 107) concerning the Protection and Integration of Indigenous and Other Tribal and Semi-Tribal Populations in Independent Countries, 26 June 1957, 328 UNTS 247 (entered into force 2 June 1959) [ILO Convention No. 107].
4 The Declaration, above n 1, art 3.
5 The Declaration, above n 1, art 46(3).
6 At art 4.

redress;[7] the right to free, prior and informed consent (FPIC);[8] and the right to the recognition, observance and enforcement of treaties.[9] I describe these rights as the self-determination framework. In addition to these breakthrough rights, there are many others that apply classic human rights to the circumstances of indigenous peoples, including the right to religion,[10] property,[11] and the right to practise and revitalize their cultural traditions and customs.[12] For example, the human right to property – which is normally directed at the right of individual ownership – is adapted to provide: indigenous peoples have the right to the lands, territories and resources which they have traditionally owned, occupied or otherwise used or acquired.[13]

Throughout the negotiations of the Declaration there were many challenges, including who are indigenous peoples for the purpose of international indigenous rights (is the Declaration for Indigenous Peoples of CANZUS states only or are indigenous rights for ethnic minorities in South Asia and Africa?);[14] whether to include the right to self-determination and other rights in the self-determination framework; the relationship between indigenous collective rights and the liberal human rights framework, including the question of whether indigenous rights themselves are in essence human rights; and the role and status of indigenous peoples in the negotiations themselves. All these issues are canvassed in this book, but the most critical is probably the right of indigenous peoples to negotiate the Declaration with states on an equal footing. This was continually contentious over the twenty-four years of negotiations. The refusal to treat indigenous peoples with equal respect led to an indigenous walk out on one occasion and many Māori advocates refused to return to the negotiation table. Typically, negotiations are governed by states with limited input from interest groups, and any subsequent disagreement about meaning requires reference back to states' negotiating positions.[15] However, due to indigenous advocates' persistence, they were effectively accorded the

---

7   At art 5.
8   At art 10, 19 and 32.
9   At art 31.
10 At art 12.
11 At art 26.
12 At art 11.
13 At art 26.
14 Albert Kwokwo Barume "Responding to the Concerns of the African States" in Claire Charters and Rodolfo Stavenhagen (eds) *Making the Declaration Work* (IWGIA, Copenhagen, 2009) (commenting on African states' opposition to the Declaration's application to peoples in Africa); See also, Benedict Kingsbury "'Indigenous Peoples' in International Law: A Constructivist Approach to the Asian Controversy" (1998) 92 Am J Int Law 414 (arguing for the Declaration's application in south Asia).
15 *Vienna Convention on the Law of Treaties,* 23 May 1969, 1155 UNTS 331, art 32 (entered into force 27 January 1980).

INTRODUCTION

same status as states with indigenous advocates sitting alongside states during negotiations and offering their views on what should be in the Declaration and why. I think this accounts for the rights in the Declaration, including the right to self-determination, which itself provides the basis ultimately for the fair treatment of indigenous peoples in negotiations.[16]

But what relevance does the Declaration have to a country like Aotearoa New Zealand – a long-established, liberal democracy with many checks and balances on governmental power, and a relatively robust set of rights aimed at promoting and respecting the rights of Māori? As is well-known, New Zealand's indigenous rights architecture is uniquely progressive in many ways. In particular New Zealand has instigated institutions in the form of the Waitangi Tribunal[17] and the Office of Treaty Settlements[18] to investigate and negotiate the settlement of historical injustices.[19] New Zealand has a Bill of Rights Act,[20] constitutional rights and conventions that act as safeguards for rights enjoyed by Māori,[21] including statutory protections of Māori interests in legislation affecting them,[22] and common law rights.[23] One challenge of course is that even states with comprehensive rights protections can fail to fully implement them or argue that the rights have been fulfilled when the case is not clear. States may prefer majority interests or elites over marginalised groups.[24] Moreover, there may be significant gaps in domestic indigenous rights architecture. As Linda Te Aho notes in her chapter, Treaty settlement policy has been largely established without the effective participation of Māori, and claimants have had to adapt their aims – and indeed their forms of political and social organisation – to what the Crown is prepared to offer and what is politically palatable. On the one hand, as Kirsty Gover has argued, this has enabled successive governments to establish

---

16   Claire Charters "The Legitimacy of the UN Declaration on the Rights of Indigenous Peoples" in Rodolfo Stavenhagen and Claire Charters (eds) *Making the Declaration Work* (IWGIA, Copenhagen, 2009).
17   See Treaty of Waitangi Act 1975.
18   Office of Treaty Settlements *Ka Tika a Muri, Ka Tika a Mua: Healing the Past and Building a Future* (2nd ed, Office of Treaty Settlements, Wellington, 2015).
19   Nicola R Wheen and Janine Hayward (eds) *Treaty of Waitangi Settlements* (Bridget Williams Books, Wellington, 2012).
20   New Zealand Bill of Rights Act 1990.
21   Constitution Act 1986.
22   See for example Resource Management Act 1991, sections 6, 7 and 9.
23   See *Attorney-General v Ngati Apa* [2003] 3 NZLR 643; *Takamore v Clarke* [2012] NZSC 116, [2013] 2 NZLR 733.
24   A useful example, and one that encouraged many indigenous advocates in Aotearoa New Zealand to pay greater attention to international human rights, was the government response to *Attorney-General v Ngati Apa* decision (above n 23) that indicated that Māori might possess exclusive property in New Zealand's coastal waters. See Claire Charters and Andrew Erueti *Māori Property Rights and the Foreshore and Seabed* (Victoria University Press, Wellington, 2007).

a unique indigenous rights framework without having to address rights-based objections.[25] On the other, it has left Māori, as a small minority, exposed to executive rule with little opportunity to intervene or object. And indeed there is a long tradition of political dealings between Māori and the settler state.[26] Practically all aspects of indigenous rights reforms have been initiated and controlled by the Executive branch of government, which exercises considerable control over Parliament – even under a Mixed Member Proportional voting system.[27] There is, for example, no legislation governing Treaty settlements, only policy established by the Executive.[28] And while Treaty settlements are ultimately given effect in legislation, there is a constitutional convention that Parliament will not re-open them when the settlements reach Parliament. Treaty settlements also exist beyond the scope of judicial review, given their non-justiciable subject matter.[29] The few judicial decisions on the Treaty have largely resulted from *statutory* references to the Treaty, given it has no legal force until legislated domestically[30] and only a few cases have resulted in success for Māori litigants. As Matthew Palmer noted in 2011, "there had been only two decisions since 1990 in which a court has found the Crown has breached the principles of the Treaty of Waitangi."[31] This control by the Executive can allow for innovation and flexibility in deal-making.[32] However, the emphasis on the political raises serious concerns about the rule of law. The extensive executive power coupled

---

25 K Gover "Settler-State Political Theory, 'CANZUS' and the UN Declaration on the Rights of Indigenous Peoples" (2015) *EJIL* 345.

26 Mark Hickford *Lords of the Land* (Oxford University Press, Oxford; New York, 2011).

27 Andrew Butler and Geoffrey Palmer *A Constitution for Aotearoa New Zealand* (Victoria University Press, Wellington, 2016) at 125, 130.

28 Baden Vertongen "Judicial Review and the Treaty Settlement Process" in Nicola R Wheen and Janine Hayward (eds) *Treaty of Waitangi Settlements* (Bridget Williams Books, Wellington, 2012).

29 *Te Runanga o Wharekauri Rekohu Inc v Attorney-General* [1993] 2 NZLR 301; *New Zealand Māori Council v Attorney-General* [2013] 3 NZLR 31 (showing deference to the Executive in resolving claims to freshwater). Compare *Mita Michael Ririnui v Landcorp Farming Limited and The Attorney-General* [2016] NZSC 62 (decisions made by the Executive in relation to land claimed by Māori were unlawful because they were made under a material mistake); *Haronga v Waitangi Tribunal* [2011] NZSC 53 (directing the Waitangi Tribunal to hear an urgency application for redress); *Proprietors of Wakatu v Attorney-General* [2014] NZCA 628, [2015] 2 NZLR 298; *Proprietors of Wakatu Inc v Attorney-General* [2012] NZHC 1461 (considering whether to uphold Māori claims to Crown breaches of fiduciary duty type obligations with respect to early land transactions). See, Claire Charters "Māori rights: Legal or Political?" (2015) Public L Rev 1.

30 *Hoani Te Heuheu Tūkino v Aotea District Māori Land Board* [1941] AC 308 (PC).

31 Matthew Palmer *The Treaty of Waitangi in New Zealand's Law and Constitution* (Victoria University Press, Wellington, 2008) at 125.

32 Kirsty Gover "Settler–State Political Theory, 'CANZUS' and the UN Declaration on the Rights of Indigenous Peoples" (2015) 26 Eur J Int Law 345.

with the fact that most of this power is sourced in the royal prerogative,[33] and the absence of an entrenched bill of rights and limited scope for judicial review means indigenous rights are largely determined by the Executive. The heavy emphasis on the politicisation of Treaty rights has resulted in high-profile calls for the entrenchment of the Treaty[34] or the establishment of a Treaty Court.[35] But there is little sign of these reforms being adopted in the near future. And given the Courts' approach to the Treaty to date, Māori would be ill advised to place all their hopes on the judiciary.[36]

As a result, international indigenous rights are important to Māori. The major advantage of the Declaration is that it sets supranational standards for evaluating domestic law and policy on indigenous rights. Like many other countries, New Zealand governments prefer to deal with indigenous rights issues domestically without outside intervention. As Natalie Baird notes in her chapter, the New Zealand government has indicated that it prefers to see the Treaty of Waitangi as the leading normative benchmark for indigenous rights reforms and not the Declaration.[37] The right to self-determination and self-government in the Declaration are said to be "aspirations", not fully-fledged human rights and the Declaration as a whole is not binding.[38] All of this points to a strong will to resolve matters within New Zealand, with the Executive determining the path of indigenous rights recognition. But this misunderstands the status of the Declaration and the fundamental object of the contemporary international human rights system. While the Declaration is not legally binding, as Claire Charters notes in her chapter, it has considerable legitimacy given the manner in which it was negotiated with indigenous peoples;[39] and there is a close connection between rights in the Declaration and classic human rights accepted by many states, including those in the ICCPR and ICESCR.[40] In addition, international indigenous rights are meant to transcend the local and particular. It is important for Māori to have access to an independent expert authority on human rights and discrimination to weigh up the competing considerations, and issue an

---

33 Another potential source is the "third source" which again has no legal basis, see Bruce Harris "Recent Judicial Recognition of the Third Source of Authority for Government Action" (2014)(1) *New Zealand Universities Law Rev*, 60. Butler and Palmer, above n 27, at 95–96 (proposing that the prerogative be abolished so that government powers have their source in law).
34 Butler and Palmer, above n 27.
35 Palmer, above n 31.
36 See, for example, Claire Charters "Māori rights: Legal or Political?" (2015) Public L Rev 1.
37 See Natalie Baird's chapter in this book.
38 New Zealand, *Hansard*, Ministerial Statements: UN Declaration on the Rights of Indigenous Peoples—Government Support (20 April 2010) 662 NZPD 10229.
39 Charters, above n 16.
40 S James Anaya *Indigenous Peoples in International Law* (Oxford University Press, Oxford; New York, 2004).

authoritative judgment. And there are now many means to raise the Declaration and evaluate domestic law and policy against its standards in international institutions, as discussed in this book.

But the Declaration signifies more than a check on executive or legal power in New Zealand. Its most compelling purpose is to offer a means of making amends for international law's complicity in the colonisation of Aotearoa New Zealand. International law has sanctioned and legitimised the creation of the New Zealand settler state in the absence of indigenous peoples' consent. Therefore, the legitimacy of the state is continually being questioned by indigenous advocates. It is widely accepted that Māori did not cede sovereignty to the British Crown under the Treaty and that power was effectively seized by the settler state.[41] By providing an international law remedy, the Declaration can do much to enhance the legitimacy of the modern state, though much turns on New Zealand's approach to the Declaration in the future.[42] The question is whether the New Zealand government will be guided by the Declaration in future reforms and open to the evaluation of reforms by international bodies.

This book is divided into three parts. Part I covers foundational issues raised by the Declaration about the basis of international indigenous rights – are they human rights or something else?; and what is the relationship between human rights and indigenous rights?.

In Chapter 1, I offer an alternative means to read the Declaration based on the politics of its negotiation. The Declaration, I argue, represents a struggle between the "North" and "South" over the conceptual basis and goals of international indigenous rights. While the orthodoxy is to read the Declaration as a human-rights instrument, I suggest that the Declaration is underpinned by two normative models. On the one hand is a "decolonization model" derived from the sovereignty-based claims made by indigenous advocates in the CANZUS states. On the other, is the human rights model which was important to these states but was crucial for indigenous peoples of Latin America, Asia and Africa. The point is that the Declaration reflects both models, but the self-determination framework is directed squarely at the indigenous peoples of CANZUS and that has implications for how the Declaration is implemented in these states.

Kirsty Gover in Chapter 2 considers the Declaration in the context of the challenges to the liberal democratic state raised by indigenous claims to collective historical rights. To date, the tensions between human rights and Treaty rights have not been fully explored in New Zealand. However, Gover argues that the Declaration has potential to introduce equality-based qualifications to indigenous

---

41 Palmer, above n 31.
42 Allen E Buchanan *Justice, Legitimacy, and Self-determination* (Oxford University Press, Oxford, 2007); Patrick Macklem *The Sovereignty of Human Rights* (Oxford University Press, New York, 2015).

rights jurisprudence in New Zealand, given the Declaration contains limitations on rights in accordance with principles of equality and non-discrimination. She explores this idea in the context of New Zealand's human rights jurisprudence as well as international and domestic responses to disputes involving conflict between indigenous collective rights and principles of non-discrimination.

Part II considers the implications of the Declaration for specific areas of New Zealand's indigenous rights architecture. In Chapter 3, Matthew Palmer and Matthew Smith consider the potential role of the Declaration in Treaty rights advocacy including its status relative to the Treaty. Linda Te Aho, in Chapter 4, evaluates Treaty settlements with a focus on recent "innovations" relating to the co-management of resources and the vesting of resources with legal personality. As Te Aho argues, while there are gains made, partly due to government adaptability and tribal negotiators' skills, ultimately iwi are required to adapt their aspirations to fit within a framework designed by the state, so that the resulting innovations fail to sufficiently address the totality of iwi claims to authority over resources. The Declaration thus offers a new normative basis for seeking greater recognition of that authority, especially the rights to self-determination and FPIC.

In Chapter 5, Sarah Down and I consider the implications of the Declaration and the UN Guiding Principles on Business and Human Rights[43] for Māori interests in "precious minerals" and the regulation of mining activities in New Zealand. While New Zealand's regulatory framework for mining includes important distinctive protections for Māori, the government has thus far failed to engage with tribes over the question of ownership of petroleum and other mineral resources and iwi have little say in the management of minerals in their traditionally owned rohe (territory). There is also a lack of clear direction by the government towards companies to respect indigenous rights. In our view the Declaration, the UN Guiding Principles and recent co-management agreements offer a path to a more equitable model for New Zealand's mineral wealth.

Claire Breen in Chapter 6 considers the Convention on the Rights of the Child and its application to indigenous children and the implications of the Declaration. As Breen notes, the Convention, while focused on the best interests of the individual child, has also been sensitive to the fact that indigenous children are connected to communities and thus in giving effect to the child's rights there must also be recognition of their cultural and historical backgrounds. Therefore, the Convention together with the Declaration – especially the Declaration's focus on collective political rights to self-determination and FPIC – offer a comprehensive package for the advancement of indigenous children's rights.

---

43 United Nations Office of the High Commissioner for Human Rights "The Corporate Responsibility to Respect Human Rights: An Interpretative Guide" (United Nations, Geneva, 2012).

Part III of the book is directed at monitoring New Zealand's compliance with the Declaration. Claire Charters in Chapter 7 draws on theories of norm implementation in international relations to argue that irrespective of the New Zealand government's resistance to the Declaration, the rights will be gradually internalised provided indigenous advocates make good use of the Declaration. 'Use it or lose it' is the message. As a case study, Charters sets out her expert testimony on the status and relevance of the Declaration provided to the Waitangi Tribunal in its inquiry into 'Whaia te Mana Motuhake' which raises fundamental issues about iwi rights to self-determination in New Zealand.[44]

In Chapter 8, Fleur Te Aho explores how the UN Special Procedures – the collection of independent experts charged by the Human Rights Council with investigating human rights violations – may help to foster implementation of the Declaration in New Zealand. Te Aho focuses especially on the work of the UN Special Rapporteur on the Rights of Indigenous Peoples. Based on empirical research, including interviews with the two former UN Special Rapporteurs and Māori rights advocates, Te Aho argues that, while there are shortcomings, the special procedures are a unique tool for advancing the rights set out in the Declaration. The special procedures promote the Declaration, not only through naming and shaming states for rights breaches, but also through creating spaces for dialogue between states and indigenous peoples, and building states and indigenous peoples' capacity for rights realisation. Te Aho draws on these techniques and her empirical work to outline strategies for mobilising the special procedures in New Zealand.

In Chapter 9, Tracey Whare discusses the UN World Conference on Indigenous Peoples held in 2014. As Whare notes, there was much at stake in particular in ensuring the Declaration was not adulterated and seeking measures in an "outcome document" that would assist with the effective implementation of the Declaration on the ground. In Whare's view these were achieved as well as upholding the indigenous right to effective participation in processes affecting them, but it required much skilled planning and advocacy.

Finally, Natalie Baird in Chapter 10 considers the way in which the Declaration has been used in the context of the UN Human Rights Council's Universal Periodic Review (UPR) mechanism, focusing on New Zealand experience. According to Baird, despite the many inherent limitations of the UPR, it has much potential to advance indigenous rights implementation if it is used as *the* framework through which to view all indigenous rights issues.

---

44 Waitangi Tribunal *Whaia te Mana Motuhake: In Pursuit of Mana Motuhake* (Wai 2417, 2015).

INTRODUCTION

Nga mihi nui

This book has its origins in a two-day symposium hosted by Te Piringa Faculty of Law, University of Waikato, in June 2014, the aim being to reinvigorate New Zealand indigenous rights politics and law by adding a new means – in addition to Treaty and cultural rights – to evaluate indigenous rights reform to date and spark ideas for further reform. The symposium was warmly supported by my colleagues at Te Piringa, especially Matiu Dickson, Linda Te Aho, Claire Breen, Robert Joseph and the Dean at the time, Brad Morse. We received funding from the New Zealand Law Foundation to bring a selection of keynote speakers to kick off proceedings – the formidable James Anaya and Mick Dodson. I would like to acknowledge the financial assistance of the Law Foundation not only in relation to the symposium but also the publication of the book. We were also able to call upon a range of New Zealand scholars working in the field of international human rights, including Moana Jackson, Aroha Mead, Edwina Hughes and Maui Solomon, which resulted in two days of fun-filled and stimulating discussion. They were unable to contribute chapters but I think that their views influenced all the speakers and are reflected in many of the chapters. Thank you also Fergus Barrowman at VUP and Madeleine Collinge for helping to get this book to print, and to Dr Megan Davis for her foreword to the book. Special thanks go to my family, Claire, Maximilian and Mia, for their continuing support and inspiration.

Poroporoaki

Our friend and colleague Matiu Dickson passed away before the book's publication and he is missed by all his colleagues (past and present) at Te Piringa. And it is fitting, given his commitment to Ngā tikanga Māori, the Treaty and indigenous rights that this book be dedicated to him. Haere atu e te rangatira. Haere ki te tua o te arai. Ki te okiokinga i o tatou tupuna. Haere, haere, haere.

I

Setting the Scene: The Declaration and Human Rights

1

1
A Mixed-Model Interpretative Approach to the Declaration

*Andrew Erueti**

A. Introduction

In this chapter, I argue that the United Nations Declaration on the Rights of Indigenous Peoples (Declaration)[1] ought to be subject to what I call a "mixed model" interpretative approach based on the political history of its negotiation as it intersected with the emergence of an international indigenous rights movement. This is a new approach that diverges from the now orthodox view that the Declaration elaborates classic human rights.[2] The Declaration does this to a large degree, but it also contains what I call the "self-determination framework" – that is, the right to self-determination;[3] self-government;[4] historical redress;[5] the right to free, prior and informed consent (FPIC);[6] and the right to the recognition, observance and enforcement of treaties[7] – and instead of elaborating human rights I suggest these rights have their basis in a "decolonisation model". Thus I present the case for viewing the Declaration as based in two normative strands. I then consider the broad implications of this mixed-model for New Zealand's indigenous rights architecture.

---

* Senior Lecturer, Faculty of Law, University of Auckland
1 *United Nations Declaration on the Rights of Indigenous Peoples*, GA Res 61/295, UNGAOR, 61st Sess, Supp No 49, UN Doc A/RES/61/295 (2007) [The Declaration].
2 See S James Anaya *Indigenous Peoples in International Law* (Oxford University Press, Oxford; New York, 1996).
3 The Declaration, above n 1, at article 3.
4 At article 4.
5 At articles 11(2) and 28.
6 At articles 19 and 32(2).
7 At article 37.

B. The Rise of an International Indigenous Movement and the Decolonisation Model

When the Working Group on Indigenous Populations (WGIP) was first established in 1982 almost all of the indigenous advocates participating represented indigenous peoples of the CANZUS or Northern states of Canada, Australia, New Zealand and the United States.[8] In this chapter, I refer to these indigenous advocates as "Northern indigenous peoples" as opposed to "Southern indigenous peoples" of Latin American, Asia and Africa. North American advocates were most prominent, but in subsequent years more Australian and New Zealand advocates began to participate. This was particularly important because it was these advocates that set out the foundational frame of argument that would prove critical in establishing core aspects of the Declaration. They emerged from the sovereignty-based movements of their countries. These were the heady days of high-profile protests and occupations by indigenous peoples but also many other social movements including the Black Power, Second Wave Feminism, and Gay and Lesbian movements. In New Zealand, there was the 1976 "Great Land March" from Te Hāpua in the far north of the North Island to the New Zealand capital in Wellington at its extreme south.[9] In Australia, aboriginal activists established the tent embassy on the lawns of Canberra's parliament in protest against the taking of aboriginal land.[10] These indigenous movements emerged practically simultaneously across the four states and they increasingly provided one another with inspiration and a sense of solidarity. Their ambitions were different to most other movements of the North. Their agenda was political power for indigenous peoples based on their prior nationhood status – in particular the restoration of indigenous historical-political institutions and territory.[11] The CANZUS governments responded with law and policy reforms leading to a new phase of indigenous rights recognition. For example, in the USA, President Nixon's 1977 "Self-Determination Policy" looked to a "new era

---

8   See the Working Group on Indigenous Population's reports, for example, *Report of the Working Group on Indigenous Populations*, UNESCOR, 1982, UN Doc E/CN.4/Sub.2/1982/33. See also the electronic copies of submissions made to the Working Group compiled by the indigenous peoples' centre for documentation, research and information (DOCIP) at docip.org.

9   Richard S Hill *Māori and the State: Crown-Māori Relations in New Zealand/Aotearoa, 1950–2000* (Victoria University Press: Wellington, 2010).

10 See, Gary Foley, Andrew Schaap and Edwina Howell *The Aboriginal Tent Embassy: Sovereignty, Black Power, Land Rights and the State* (Routledge, Oxford, 2013).

11 For example, referring to the Treaty of Waitangi of 1840, Māori activists in New Zealand called for sovereign control over their communities and lands alongside the sovereign power of the state. Andrew Sharp *Justice and the Māori: Māori Claims in New Zealand Political Argument in the 1980s* (Oxford University Press, Melbourne; Auckland, 1990).

in which the Indian future is determined by Indian Acts and Indian decisions."[12] Yet Indian activists, particularly the more radical elements, were frustrated at their relatively weak bargaining power and the slow pace of reforms. A perennial problem for indigenous peoples was the unilateral manner in which reforms were determined. This had been a problem throughout the history of indigenous-settler state relations. But it continued to plague policy making in the new era of indigenous rights recognition. As with other social movements of the time, reform was neither fast enough nor radically transformational.[13]

Northern indigenous advocates saw promise in the UN system. The US-based International Indian Treaty Council (Treaty Council) especially was a key player in establishing a space in the international arena.[14] Lobbying by the Treaty Council and the Canadian-based World Council of Indigenous Peoples together with support from within the UN[15] and sympathetic states[16] led to the establishment of the Working Group on Indigenous Populations (WGIP), which was given the task of focusing on "the evolution of standards concerning the rights of indigenous populations."[17] This was clearly intended to be a human rights project. The working group was located in the human rights division of the UN as a subsidiary body beneath the Sub-Commission on the Prevention of Racial Discrimination, which was itself a subsidiary body of the UN Commission on Human Rights (now the Human Rights Council). In this international context, there were several models available to indigenous peoples, including the human rights and minority rights models. These were the models preferred by

---

12   Richard Nixon, President of the United States "Special Message on Indian Affairs" (July 8, 1970) at 564. See also the Alaska Native Claims Settlement Act (ANCSA), 1971, which sought to resolve the long-standing issues surrounding aboriginal land claims in Alaska. In Australia, State and National land laws were passed leading to major land returns to aboriginal peoples including large areas of the Northern Territory. See Marcia Langton *Settling with Indigenous People: Modern Treaty and Agreement-making* (Federation Press, Sydney, 2006).
13   Derek Bell *And We Are Not Saved: The Elusive Quest For Racial Justice* (Basic Books, New York, 1989).
14   The Treaty Council was formed in June 1974, at the first International Indian Treaty Conference, by the American Indian Movement (AIM) and traditional leaders of the Sioux Nation. Roxanne Dunbar Ortiz *Indians of the Americas: Human Rights, and Self-Determination* (Zed Books, London, 1984).
15   See for example ECOSOC Resolution 1589(L), 21 May 1971, UN. ESCOR, 50th Sess., Supp. No.1 at 16, UN Doc E/5044 (1971) (authorising the Sub-Commission to conduct a general and complete study into the problem of discrimination against indigenous populations and to suggest the necessary national and international measures by which to eliminate this).
16   The Nordic states, Norway, in particular, lobbied for the establishment of the WGIP, see Asbjorn Eide, UN Action on the Rights of Indigenous populations in *The Rights of Indigenous Peoples in International Law: Selected Essays on Self-Determination* (University of Saskatchewan, Saskatoon, 1987) at 31.
17   *Study of the Problem of Discrimination against Indigenous Populations*, ESC Res 1982/34, UNESCOR, 28th Plen Mtg, UN Doc E/RES/1982/34.

states.[18] They reflected what many states had already instituted in their legal systems. However, human rights did not fit well with the core concerns of the emergent international movement. The Universal Declaration of Human Rights (1948)(UDHR) drafted by Western states with an emphasis on individual rights held universally, irrespective of the person's cultural, religious or political connections, failed to address those matters that were of most importance to Northern indigenous peoples – political sovereignty and territory.[19] The same could be said for the two treaties that give effect to the UDHR, the International Covenant on Civil and Political Rights[20] and the International Covenant on Economic, Social and Cultural Rights.[21] More fundamentally for indigenous advocates, human rights were closely attached to the construction of, and implied fidelity to, the modern liberal democratic state. As Samuel Moyn notes, rights established the boundaries of citizenship as a means of solidifying state power.[22] The minority rights model was not a good fit either, being notoriously weak – in large part because states are concerned about internal minorities seeking greater autonomy and possibly independence.[23] Hence the emphasis on human rights in the UN Charter and no mention of minority rights in the UDHR and the post-war regional human rights instruments.[24] Article 27 of the ICCPR guarantees the right to culture, but is expressed as a right held by individual members of minorities rather than of the minority as a collective. The Convention concerning the Protection and Integration of Indigenous and Other Tribal and Semi-Tribal Populations in Independent Countries (ILO Convention

---

18 According to CANZUS states, the clear plight of indigenous peoples suggested that the priority should be the basic human rights set out in the International Covenants. See, for example, New Zealand "New Zealand Statement under Item 5" (31 July–4 August 1989) doCip Doc. 200284_1 (on file with author) (Referring to UN Resolution 21/120 and the need to "ensure compatibility with existing human rights instruments") at 2. See also Australia, (22 July 1983) UN Doc E/CN.4/Sub.2/1983/2/Add.2 at 2 ("The standards evolved by the group should harmonize with existing human rights enunciated in the relevant international legal instruments.").
19 *Universal Declaration of Human Rights*, GA Res 217A (III), UNGAOR, 3rd Sess, Supp No 13, UN Doc A/810 (1948) 71.
20 International Covenant on Civil and Political Rights, 16 December 1966, 999 UNTS 171 (entered into force 23 March 1976) [ICCPR].
21 International Covenant on Economic, Social and Cultural Rights, 16 December 1966, 993 UNTS 3 (entered into force 3 January 1976) [ICESCR].
22 Samuel Moyn *The Last Utopia: Human Rights in History* (Harvard University Press, Cambridge, 2010), ch 1.
23 Will Kymlicka *Multicultural Odysseys: Navigating the New International Politics of Diversity* (Oxford University Press, New York, 2007).
24 *Convention for the Protection of Human Rights and Fundamental Freedoms*, 4 November 1950, 213 UNTS 221 (entered into force on 3 September 1953); OAS, Conference of American States, *American Declaration on the Rights and Duties of Man*, OEA/Ser.L/V/II. 82/Doc. 6/Rev. 1 (1948); *American Convention on Human Rights*, 22 November 1969, 1144 UNTS 123 (entered into force 18 July 1978).

107),[25] adopted in 1957, and Convention (No 169) concerning Indigenous and Tribal Peoples in Independent Countries (ILO Convention 169),[26] adopted in 1989, broadly provide for a range of civil, political, economic, social and cultural rights for two categories of peoples: indigenous peoples of the settler states; and tribal peoples of Asia, Africa and the Middle East. The latter category comprised culturally distinctive marginalised communities like the hill-tribal peoples of east, and south east and southern Asia. However, ILO Convention 107's intention was to ultimately "integrate" indigenous/tribal peoples by making them more productive workers.[27] ILO Convention 169, on the other hand, was directed towards the promotion of indigenous/tribal rights, in keeping with the prevailing views at the time of its adoption in 1989. However it did not incorporate the rights in the self-determination framework, even though indigenous advocates (mostly Northern) lobbied for their inclusion during the convention's negotiation.

But the decolonisation model best matched the ideals behind indigenous sovereignty. For several decades following the Second World War, the UN-directed decolonisation project had been the dominant international movement for the freedom of peoples.[28] The UN Charter had offered the promise of independence by referring to the "self-determination of peoples."[29] However, the founding states of the UN, most of them Imperial Powers, were ambivalent about decolonisation and self-determination. Mark Mazower notes:[30]

> One can view the Charter and especially its preamble, along with the UDHR and the Genocide Convention, as testifying to the foundational imperatives of the new world order established in the fight against Nazism. Or one can read them as

---

25 Convention (No. 107) concerning the Protection and Integration of Indigenous and Other Tribal and Semi-Tribal Populations in Independent Countries, 26 June 1957, 328 UNTS 247 (entered into force 2 June 1959) [ILO Convention No. 107].

26 Convention (No. 169) concerning Indigenous and Tribal Peoples in Independent Countries, 27 June 1989, 28 ILM 1382 (entered into force 5 September 1991). [ILO Convention No. 169].

27 ILO Convention No. 107, above n 25. See, Article 2(1) ("Governments shall have the primary responsibility for developing co-ordinated and systematic action for the protection of the populations concerned and their progressive integration into the life of their respective countries"). For discussion on drafting of ILO Convention 107, see Luis Rodríguez-Piñero *Indigenous Peoples, Postcolonialism, and International Law: the ILO regime (1919-1989)* (Oxford University Press, New York, 2005).

28 In fact, Moyn argues that human rights struggled to emerge from the shadow cast by the decolonisation movement. The notion of human rights in the sense of supranational standards of protection did not fully emerge until the mid-1970s with the demise of anti-colonialism. See Moyn, above n 22.

29 *Charter of the United Nations*, 26 June 1945, Can TS 1945 No 7; Article 1(2) lists as one of the UN purposes: "To develop friendly relations among nations based on respect for the principle of equal rights and self-determination of peoples, and to take other appropriate measures to strengthen universal peace."

30 Mark Mazower *No Enchanted Palace: The End of Empire and the Ideological Origins of the United Nations* (Princeton University Press, New Jersey, 2009) at 8.

promissory notes that the UN founders never intended to cash.

Like the League of Nations, the UN was a club of Western states concerned about shoring up and maintaining their power.[31] However, as Mazower notes, a shift occurred due to a battle of ideas about the protection of minorities and agitation from former colonial nations who were early entries into the UN system. India's Prime Minister, Jawaharlal Nehru, led his country's protests at the South African treatment of its Indian population and found a receptive audience despite the UN's formal prohibition on intervening in internal matters.[32] This triggered a major change in direction for the UN from its initial project of protecting imperialism to the active promotion of decolonisation. The decolonisation project succeeded in making the UN an instrument for the emancipation of colonial peoples throughout the world. Self-determination then, moved from a principle of international law to a widely accepted legal right. This movement and the process of decolonisation radically shifted international politics.[33] While at its inception in 1945 the UN consisted of fifty-one states, mostly representative of the Americas, Western Europe and with minimal representation from Asia and Africa, by 1970 there were over seventy new member states.[34] These additions were almost all newly decolonised nations of Asia and Africa. In 1960 alone, seventeen African states joined the UN.[35] In fact, the decolonisation movement was so powerful that the reference to self-determination in the International Covenants was largely due to this democratisation of the UN. When the UN organs debated the International Covenants in the 1950s, the post-colonial states insisted that they contain the right of peoples to self-determination as the threshold right.[36] In this, they found support from the Soviet Union and Communist bloc countries.[37]

---

31 At 8.
32 At 8.
33 David A Kay "The Politics of Decolonization: The New Nations and the United Nations Political Process" (1967) 21:4 Int Organ 786; Thomas D Musgrave *Self-determination and National Minorities* (Oxford University Press, Oxford, 2000) at 67–68.
34 See Moyn, above n 22.
35 The countries were Cameroun, Central African Republic, Chad, Congo (Brazzaville), Congo (Leopoldville), Cyprus, Dahomey, Gabon, Ivory Coast, Malagasy Republic, Mali, Niger, Nigeria, Senegal, Somalia, Togo, Upper Volta.
36 Antonio Cassese *Self-Determination of Peoples: A Legal Reappraisal* (Cambridge University Press, Cambridge, 1998) ("The socialist countries – soon joined, at least at the political level, by an increasing number of freshly independent Third World countries – were the most active advocates of anti-colonial self determination. They adopted and developed Lenin's thesis that self determination should first and foremost be a postulate of anti-colonialism" at 44); Moyn, above n 22 at 97–98.
37 Cassese, above n 36 at 47–52 (noting how in 1950 the Soviet Union proposed a provision regarding self-determination in the International Covenants – "the primary concern was the right of self-determination of colonial peoples" at 48); Musgrave, above n 33 at 67–68. Lenin had long advocated for the self-determination of colonised peoples as did subsequent Soviet

Western states, on the other hand, opposed inclusion of a right to self-determination. Alternatively, if self-determination was to be included, they argued that it should not be confined to colonial situations but should also apply to the peoples of sovereign states oppressed by their own governments.[38] Thus, the West sought to define the right of self-determination in terms of their political tradition of popular sovereignty and representative government.[39] But the West was also concerned about its colonial interests and control over investment in developing countries.[40] The post-colonial states ultimately prevailed. Common article 1 of the International Covenants thus provides:[41]

> All peoples have the right of self-determination. By virtue of that right they freely determine their political status and freely pursue their economic, social and cultural development.

The post-colonial states also sought recognition of the right to self-determination and its connection with decolonisation in a series of UN General Assembly resolutions, including the 1960 Declaration on the Granting of Independence to Colonial Countries and Peoples.[42] This stressed "the necessity of bringing to a speedy and unconditional end colonialism in all its forms and manifestations."[43] Many of the imperial powers abstained from the Declaration vote.[44] However Western states did support the later 1970 Declaration on Principles of International Law Concerning Friendly Relations and Co-operation Among States in Accordance with the Charter of the United Nations (Friendly Relations Declaration).[45] This was adopted without vote by consensus, but only

---

political leaders. See, Cassese, above n 36 at 14–19 (although as Cassese notes "the Soviet leader championed self-determination more to further his ideological and political objectives than to safeguard peoples" at 18).

38 Cassese, above n 36 at 47–52.
39 At 19–23.
40 At 49–50 ("By and large, it can be contended that Western countries opposed the provision on self-determination either on account of their colonial interests, or out of fear that the paragraph relating to the free disposition of natural resources imperiled foreign investments and enterprises in developing countries" at 50).
41 ICESCR, above n 21.
42 Declaration on the Granting of Independence to Colonial Countries and Peoples, GA Res 1514, UNGAOR, 15th Sess, Supp No. 16/15, UN Doc A/4684 (1960), [1960 Declaration on the Granting of Independence]. There were in fact earlier resolutions aimed at anti-colonialism, for example Resolution 637 (VII) of 16 December 1952 which asked UN members to "recognize and promote the realization of the right to self-determination of the peoples of non-self-governing and trust territories who are under their administration." Musgrave, above n 33 at 67–68.
43 1960 Declaration on the Granting of Independence, above n 42.
44 Eighty-nine states voted in favour of the Declaration; there were nine abstentions. Those abstaining were the United States, United Kingdom, Belgium, Australia, Portugal, Spain, South Africa, the Dominican Republic and France. See Cassese, above n 36 at 71.
45 *Declaration on Principles of International Law Concerning Friendly Relations and Co-*

because it contained a clear compromise between the demands of the post-colonial states/Soviet Bloc and the West. The Friendly Relations Declaration endorsed self-determination and, like the 1960 Declaration, noted the need to bring "a speedy end to colonialism."[46] It also upheld the right of states to territorial integrity in the penultimate paragraph.[47] The right to territorial integrity is significant because the right affirms state borders and independence and acts as a counterbalance to any domestic claim to independence by internal secessionist groups and foreign intervention into domestic affairs.[48] However, to appease the West, the reference to territorial integrity was conditioned by the requirement that states comply with the principle of equal rights and representative government. This was a response from Western states concerned about human rights violations within the Soviet and post-colonial states. It also met with a long-term agenda to promote democracy and representative government. Subsequently scholars have argued that the Declaration's reference to equality should be read as granting a right to independence in cases of gross abuses of human rights.[49] It is commonly said to endorse a "human rights approach" to self-determination.[50]

Decolonisation was probably *the* social liberation movement of the 20th century but it was denied to indigenous peoples. According to the so-called blue- or salt-water thesis adopted by the UN General Assembly in 1960, the right to self-determination and decolonisation only applied to *overseas* colonial possessions.[51] There had to be blue- or salt-water between the colonising country and the colony or at least a geographically discrete set of boundaries. This thesis excluded indigenous peoples of the Americas and Australasia from decolonisation.

---

operation Among States in Accordance with the Charter of the United Nations, GA Res 2625, UNGAOR, 25th Sess, Supp No. 28, UN Doc. A/8082 (1970) [1970 Declaration on Friendly Relations].

46 Unlike most other UN General Assembly resolutions concerning self-determination, it made no reference to Resolution 1514. Musgrave notes "Had Third World states insisted on this, agreement from Western States would not have been forthcoming and consensus would not have been possible." Musgrave, above n 33 at 75.

47 1970 Declaration on Friendly Relations, Paragraph 7.

48 Cassese, above n 36.

49 Cassese, above n 36 at 118–120; Allen E Buchanan *Justice, Legitimacy, and Self-determination: Moral Foundations for International Law* (Oxford University Press, Oxford, 2007); Musgrave, above n 33. However, it is not clear in international law that this creates an additional legal category to classic colonialism. See, Accordance with International Law of the Unilateral Declaration of Independence in respect of Kosovo (Kosovo Opinion), Advisory Opinion, [2010] ICJ Rep 403 at 436.

50 As Cassese notes, Western states had originally sought language in the Declaration that would explicitly equate self-determination with representative democracy. Soviet and Southern states objected and this "savings clause" was a compromise. Cassese, above n 36 at 109.

51 *Principles which should guide members in determining whether or not an obligation exists to transmit the information called for under Article 73e of the Charter*, GA Res 1541(XV), UNGAOR, 15 Sess, UN Doc A/RES/1541(XV) (1960), Principle IV [GA Res 1541(XV)].

This was the setting in which indigenous peoples found themselves when they commenced negotiations in the WGIP. Their choices were human rights, minority rights or anti-colonialism.[52] During the first working group meetings, the Treaty Council and other prominent Northern indigenous organisations provided the working group with their idealised model Declarations. These do not resemble human rights instruments so much as mini-declarations of independence. The Treaty Council's model Declaration provided:[53]

> Article 1. Indigenous populations are subject to an economic and/or political and/or social domination which is alien and colonial or neo-colonial in nature.
> Article 2. Indigenous populations are composed of nations and peoples which are collective entities entitled to and requiring self-determination. The Working Group should, therefore, develop a definition of the ultimate goals of self-determination, appropriate to indigenous populations, and procedures for achieving those goals.
> Article 3. Indigenous nations and peoples *who so desire* should be granted the full rights and obligations of external self-determination.
> Article 4. Indigenous nations and peoples *who wish to limit* themselves to the exercise of internal self-determination only should be granted the freedom to do so. The rights of internal self-determination should include, but not be limited to, the right to:
> (a) control their own economies;
> (b) freely pursue their economic, social and cultural development in conformity with their tradition, custom and social mores;
> (c) engage in foreign relations and trade if they so desire;
> (d) restore, practise and educate their children to their cultures, languages, traditions and way of life;
> (e) and the right to the ownership of land as the territorial base for the existence of indigenous populations as such. (emphasis added)

Few indigenous advocates actually sought full independence. Articles 3 and 4 of the Treaty Council's model Declaration, for example, grant indigenous peoples the choice of either internal and external self-determination. But it is clear that the option of independence was important to many and that self-determination would provide support for this right should indigenous peoples and states fail to negotiate their terms of co-existence.[54] Self-determination thus provided

---

52 Compare, Benedict Kingsbury "Competing Conceptual Approaches to Indigenous Group Issues in New Zealand Law" (2002) 52 Univ Tor Law J 101.

53 See *Information received from NGOs, International Indian Treaty Council, "Draft Principles for Guiding Deliberations of the Working Group"*, 1982, UN Doc E/CN.4/1983/5/Add.2 (emphasis added).

54 The Working Group Chair, Erica-Irene Daes, referred to this as "a kind of belated State-building, through which indigenous peoples are able to join with all the other peoples that make up the State on mutually-agreed and just terms, after many years of isolation and exclusion." See, Erica-Irene Daes "Some Considerations on the Right of Indigenous Peoples to Self-Determination" (1993) 3 Transn'l L. & Contemp. Probs 1 at 9.

indigenous peoples with significant leverage in these negotiations. In support of this argument, Northern indigenous peoples pointed to treaty-making with European states, and a long-established practice of recognition of indigenous peoples as first peoples with a sui generis political-legal status.[55] Human rights were obviously significant to indigenous advocates. Indigenous peoples in the North occupied the margins of social and economic life and few participated meaningfully in civic life. However, the human rights model was most important to the extent it supported decolonisation.[56] Equality meant that all peoples, not just those in blue-water states, should be entitled to self-determination and decolonisation. As noted by the indigenous organisation, The Four Directions Council, in the Working Group:[57]

> Looking around the world today, we observe a curious phenomenon. Peoples of every race, with one exception, have been achieving self-determination and decolonization under the auspices of the UN. There are independent States today of every colour, save one. Is this a temporary oversight, or the result of institutionalized discrimination?

Equality was also used to stave off states' demands that any reference to self-determination in the Declaration be conditioned by states' rights to territorial integrity. Indigenous peoples argued in response that common article 1 in the International Covenants was not subject to territorial integrity. This decolonisation model was influential. When the early drafts of the Declaration emerged, they contained statements of classic human rights and minority rights, though adapted to indigenous peoples. But several years into the negotiations, there was a major shift. The 1989 draft contained a reference to historical redress for dispossession of land, and a collective right to autonomy.[58] Gradually references to FPIC and self-government were inserted so that by 1993, the year of the final WGIP meeting, the Declaration was comprised of a preamble with 19

---

55 For an account of this practice of indigenous-states relations, see Kirsty Gover *Tribal Constitutionalism* (Oxford University Press, Oxford, 2010).

56 Human rights were important but to focus too much on basic human rights or poverty would divert attention from the Indigenous advocates' decolonisation model. Human rights in the abstract supported the goals of popular or collective liberation – just as they had with the anti-colonialism movement. See, Moyn, above n 22 at 85.

57 See, Four Directions Council "Statement Concerning Racism in the Application of the Principles of Self-determination and Legal Equality of States" (9 August 1983) doCip Doc. 200479_2 (on file with author). See also Venne (1984) doCip Doc. 200479_2 (on file with author) (urging the Working Group on Indigenous Populations to consider a recommendation to the Sub-Commission that: "The standards and obligations enunciated in the UN Charter on non-self-governing and trust territories, chapter 11, Article 73 must apply to self-determining Indigenous peoples.").

58 *Report of the Working Group on Indigenous Populations*, UNESCOR, 1989, UN Doc E/CN.4/Sub.2/1989/36 at Annex II "First revised text of the draft Universal Declaration on the Right of Indigenous Peoples, as presented by the Chairman/Rapporteur Ms Erica-Irene Daes".

paragraphs and 45 articles, and contained the self-determination framework.[59] The Declaration contained a reference to self-determination in almost identical terms to the rights as expressed in common article 1 of the International Covenants. Article 3 of the Declaration provided:

> Indigenous peoples have the right of self-determination. By virtue of that right they freely determine their political status and freely pursue their economic, social and cultural development.

There was no reference to territorial integrity. It is the decolonisation model that accounts for the self-determination framework in the Declaration. As state-like peoples subjected to colonisation, equality demanded that indigenous peoples be entitled to self-determination alongside other peoples. The resulting standards established by the decolonisation model set a precedent that would prove to be enormously difficult for states to dis-assemble in subsequent negotiations.

C. Emergence of the Human Rights Model of Indigenous Rights

The Declaration produced by the WGIP was a breakthrough for indigenous peoples, but states objected to the self-determination framework. The WGIP sat below the Sub-Commission on the Prevention of Racial Discrimination, which provided it with flexibility and a degree of independence. The WGIP members were not state representatives but independent human rights experts chosen from the Sub-Commission. But when the Declaration came before the Sub-Commission's parent body, the UN Commission on Human Rights, which is comprised of state representatives, the Commission directed the Declaration to a new working group for further negotiation.[60] In this Working Group of the Draft Declaration (WGDD), which met from 1995 to 2006, there was a shift in focus away from the decolonisation model towards a human rights model whereby all of the rights in the Declaration were considered to be elaborations of human rights.[61] Northern indigenous peoples resisted this. However, eventually the human rights model became the prominent model. It has effectively become the mantra of the international indigenous rights movement.[62]

---

59 *Report of the Working Group on Indigenous Populations*, UNESCOR, 1993, UN Doc E/CN.4/Sub.2/1993/29 at Annex 1 "Draft Declaration as agreed Upon by the members of the Working Group on the Declaration at its Eleventh Session".
60 *Establishment of a Working Group of the Commission on Human Rights to Elaborate a Draft Declaration*, ESC Res 1995/32, UNESCOR, 52nd Sess, Supp No 2, UN Doc E/CN.4/1996/177 (1995).
61 For the classic statement of this human rights model, see Anaya, above n 2.
62 See, for example, the essays in Paul Joffe, Jackie Hartley and Jennifer Preston *Realizing the UN Declaration on the Rights of Indigenous Peoples: Triumph, Hope, and Action* (Purich Publishing, Vancouver, 2010); and Claire Charters and Rodolfo Stavenhagen *Making the Declaration Work* (IWGIA, Copenhagen, 2009).

Karen Engle has offered a strong critique of this shift.[63] She attributes it to a decision made by indigenous advocates to adapt to the realities of working within the UN human rights system. Many indigenous advocates saw strong claims to self-determination as a "futile attempt to affect international law too dramatically."[64] She cites James Anaya as one of the lead proponents of this shift in strategy.[65] She also notes that the human rights model was the preferred approach of indigenous advocates of the former Spanish colonies of Latin America where claims to political sovereignty were not realistic – given the presence of repressive regimes – or aligned with the aims of the Latin American indigenous movement.[66] When Latin American indigenous advocates did participate, their focus, as she shows, tended not to be political independence, but cultural autonomy and basic human rights.[67] Conceiving indigenous rights as human and cultural rights, Engle argues, has led to the simplification and reification of indigenous identities.[68] It has also "largely displaced or deferred many of the economic and political issues that initially motivated much indigenous advocacy: issues of economic dependency, structural discrimination, and lack of indigenous autonomy".[69] The movement has drifted from its moorings in self-determination towards matters of culture, consultation and land rights. She describes this as the "soft edge" of the claims of indigenous peoples, resulting in less of a threat to the state, and cites ILO Convention No 169 as "both representative of and central to the move to protect indigenous rights under a human rights framework, particularly through the right to culture."[70] All this jurisprudence as she notes is based on human rights and especially the right to culture.[71]

Anaya has indeed played a key role in the shift towards a human rights model. All rights in the Declaration, are "a contextualized elaboration of general human rights principles and rights as they relate to the specific historical, cultural and

---

63 Karen Engle *The Elusive Promise of Indigenous Development: Rights, Culture, Strategy* (Duke University Press, Durham, 2010).
64 At 2.
65 At 98.
66 At 55–66.
67 At 67.
68 Here, Engle is channeling Nancy Fraser. See Nancy Fraser and her critique of the prominence of the politics of recognition at the expense of the politics of distribution. Nancy Fraser and others *Adding Insult to Injury: Nancy Fraser Debates Her Critics* (Verso, London, 2008).
69 Engle, above n 63 at 3.
70 At 5. This "soft approach", Engle argues, is evident also in the decisions of UN and Inter-American human rights treaty bodies. Advocates have largely couched their demands in terms of cultural rights as treaty bodies have proven increasingly receptive to these arguments. Here, Engle dwells especially on the Inter-American Court of Human Rights which has upheld indigenous rights to consultation, land and resources, and FPIC. At ch 4.
71 Engle, above n 63 at 123–132.

social circumstances of indigenous peoples."[72] When he introduced this approach, Anaya was part of a new school of thought about self-determination and human rights.[73] But contrary to Engle, Anaya's human rights model delivers much more than rights to land and culture. Anaya's model, in theory, could support the self-determination framework and deliver significant autonomy for indigenous groups vis-à-vis the state.[74] But it is a human rights reading of self-determination and that is different from a decolonisation reading.[75] The decolonisation model speaks to a nation-to-nation relationship between Northern indigenous peoples and CANZUS states, whereas a human rights model applies, and in fundamental ways depends on, existing configurations of state power.[76] The decolonisation model indicated that self-determination in the Declaration offered indigenous peoples the option of independence should indigenous peoples and states fail to negotiate their terms of co-existence. However, it is easy to appreciate the human rights model's appeal as a means of thinking about indigenous rights. At its heart it is an appeal to the universal right of equality. Indigenous peoples as equal and free citizens ought to be entitled to those rights available to other peoples.[77] Such a broad justification meant the Declaration could encompass both the Northern and Southern movements. Cast as a human rights instrument – or the elaboration of widely ratified human rights including the International Covenants – the rights in the Declaration would also possess "binding qualities", despite its technical

72 See, *Report of the Special Rapporteur on the Situation of Human Rights and Fundamental Freedoms of Indigenous People* UNHRCOR A/HRC/9/9 (2008) at 86.
73 During the early 1990s, leading international law scholars were discussing self-determination in a human rights sense in terms of promoting representative government and democratic governance. See, for example, Hurst Hannum "Rethinking Self-Determination" (1993) 34(1) Va J Int Law 1; Thomas M Franck "The Emerging Right to Democratic Governance" (1992) 86(1) Am J Int Law 46; and Robert McCorquodale "Self-Determination: A Human Rights Approach" (1994) 43 International and Comparative Law Quarterly at 857–885.
74 Although Engle concedes "indigenous peoples sometimes make relatively strong redistributive claims under the right to culture, or with the claim that particular human rights (like the right to property) protect their culture." Engle, above n 63 at 3.
75 See, for example, James Anaya "Divergent Discourses about International Law, Indigenous Peoples, and Rights over Lands and Natural Resources: Toward a Realist Trend" (2005) 16 Colo. J. Int'l Envtl. L. & Pol'y 237.
76 For an example of how a human right to self-determination interpretative approach may be reduced to effective participation in democratic life, see the Statement in the working group by Colin Milner on behalf of the Australian delegation (24 July 1992). doCip Doc. 960255_3 and 960255_34 (on file with author): "Realization of the right to self-determination is not limited in time to the process of decolonization nor is it accomplished by a single act or exercise. Rather it entails the continuing right of all peoples and individuals within each state to participate fully in the political process by which they are governed. Clearly enhancing popular participation in this decision-making is an important factor in realizing the right to self-determination. It is evident that, even in some countries which are formally fully democratic structural, attitudinal and procedural barriers exist which inhibit the full democratic effective participation of particular groups."
77 Anaya, above n 2 at 75–76.

status as a non-binding instrument. And it enabled indigenous peoples to access the extensive international and regional institutional mechanisms available to advance human rights, including the UN human rights supervisory functions and the global network of human rights NGOs.[78] Furthermore, the human rights model could accommodate a reference to territorial integrity, as it assumes indigenous peoples will continue to be citizens of the modern state.

I agree with Engle that many Northern indigenous peoples shifted from the decolonisation to the human rights model for strategic reasons. But many advocates stayed the course and continued to rely on the decolonisation model right up to the point of the Declaration's UN General Assembly's endorsement. However, I argue that the most significant reason for the shift to human rights was the increased participation of indigenous peoples from the South – and not simply Latin America as identified by Engle – but especially the participation of indigenous peoples of east, south eastern and southern Asia and Africa, where there were different agendas more disposed to human rights-based models.[79] The inclusion of Asian and then African indigenous peoples in the Declaration negotiations is largely due to the advocacy efforts of activist-anthropologists working with tribal peoples in the South. Survival International, Anti-Slavery and International Work Group for Indigenous Affairs (IWGIA) attended the Declaration negotiations and spoke about the struggle of Jumma tribal peoples of Bangladesh and the Indian scheduled tribes of India. They placed particular emphasis on culture and human rights because this established common cause with indigenous peoples of the North. While Northern Indigenous Peoples focused on decolonisation, human rights were also a primary concern. It was also an effort to defuse anxiety held by Southern states over minority security and stability issues. Asian and African states were particularly concerned with the right to self-determination in the Declaration because it suggested that local communities could seek secession or at least strong forms of internal autonomy. They argued that their states contained no indigenous peoples, only minorities, and insisted that the Declaration provide a definition of indigenous peoples that made clear that it only applied to indigenous peoples of the settler states of Australasia and the Americas. In response, Asian indigenous advocates held themselves out as "harmless" communities of remote, mountain and hilltop areas seeking cultural survival in the face of unrelenting Western development and culture (not secession). Indeed, Asian and African indigenous peoples could not credibly advance the decolonisation model. They could only benefit from alternatives to the decolonisation model.

---

78 On this, see the chapters by Fleur Te Aho and Natalie Baird in this book.
79 For the full argument about the impact of the participation of Asian and African indigenous advocates in the Declaration negotiations, see A Erueti "UN Declaration on the Rights of Indigenous Peoples: A Mixed- Model Interpretative Approach" (SJD thesis, University of Toronto, 2016).

Asian and African indigenous peoples quickly became active participants in the Declaration negotiations. Once they gained a foothold in the negotiations, new movements also emerged from the Soviet Union and Middle East. All of these Southern movements provided argument and an empirical basis to support the inclusion of the basic human rights in the Declaration. And in some respects their argument was more powerful than the human rights arguments made by Northern indigenous peoples. Many of the Latin American, Asian and African indigenous advocates came from countries widely recognised as failed or failing states. The issues raised in the South tended to underscore the urgency of the project of adoption of the Declaration by the UN General Assembly. Issues of life and liberty, and the impacts of extractive industry in the South provided a more immediate and perhaps compelling motivation than the Northern-based historical-centric arguments. In relation to Asian indigenous peoples in particular, their sheer numbers (most UN estimates are two million) provided a compelling case for international action. These southern advocates through their participation and argument vested the human rights in the Declaration with political legitimacy and authority. Thus it is clear Southern indigenous peoples served an important purpose in generating attention towards the Declaration and ensuring that it was adopted by the UN. Thus Southern indigenous peoples not only provided a human rights argument, but they also contributed considerable momentum in the negotiations and lifted the profile of the Declaration, thereby advancing the aims of the Northern movement and vesting the overall project with significant authority.

However, this presented real difficulties for the Northern indigenous peoples because once Asian and African indigenous peoples themselves began to attend the Declaration negotiations and hold themselves out as indigenous peoples, Asian and African states began to oppose strong statements of indigenous rights in the Declaration. This placed pressure on the Northern movement to drop the decolonisation model. However, I disagree with Engle's view that "strong forms of self-determination" were abandoned in favour of the human rights model. The decolonisation model was, in fact, consistently maintained throughout by the Treaty Council and other prominent indigenous advocates of the North. They did not want to compromise their core roots in radical sovereign tribal politics. And this persistence from the North had an impact. There were changes made to the Declaration, but the final version of the Declaration produced by the WGDD continued to contain the self-determination framework and contained no reference to territorial integrity. The exclusion of the state right to territorial integrity was significant to indigenous peoples because it supported their decolonisation model and the option of independence sought by them.

It is the persistence in advancing the decolonisation model that accounts for this outcome. Of course, territorial integrity was added to the Declaration but only at the eleventh hour after strong opposition to the Declaration in the UN Third Committee from the African Group of States.[80] Just before the Declaration was to be sent to the UN General Assembly, the African Group, prompted by the Northern states, refused to vote for the Declaration in the General Assembly unless the self-determination framework was removed.[81] Eventually, the African Group agreed to support the Declaration provided it contained a reference to territorial integrity.[82] This was a great disappointment to Northern indigenous peoples after more than twenty years of effort to avoid any reference to territorial integrity. But I do not think this last-minute change undermines the longstanding connection between the decolonisation model and self-determination in the Declaration. It would seem to rule out the option of independence sought by indigenous peoples. But the Declaration's right to self-determination is still imbued with strong decolonisation overtones. This political narrative of the Declaration drafting indicates that there are two forms of argument underlying the indigenous rights in the Declaration. As I noted above and develop below, this insight calls for a mixed-model reading of the Declaration that stands apart from the current human rights model.

D. A New Mixed-Model Interpretative Approach to the Declaration

Whereas the Northern indigenous movement initiated the UN-based activity that led to the adoption of the Declaration, it was the project's extension to the Southern movement – the Declaration's globalisation – that provided it with significant momentum. While Engle emphasises the great material cost of globalisation for the North, she argues against a focus on human rights and thus necessarily excludes the Southern movement. In contrast, I offer an account of the Declaration that seeks fully to reflect – and respect – the impact of both Southern and Northern indigenous peoples. On this account, the political history of the Declaration led it to carry two normative strands. I propose that the Declaration be read as containing two normative themes for different categories of peoples. On the one hand, the Declaration can be read as an instrument for Northern indigenous peoples; it contains human rights but also the self-determination framework which is supported by their decolonisation model. On the other, the Declaration can be read as a human rights instrument for Southern indigenous peoples. The benefit of this model is that it is not a zero sum game for the Northern and Southern movements.

80 Albert Kwokwo Barume "Responding to the Concerns of the African States" in Claire Charters and Rodolfo Stavenhagen (eds) *Making the Declaration Work* (IWGIA, Copenhagen, 2009).
81 At 34.
82 At 35.

It enables both the Northern and Southern indigenous movements to gain the rights they seek from the Declaration. This interpretation of the Declaration enables indigenous peoples of Africa and Asia (as well as Latin America) to access the rights in the Declaration that mean most to them and are grounded in their particular experience. These include the rights to practise and revitalise their cultural traditions and customs (Article 11); the right to manifest, practise, develop and teach their spiritual and religious traditions, customs and ceremonies (Article 12); and the right to determine and develop priorities and strategies for exercising their right to development (Article 23). But there are many more, indeed, almost all the 46 Articles in the Declaration. This could conceivably include self-determination itself, though in the sense of promoting the right to effective participation in public life and local autonomy.

However, the self-determination framework – the right to self-determination, self-government, historical redress, treaty rights and FPIC – resulted from the decolonisation model. Indigenous peoples are first peoples, prior to the current state, and entitled to recognition of their inherent sovereign status. For indigenous peoples of the CANZUS states, this interpretative approach highlights the normative power of the decolonisation model and demonstrates that the self-determination framework is in the Declaration to address their specific circumstances. Northern indigenous peoples would of course claim the basic human rights outlined in the Declaration. These are important to them, albeit, their first priority was decolonisation and self-determination. As I say, both the Northern and Southern movements benefit from this mixed-model. The mixed-model, I argue, can substantially benefit the Southern movements, particularly the Asian and African movements, by removing state concerns with the category of indigenous peoples and the self-determination framework. It would also emphasise the political legitimacy that these rights have for Southern indigenous peoples. In the North, the decolonisation model can be applied to counter the trend among states to interpret the Declaration as a human rights model. By revealing the place of the decolonisation model in the political history and thereby in the text of the Declaration, I seek to position indigenous advocates to re-assert the decolonisation model to counter-act the effects of the dominant human rights model. The challenge of my mixed-model approach is to avoid the decolonisation model being absorbed by the human rights model through the practices of interpretation. And that can be met if Northern Indigenous advocates recognise the relevance and normative significance of the self-determination framework and apply it in their Indigenous rights advocacy (which has generally not been the case to date).

E. New Zealand and the Mixed-Model

What are the implications of this mixed-model for New Zealand's indigenous rights architecture? The significance lies in the connection between the self-determination framework and the decolonisation model. The Declaration, according to the New Zealand government, contains both "accepted international human rights" and "new, and non-binding, aspirations."[83] The aspirational elements are clearly a reference to the self-determination framework as a set of rights that step beyond the classic or "accepted" set of human rights. According to the government, the aspirational elements of the Declaration are to be defined within the bounds of New Zealand's existing legal and constitutional frameworks through its "distinct", well-established domestic processes for resolving Treaty claims.[84] According to this interpretative approach, then, the implementation of the "aspirations" set out in the self-determination framework are to be determined according to the discretion of the state, disconnected from any international context and normative model. The New Zealand government is aware of this. It is the prospect of meaningful autonomy and territorial rights that is of most concern to New Zealand. This is why New Zealand sought to weaken the self-determination framework and insist on a reference to territorial integrity.[85] And the government continued to refuse to endorse the Declaration, even after a reference to territorial integrity was inserted in the Declaration. Indeed, New Zealand's indigenous rights architecture has always sought to avoid the issue of political authority.[86] Iwi may have greater rights of participation in public life, recognition of cultural rights in the form of co-management of resources of significance and material gains from transfer of lands, and other forms of redress through Treaty settlements. However by emphasising the connection between the decolonisation model and the self-determination framework in the Declaration, indigenous advocates in New Zealand have a solid foundation for seeking rights that recognise Māori political authority.

---

83 NZ, *Hansard,* Ministerial Statements: UN Declaration on the Rights of Indigenous Peoples—Government Support (20 April 2010) 662 NZPD 10229.

84 At 4 ("In moving to support the Declaration, New Zealand both affirms those [human] rights and reaffirms the legal and constitutional frameworks that underpin New Zealand's legal system. Those existing frameworks, while they will continue to evolve in accordance with New Zealand's domestic circumstances, define the bounds of New Zealand's engagement with the aspirational elements of the Declaration").

85 See also Minister Macklin who said when Australia endorsed the Declaration in 2009, "Australia's position in relation to self-determination is that it recognizes the right to participate in public life, self-management and the entitlement of Indigenous peoples to have control over their destiny and to be treated respectfully." See Jenny Macklin, 'Statement on the United Nations Declaration on the Rights of Indigenous Peoples' (speech, Australian Parliament, Canberra, Australia, 3 April 2009) at: <http://www.un.org/esa/socdev/unpfii/documents/Australia_official_statement_endorsement_UNDRIP.pdf>.

86 Andrew Erueti "Conceptualising Indigenous Rights in Aotearoa New Zealand" (2017) 27(3) NZULR 715.

F. Conclusion

Based on the political history of the Declaration's negotiation, it has to be read as being underpinned by two normative forces, anti-colonialism and human rights. And while human rights are essential to Māori, given their social and economic status in New Zealand, what has been overlooked with the Declaration so far is the decolonisation model, its connection with the self-determination framework and the implications of this for reform in New Zealand that gives effect to iwi political authority.

2
The Treaty and Human Rights in New Zealand Law: Can We Add the Declaration and Stir?

Kirsty Gover[*]

A. Introduction

The United Nations Declaration on the Rights of Indigenous Peoples (Declaration)[1] adds to a rather complex set of existing presumptions governing Māori interests in New Zealand law. In the absence of a legislative "Treaty clause", distinctive collective Māori interests may be advanced or protected by New Zealand courts in statutory interpretation by reference to the following: the principle of legality and the set of fundamental common law rights it protects; the "Treaty of Waitangi presumption"; the presumption of consistency with international law; or, finally, through the legislative framework offered by the New Zealand Bill of Rights Act (BORA), (specifically its s 6 direction on statutory interpretation,[2] coupled with

---

[*] Associate Professor, Melbourne Law School. Thanks to participants at the *Symposium on the UN Declaration on the Rights of Indigenous Peoples*, (24–25 July 2014, Te Piringa Faculty of Law, University of Waikato); *Public Law in Three Nations Symposium* (9–10 December 2015, Melbourne Law School) and *175 Years of Interpreting the Treaty of Waitangi – Legal, Historical, and Political Dimensions of Interpreting the Treaty Through Time* (15 February 2016, Victoria University of Wellington Law Faculty). Special thanks to Natalie Baird, Claire Charters, Andrew Erueti, Janet McLean, Paul Rishworth, Hanna Wilberg, Jason Varuhas, Lael Weiss and David Williams for advice on materials and helpful comments on earlier drafts. This chapter draws in part on analysis included in Kirsty Gover "The Treaty and Human Rights in New Zealand Law" in Matthew Groves and Dan Meagher (eds) *The Principle of Legality in Australia and New Zealand* (Federation Press, Sydney, 2017), 209–236.

[1] United Nations Declaration on the Rights of Indigenous Peoples, GA Res 61/295, UN GAOR, 61st sess, 107th plen mtg, Supp No 49, UN Doc A/RES/61/295 (13 September 2007) [Declaration].

[2] New Zealand Bill of Rights Act 1990 [BORA], s 6: "Wherever an enactment can be given a meaning that is consistent with the rights and freedoms contained in this Bill of Rights, that meaning shall be preferred to any other meaning."

its affirmative action[3] and minority rights protections).[4] To date New Zealand judges have tended to consider the common law presumptions together, alongside the BORA, without addressing the possible inconsistencies between them. This feature of New Zealand judicial reasoning may make Māori rights vulnerable, by allowing non-discrimination principles to be deployed in statutory interpretation where the Treaty presumption should arguably be determinative on its own terms. It is not difficult to imagine how the presumptions might yield competing interpretative principles, for example, in a case where a statute conferring a benefit on Māori is challenged by a non-beneficiary as a discriminatory measure violating s 19(1)[5] of the BORA. In Part B, I consider how the presumptions might play out in the context of a BORA challenge. Part C outlines international and domestic responses to disputes involving conflict between indigenous collective rights and principles of non-discrimination. In Part D, I discuss the Treaty presumption and its relation to the other common law presumptions in New Zealand law. In Part E, I address the degree of resonance between the Treaty presumption, the Declaration and rights included in the BORA, and consider the ways that this correlation has been understood in New Zealand courts. I conclude in Part F by offering an example of how the presumptions and the Declaration might come together in a BORA dispute where the status of children adopted by Māori parents is in question.

B. *The BORA and the Common Law Presumptions*

The presumptions discussed in this chapter are principles informing judges in the interpretation of statutes and the development of the common law. This chapter does not traverse the growing body of scholarship dealing with the contours and scope of these presumptions in New Zealand law, but is focused on the intersections between them where Māori interests are at stake. In brief, in common law jurisdictions, the principle of legality refers to the presumption that legislatures do not intend to legislate contrary to fundamental common law rights, so that general or ambiguous words in legislation should be given a reading that does not abrogate those rights. There is no consensus on the content of the

---

3 BORA, s 19(2): "Measures taken in good faith for the purpose of assisting or advancing persons or groups of persons disadvantaged because of discrimination that is unlawful by virtue of Part 2 of the Human Rights Act 1993 do not constitute discrimination."
4 BORA, s 20: "A person who belongs to an ethnic, religious, or linguistic minority in New Zealand shall not be denied the right, in community with other members of that minority, to enjoy the culture, to profess and practice the religion, or to use the language, of that minority."
5 Section 19(1): "Everyone has the right to freedom from discrimination on the grounds of discrimination in the Human Rights Act 1993." See also Human Rights Act 1993, s 20L(2): Race and "ethnic or national origins" are prohibited grounds under the Human Rights Act 1993, s 21(1)(f) and s 21(1)(g) respectively.

"common law bill of rights" protected by the principle of legality, but in most jurisdictions it is accepted that it contains some interests, such as property rights, even where these are not protected as "human rights" in relevant legislative, constitutional or international human rights instruments. The presumption that legislation ought to be interpreted consistently with international law obligations extends in New Zealand to unincorporated treaties, and has been most developed in relation to international human rights treaties, but has also included treaty commitments not relating to human rights protections.[6] In New Zealand, the principle of legality and presumption of consistency with international law cover much of the same ground where human rights are in question, and both presumptions are brought to bear in the implementation of the BORA, which requires judges to give challenged legislation a meaning consistent with the terms of the BORA.[7] The Treaty presumption relates to both the principle of legality and the presumption of consistency with international law, because of the Treaty's unique status as an expression of the fundamental common law rights of Māori (especially their property rights), and of an international agreement, whatever its precise status in international law, an analogy which has been given extra resonance by New Zealand's endorsement of the Declaration in 2010.[8] The Treaty presumption, while in a nascent stage in its development, gives expression to the idea that legislation impacting on certain Māori interests should be given a reading consistent with the Treaty of Waitangi. The fundamental rights and interests of Māori protected by the Treaty presumption are not identical to those protected by the principle of legality, nor do they correspond with New Zealand's international human rights commitments, including non-binding provisions of the Declaration.

Crucially, for the purposes of this chapter, the content of the presumptions and the body of rights they protect are imperfectly aligned. They form something like a Venn diagram, in which, depending on the right asserted and the rights with which it is in "competition" or "company", some rights will be supported and others qualified or read down. Efforts to predict how the presumptions may influence or condition one another when deployed by a judge to interpret legislation

---

6   See for example *Sellers v Maritime Safety Inspector* [1999] 2 NZLR 44, discussed in J S Davison "Freedom of Navigation on the High Seas: Sellers v Maritime Safety Inspector" (1999) 14 Int'l J. Marine & Coastal L. 435. See also Claudia Geiringer "Tavita and All That: Confronting the Confusion Surrounding Unincorporated Treaties and Administrative Law" (2004) 21 NZULR 66. Also, *New Zealand Airline Pilots Association Inc v Attorney-General* [1997] 3 NZLR 269, 289 (CA).

7   BORA, s 6.

8   Ministerial Statements, UN Declaration on the Rights of Indigenous Peoples – Government Support, (20 April 2010) 662 NZPD 19676 <http://www.parliament.nz/en-nz/pb/debates/debates/49HansD_20100420_00000071/ministerial-statements-—-un-declaration-on-the-rights-of>.

impacting on Māori rights requires attention to one very important issue: some of the presumptions contain or protect Māori collective-historic rights alongside principles of non-discrimination, while other presumptions address Māori rights independently of these principles. Consequently, the resonance between the presumptions in any given case may enlarge Māori interests or qualify them, depending on the methodology used to reconcile Māori collective-historic rights with the human rights and interests of non-Māori individuals and the public in statutory interpretation. This reconciliation must occur both "within" and "among" the common law presumptions. The question I broach in this chapter is whether and how the Declaration could affect the way these different sets of rights are characterised and ranked by New Zealand courts.

As will soon be clear, my central concern is that the Declaration, or certain of its provisions, could be used to justify the reading down of Treaty rights and guarantees that might otherwise be brought to bear in an unqualified way on relevant legislation. The Declaration is a compendium of individual and collective rights for indigenous peoples, including rights to self-determination, intellectual property, language and culture, lands and resources, autonomy and self-governance, political participation, consultation and particular rights related to the use of traditional lands (for example in provisions prohibiting forced relocation, or the storage of hazardous materials on indigenous land). It is however, book-ended by measures that admit limitations on Declaration rights in accordance with principles of equality and non-discrimination,[9] and contains some provisions that are internally qualified by references to "international human rights".[10] To foreshorten complex debates about the meaning of the Treaty articles and principles, I will simply note here that the rights of Māori under Article 2 of the Treaty to tino rangatiratanga and property are not expressly qualified by the rights of non-Māori.[11] Article 2 rights stand instead in relation to the Crown's sovereignty or kāwanatanga in Article 1 and the guarantee of equal citizenship rights to Māori in Article 3. The conduct of both parties to the Treaty is to be governed by Treaty principles developed by the courts.[12] While it is clear that the Crown's Treaty obligations to Māori are not "absolute and unqualified",[13] and that the Crown has "other responsibilities as the government

---

9   See the Declaration, arts 1 and 2, and arts 46(2) and 46(3), addressed below.
10 For example, arts 34 and 40.
11 See the authoritative translation of the Treaty of Waitangi by I H Kawharu in appendix to I H Kawharu (ed) *Waitangi: Māori and Pākeha Perspectives of the Treaty of Waitangi* (Oxford University Press, Auckland, 1989) at 319.
12 Including a duty of "reasonable cooperation" (*New Zealand Maori Council v Attorney-General* [1987] 1 NZLR 664, (*Lands*), per Cooke P) and the obligation on each party "to act in good faith, fairly, reasonably, and honourably towards the other" (*Te Runanga o Wharekauri Rekohu Inc v Attorney-General* [1993] 2 NZLR 301, 305 per Cooke P.)
13 *New Zealand Maori Council v Attorney-General (Broadcasting Assets)* [1994] 1 NZLR 513, 517.

of New Zealand", Treaty jurisprudence to date has not suggested that the Crown's obligations to Māori are limited by the rights of other citizens to be free from discrimination.[14] The question posed by the Declaration is whether, given the absence of a BORA reference to the Treaty, in a case involving the right of a non-Māori New Zealander to be free from discrimination, the Declaration could assist to prevent a reading that would undermine or "trump" a Treaty-based interpretation of relevant legislation. Whether in such a case the Declaration, engaged via the presumption of consistency with international law, would bolster the Treaty presumption or give support to non-discrimination principles in the presumptions and BORA remains an open question. The few references to the Declaration so far made in New Zealand jurisprudence seem to me to point in both directions.

Returning to the example flagged earlier, if a BORA discrimination challenge were brought in respect of an ambiguously worded statute directed to the protection of Māori or iwi interests, the methodology used by courts to date suggests the inquiry would be comprised of two stages of statutory interpretation: the first directed to the interpretation of the challenged measure and its impact on BORA rights, and the second directed to interpretation of the measure in accordance with s 6 of the BORA (in order to give it, where possible, a BORA-consistent meaning). In the first stage, the ordinary or natural meaning of the impugned provision would be identified in accordance with ordinary principles and presumptions of purposive statutory interpretation, in order to determine whether it imposed a prima facie limit on the right to freedom from discrimination guaranteed by s 19(1).[15] This process would require in the first instance, an assessment of whether the provision effected differential treatment between groups in "analogous or comparable situations"[16] on the basis of a prohibited ground (which, if found, is likely to be race[17] or "ethnic or national origins"[18]), and whether it imposed a material disadvantage on the group differentiated against.[19] New Zealand jurisprudence suggests that a court would

---

Nor are they insensitive to context. President Cooke has noted that "the Treaty obligations are ongoing. They will evolve from generation to generation as conditions change." *Te Runanga o Muriwhenua Inc v Attorney-General*, [1990] 2 NZLR 641 at 656.

14   *Broadcasting Assets* above n 13 at 517. In the fulfilment of its Treaty obligations the Crown is not required to "go beyond taking such action as is reasonable in the prevailing circumstances". In this case, the Privy Council noted that while "in times of recession" it may be reasonable for the Crown to avoid "becoming involved in heavy expenditure in order to fulfill its obligations although this would not be acceptable at a time when the economy was buoyant."

15   *Child Poverty Action Group Inc v Attorney-General* [2013] NZCA 402 (CPAG) at [40] and [92].

16   *Ministry of Health v Atkinson* [2012] NZCA 184, [2012] 3 NZLR 456 (Atkinson) at [55].

17   Human Rights Act 1993, s 21(1)(f).

18   Human Rights Act 1993, s 21(1)(g).

19   *CPAG* above n 15 at [43], also *Atkinson* above n 16 at [55] and [109].

undertake to read s 19(1) as broadly as possible, consistently with the fact that the text of the section does not qualify the term "discrimination" on its face,[20] and would adopt a "purposive and untechnical approach" to its interpretation.[21] The interpretation of the impugned statute would proceed in accordance with relevant presumptions of statutory interpretation. This would entail a further inquiry into whether fundamental common law rights were affected by the measure in question (rights for example, to non-discrimination,[22] property[23] or minority rights[24]). If so, the statute's "general words" should be given an interpretation that does not abrogate those rights.[25] This could put the Treaty presumption and the principle of legality in competition. The "principle of legality" analysis could yield a balancing or proportionality test of its own (for instance to balance conflict between anti-discrimination rights and minority rights), but the form of such a test has not been addressed in the jurisprudence.[26] Finally the application of the international law presumption would import proportionality measures, by reference to New Zealand's obligations under the International Covenant of Civil and Political Rights (ICCPR)[27] on which the BORA is based (and possibly to the jurisprudence of the UN Human Rights Committee (HRC))[28] and of course, to the Declaration itself.[29]

The central ambiguity at this stage is the role to be played by BORA's s 19(2) (allowing measures that assist or advance groups disadvantaged by discrimination)[30] or s 20 (protecting the rights of minorities)[31] in determining whether the measure imposes a prima facie limit on a s 19(1) right. The method proposed in *Hansen*[32] suggests that if a measure benefitting Māori or iwi was found to be supported by s 19(2), the section could operate as an ex ante defence

---

20 *Atkinson*, above n 16 at [113].
21 *Air New Zealand Ltd v McAlister* [2009] NZSC 78, [2010] 1 NZLR 153 at [51] per Tipping J "McAlister", followed in *CPAG*, above n 15 at [48].
22 Butler and Butler suggest the right to be free from discrimination is part of New Zealand's "common law Bill of Rights": see Andrew Butler and Petra Butler *The New Zealand Bill of Rights Act: A Commentary* (LexisNexis, Wellington, 2005), at [3.3.11-3.3.12].
23 See discussion below.
24 See *Ngati Apa Ki Te Waipounamu Trust v The Queen* [2000] 2 NZLR 659 (CA) at [82] per Elias CJ.
25 See for example the method used in *Cropp v Judicial Committee* [2007] NZCA 423; [2008] NZAR 50, at [27].
26 Hanna Wilberg "Justified Limits on Common Law Rights Protection via the 'Principle of Legality'?" in Matthew Groves and Dan Meagher (eds) *The Principle of Legality in Australia and New Zealand* (Federation Press, Sydney, 2017).
27 *International Covenant on Civil and Political Rights*, opened for signature 16 December 1966, 999 UNTS 171 (entered into force 23 March 1976).
28 *CPAG* above n 15 at [50] noting that these determinations have "persuasive authority".
29 Declaration, above n 1.
30 BORA, s 19(2).
31 BORA, s 20.
32 For example, *R v Hansen* [2007] NZSC 7, [2007] 3 NZLR 1 (Hansen) at [92] per Tipping J.

of the measure, and so avoid a s 5 justification inquiry into whether the limit is "demonstrably justified in a free and democratic society".[33] The measure would not constitute discrimination, even if it differentiated on a prohibited ground and imposed material disadvantage on the group differentiated against. Such an approach, taken in respect of measures benefitting indigenous peoples, would accord with that taken by the Canadian Supreme Court in *R v Kapp*, as discussed below.[34] Questions remain however, about whether the successful invocation of s 19(2) at the outset of the court's inquiry would obviate the need to engage in an initial analysis of whether the measure would otherwise be discriminatory (the approach taken in *R v Kapp*), or whether s 19(2) would function as an ex post exception, allowing discriminatory measures that have the requisite purpose of ameliorating disadvantage (this is closer to the approach taken by the Australian High Court, as discussed below).[35] In either case, the purposive reading of the impugned provision in its legislative context could entail reference to the Treaty presumption to bolster a reading affording a high degree of protection for Māori or iwi interests under s 19(2) or s 20, if the legislation could be shown to have been enacted with intent to ameliorate disadvantage or protect the rights of a Māori minority to "enjoy the culture ... of that minority". As discussed below, however, there is an uneasy relationship between affirmative action measures, minority rights protections and the historic-collective rights of indigenous peoples. Some Māori rights will not easily generate a justification in the terms offered by s 19(2) or s 20. It is important in this context to note also that neither s 19(1), s 19(2) or s 20 has (to my knowledge) been used to advance or protect the collective claims of Māori.[36]

---

33 BORA, s 19(2) and s 5. See *CPAG* above n 15 at [31] fn 31. "Affirmative action measures do not constitute discrimination: Human Rights Act 1993, s 19(2) [sic]." I am grateful to Hanna Wilberg for encouraging me to think more carefully about this point.

34 *R v Kapp* [2008] 2 SCR 483.

35 See *Gerhardy v Brown* (1985) 159 CLR 50 and *Maloney v The Queen* (2013) 252 CLR 168.

36 See Fleur Adcock "Maori and the Bill of Rights Act: A Case of Missed Opportunities?" (2013) 11 NZJPIL 183 at 199. Also, *Amaltal Fishing Co Ltd v Nelson Polytechnic* [1996] NZAR 97 (Complaints Review Tribunal). This remains the case even legislative proposals seem clearly to imply racial discrimination against Māori. For example, the CERD Committee issued a decision under its early warning and urgent action procedure finding that the Foreshore and Seabed Act 2004 appeared to "contain discriminatory aspects against the Maori". Committee on the Elimination of Racial Discrimination, *Decision 1 (66) – New Zealand Foreshore and Seabed Act 2004*, 66th sess, UN Doc CERD/C/DEC/NZL/1 (27 April 2005) at [6]. Likewise, the Attorney-General's advice on the consistency of the Foreshore and Seabed Bill with the BORA accepted that there was "a significant argument for a prima facie breach of section 19", concluding that any limit could nonetheless be justified under s 5. Attorney-General, Foreshore and Seabed Bill, (6 May 2004) at [56], [79] and [103]. Claire Charters discusses the continuing reluctance of New Zealand courts to have reference to human rights principles in cases involving Māori interests, even when the facts would support such a reference. Claire Charters "Maori Rights: Legal or Political?" (2015) 26 PLR 1 at 4.

If not invoked in order to determine whether the provision constitutes a prima facie limit on the right to be free from discrimination under s 19(2) and 20 of BORA, reference to the Treaty could of course find its way into the BORA analysis by way of s 5. Having identified the meaning of the measure by reference to general methods and presumptions of statutory interpretation, and having found that it was "prima facie discriminatory", the court would then assess whether the limit imposed on s 19(1) rights was nonetheless "demonstrably justified", as permitted by s 5 of the BORA. This would entail consideration of whether the purpose of the measure was "sufficiently important" to supply a justification and whether the limiting measure was proportionately connected to furtherance of that purpose.[37] In a challenge to a measure beneficial to Māori, one would expect that a s 5 analysis would include reference to the Crown's obligation to uphold the Treaty partnership, protect Māori Treaty rights or redress past breaches of the Treaty. It may conceivably also refer to the government's obligations under the (non-binding) Declaration.[38] In assessing compliance with s 5 in a case involving protection of Māori interests, a court would accord greater leeway to political decision-making than it would in other circumstances, since the measure is likely to be characterised as one involving a "complex interaction of a range of social, economic, and fiscal policies",[39] "social and economic policy"[40] that implicates "major political, social or economic decisions".[41] The New Zealand courts' traditional deference to the political branches in matters relevant to Treaty settlements might also be a factor in an inquiry of this kind.[42] Much would depend on how the measure is viewed by the government of the day and its legal advisors, and the political interests served (or not served) by seeking to invoke the Treaty to justify a limit on s 19(1).[43]

If, after the s 5 analysis, the right to freedom from discrimination was found to be unjustifiably limited, then by virtue of s 6[44] the court would then be required to prefer an interpretation of the impugned provision that is consistent with the BORA over one that is not.[45] As noted, the BORA s 6 analysis would

---

[37] *Hansen* above n 32 at [104] as deployed in *Atkinson*, above n 16 at [143].
[38] See for example Crown Law Office, Consistency with the New Zealand Bill of Rights Act 1990: Te Ture Whenua Māori Bill (4 April 2016) at [20] <https://www.justice.govt.nz/assets/Documents/Publications/te-ture-whenua-maori-bill.pdf>.
[39] *CPAG* above n 15 at [91].
[40] *Atkinson* above n 16 at [172].
[41] *Hansen* above n 32 at [116] per Tipping J, discussed in *CPAG* above n 15 at [80].
[42] Claire Charters suggests that the Supreme Court's decision in *Haronga v Attorney General* [2012] 2 NZLR 53, is a move away from orthodox deference to Treaty settlements policy, while noting that the case involved the Tribunal's compulsory powers rather than Treaty policy *per se*. Claire Charters, "Maori Rights: Legal or Political?" (2015) 26 PLR 1 at 3.
[43] See for example, Adcock above n 36 at 196.
[44] BORA, s 6.
[45] *Hansen,* above n 32 at [104].

likely be accompanied by an assessment of whether the measure protects the BORA rights of the relevant Māori group under s 19(2) or s 20 or whether it could otherwise be read down so as to render it compliant with the BORA by removing its discriminatory effect. If not, the provision would be characterised as an unjustified limit on a s 19(1) right, and the court could make a declaration of inconsistency.[46] In short, the tensions between non-discrimination, special measures, minority rights and the Treaty are not resolved within the BORA, and the issue has never been squarely raised in a BORA case, a point noted with concern by Paul Rishworth.[47] The field is therefore open for innovation. The common law presumptions are an important vehicle for judicial support of political action in the service of the Treaty relationship and Māori rights, including the international law presumption that could lend support to that relationship by emphasising the intent and purpose of the Declaration. The question would be in any case, whether a Treaty-consistent reading could assist to support a finding that the challenged measure does not differentiate on a prohibited ground; does not impose a material disadvantage on a non-beneficiary; does not constitute a prima facie limitation on a s 19(1) right or, notwithstanding the lack of such findings, in any case constitutes a justified limit on the right in terms of s 5.

In light of all this, it matters a great deal that there is no reference to the Treaty in the BORA. A provision affirming the protection of Māori Treaty rights was, however, proposed in the White Paper that preceded the development of the Act. The proposed text referred to the English and Māori text of the Treaty in the bill's schedule, and provided that:[48]

(a) The rights of the Maori people under the Treaty of Waitangi are hereby recognised and affirmed.
(b) The Treaty of Waitangi shall be regarded as always speaking and shall be applied to circumstances as they arise so that effect may be given to its spirit and true intent.

The inclusion of this provision was opposed by Māori who did not want the Treaty to appear alongside human rights in ordinary unentrenched legislation.[49]

---

46 BORA, s 7.
47 Paul Rishworth "Common Law Rights and Navigation Lights: Judicial Review and the New Zealand Bill of Rights" (2004) 15 PLR 103 at 119.
48 Geoffrey Palmer "A Bill of Rights for New Zealand: A White Paper" [1985] 1 AJHR A6 at 11.
49 K J Keith "The New Zealand Bill of Rights Act 1990 – An Account of its Preparation" (2013) 11 NZJPIL 1 at 12. See also Geoffrey Palmer *New Zealand's Constitution in Crisis: Reforming our Political System* (McIndoe, Dunedin, 1992); and K J Keith "'Concerning Change': The Adoption and Implementation of the New Zealand Bill of Rights Act 1990" (2000) 31 VUWLR 721 at 722–726; P G McHugh "'Treaty Principles': Constitutional Relations Inside a Conservative Jurisprudence" (2008) 39 VUWLR 39 at 67: "Maori lost an important opportunity when their representatives rejected inclusion of a Treaty principles clause in the Bill of Rights Act 1990 (BORA). This would have given those principles a clear application throughout the public

Māori commentators worried that any Treaty provision included in the BORA would be read restrictively by judges, and that via such provisions, Treaty protections or the Treaty itself would be made subject to the Act's s 5 "reasonable limitations" provision.[50] The Declaration does, however, put collective-historic rights alongside individual human rights and principles of non-discrimination. What should be made of this distinction?

The 1980s debates about the Treaty and human rights that preceded the enactment of the BORA made one thing very clear; while the frameworks and approaches offered by the BORA, the principle of legality and the presumption of consistency with international law are ones we share with our common law peer jurisdictions, the Treaty and its principles are entirely a New Zealand creation (one that in fact created New Zealand, the polity and state). As Paul Rishworth has noted, "with Treaty rights we are largely on our own".[51] Lord Cooke of Thorndon put it in even stronger terms in his 1993 comment on the (then draft) Declaration:[52]

> ... the message I want to convey is that we have a precious thing, a truly distinctive thing, in our Treaty of Waitangi and the principles of partnership that have been developed from it. Let us cling to that. No doubt the international Declaration is useful, and some inspiration may be obtained from it, but it is the Treaty that is central to our community and our way of life.

Hence Māori and non-Māori New Zealanders are free to make of the Treaty whatever our shared and evolving concepts of justice and legitimate governance demand. Our inheritance as a liberal democracy is much enriched by the possibilities the Treaty allows. We should be wary, therefore, of subsuming it within (or subordinating it to) human rights methods, including those animating the common law presumptions, the BORA and the Declaration.

C. *The Challenge of Historic-Collective Indigenous Rights: International and Domestic Responses*

The Declaration's Article 46 encompasses both an "interpretative" provision and a "limitations" provision. Art 46(3) provides that the Declaration "shall be interpreted in accordance with the principles of justice, democracy, respect for human rights, equality, non-discrimination, good governance and good faith". Article 46(2) specifies that "[i]n the exercise of the rights enunciated in

---

sector"; Palmer above n 48 at [10.391].
50 Paul Rishworth and others *The New Zealand Bill of Rights Act* (Oxford University Press, Oxford, 2006) at 410.
51 Paul Rishworth "The Treaty of Waitangi and Human Rights" [2003] NZ L Rev 381 at 381.
52 Lord Cooke of Thorndon "A Postscript" in Alison Quentin-Baxter (ed) *Recognising the Rights of Indigenous Peoples* (Institute of Policy Studies, Wellington, 1998) at 199.

the present Declaration, human rights and fundamental freedoms of all shall be respected" and admits that limitations may be imposed on the exercise of the rights contained in the Declaration, but only where those limitations "are determined by law and in accordance with international human rights obligations", and are "non-discriminatory and strictly necessary solely for the purpose of securing due recognition and respect for the rights and freedoms of others and for meeting the just and most compelling requirements of a democratic society." The relationship between Article 46 and the other rights enumerated in the Declaration is a matter of considerable controversy. Karen Engle, for example, worries that the article unreasonably enables states to circumvent their obligations under the Declaration:[53]

> Paragraphs (2) and (3) of Article 46 ... threaten to function in the same way as the repugnancy clause. By subjecting the rights contained in the declaration to the vague standards of "international human rights obligations" and "justice, democracy, respect for human rights, equality, non-discrimination, good governance and good faith", the provisions offer states a way to define certain indigenous claims out of these categories, and to deny them accordingly. In attempting to reconcile human rights and indigenous rights, they also reinforce the tensions between them.

It is important to note that Articles 46(2) and 46(3) of the Declaration were added at the last stages of the Declaration's passage to the UN General Assembly. A brief history will assist to show the significance of this point. The first phase of the drafting of the Declaration (1985–1995) was a mostly inter-indigenous exercise.[54] The completed draft text was handed over in 1995 to an intergovernmental drafting group (the Working Group on the Draft Declaration, WGDD), which was given a ten-year mandate to "elaborate" a Declaration, with continuing indigenous participation, in order to secure a consensus among states on its content.[55] An impasse between states and the WGDD's indigenous caucus, however, quickly emerged. At the end of the WGDD's mandate in 2005, only two articles of the draft Declaration had been provisionally adopted and states had reached a consensus on less than half of the draft articles overall. One extra WGDD session was secured, but states failed again to achieve a consensus. To facilitate the submission of the draft text to the General Assembly, the Chairperson-Rapporteur prepared a "compromise text" for submission to the

---

53 Karen Engle "On Fragile Architecture: The UN Declaration on the Rights of Indigenous Peoples in the Context of Human Rights" (2011) 22 EJIL 141 at 162.
54 *Study of the problem of discrimination against indigenous populations*, ECS Res 1982/34, UNECSOR, 28th Plen Mtg, UN Doc E/RES/1982/34.
55 *Establishment of a working group of the Commission on Human Rights to elaborate a draft declaration in accordance with paragraph 5 of General Assembly resolution 49/214*, ESC 1995/32, UNESCOR, 52nd Plen Sess (1995).

first session of the newly-established UN Human Rights Council (HRC) in 2006, based on proposals he had earlier circulated and on the contributions of states and indigenous representatives in the preceding sessions of the WGDD.[56] The "compromise text" was designed to " ... include the necessary balance for achieving a consensus or, at least, for making it acceptable to the majority."[57] Among the Chair's 2005 changes to the text were the new sub articles 46(2) and 46(3). Sub-Article 46(1), protecting the territorial integrity and political unity of states, was then added in 2007 in order to secure the support of the "African Group" of states ahead of the 2007 General Assembly vote.[58] All of this is to say, that the omnibus "limitations clause" of Article 46 was not proposed by indigenous peoples (although it was arguably accepted by indigenous representatives in the lead up to the 2006 submission of the draft to the Human Rights Council), and was added after intergovernmental discussions had concluded, so that it was not debated in the WGDD along with the other substantive provisions of the Declaration.[59]

The connection between Article 46 and the collective rights protections in the Declaration, then, goes to the very heart of the political theory constituting liberal democratic settler states. The tension between historic-collective indigenous rights and individual human rights is a long-standing and difficult one. Historic indigenous rights are not claims to an equitable share of primary goods on terms equal to those of other individuals, but to particular property and powers, those that were held by the predecessors of indigenous communities and have been or should have been inherited by their descendants. These rights are not necessarily, or as a matter of principle, "capped" by concepts of equality and non-discrimination. They depend for their justification on the existence of indigenous arrangements of power, property and law that preceded the establishment of the settler state, and propose a counterfactual modelling of what a just society might have looked like had those arrangements been inviolable, so that only changes consented to would be legitimate. In other words, what is sought is the distribution of primary goods in accordance with a hypothetically just, consensual agreement between indigenous and settler peoples, and their

---

56 Luis Enrique Chávez "The Declaration on the Rights of Indigenous Peoples, Breaking the Impasse: The Middle Ground" in Claire Charters and Rudolfo Stavenhagen (eds) *Making the Declaration Work: The United Nations Declaration on the Rights of Indigenous Peoples* (IWGIA, Copenhagen, 2009) 96 at 103.

57 At 102.

58 For a more in-depth discussion of this process, see Kirsty Gover "Settler–State Political Theory, 'CANZUS' and the UN Declaration on the Rights of Indigenous Peoples" (2015) 26(2) EJIL 345.

59 As recalled by Luis Alfonso De Alba. See Luis Alfonso De Alba "The Human Rights Council's Adoption of the United Nations Declaration on the Rights of Indigenous Peoples" in Claire Charters and Rudolfo Stavenhagen (eds) *Making the Declaration Work: The United Nations Declaration on the Rights of Indigenous Peoples* (IWGIA, Copenhagen, 2009) 108 at 117.

respective governments. Certain indigenous rights then, have a justificatory base that is premised on the principle of continuity of collective historical rights, rather than on concepts of equality. This makes it difficult to shoe-horn them into prospective liberal human rights frameworks, at least, as I hope to show, without doing damage to some of their most essential attributes.

The task of reconciling these differently-justified rights falls to states and indigenous peoples in all liberal democratic settler societies. Chief Justice Lamer (as he then was) of the Canadian Supreme Court has described this exercise elegantly in the course of considering Aboriginal claims under s 35 of the Canadian Constitution Act[60] (which protects "existing Aboriginal and Treaty rights"):[61]

> In the liberal enlightenment view, reflected in the American Bill of Rights and, more indirectly, in the [Canadian] Charter [of Human Rights and Freedoms], rights are held by all people in society because each person is entitled to dignity and respect. Rights are general and universal; they are the way in which the "inherent dignity" of each individual in society is respected ... Aboriginal rights cannot, however, be defined on the basis of the philosophical precepts of the liberal enlightenment. Although equal in importance and significance to the rights enshrined in the Charter, aboriginal rights must be viewed differently from Charter rights because they are rights held only by aboriginal members of Canadian society. They arise from the fact that aboriginal people are aboriginal.

New Zealand, like Canada and the other settler states, has to grapple with and try to reconcile two forms of liberalism. The first is classical liberalism, which is largely forward-looking, and directed to the maintenance of equality and non-discrimination norms, the rule of law, and the just allocation of resources and primary goods amongst members of the society. The second form of liberalism has a more reparative and constitutive aspect, looking back to the establishment of the state to address the liberal concept of "consent", the idea of the social contract that is thought in some accounts to underpin legitimate governance, and the identity of "the people" in whom popular sovereignty vests. The historic and persistent lack of indigenous consent to settler governance, and to inclusion in the settler body politic, undermines the premises of the settler state's claim to be a liberal democratic polity comprised of a single sovereign people governed by a legitimate government.[62] The restoration of indigenous property and governance authority offers a way for settler states to negotiate indigenous consent, but entails the redistribution of primary goods in a way that

---

60 *Canadian Charter of Human Rights and Freedoms. Canada Act 1982* (UK), s 35.
61 *R v Van der Peet* [1996] 2 SCR 507 at [18]-[19] per Lamer CJ.
62 A similar idea is discussed in Steven Curry, "Indigenous Rights" in Tom Campbell, Jeffrey Goldsworthy and Adrienne Stone (eds) *Protecting Human Rights: Instruments and Institutions* (Oxford University Press, Oxford, 2003) at 307.

can appear, within a human rights framework, to discriminate against non-indigenous individuals and communities, and against persons denied access to those goods. The mechanisms used to further prospective and constitutive liberalism in settler societies may partly conflict, a tension which is evident in efforts to reconcile human rights and indigenous rights in international and domestic fora.

From time to time, then, government efforts to secure indigenous rights, protect indigenous interests or to otherwise differentiate between indigenous and non-indigenous citizens, have been challenged as racially discriminatory measures.[63] Courts have adopted various responses to these challenges, but none entirely escapes or resolves the tension between anti-discrimination norms and historic wrongs (broadly, the exercise of coercive governmental powers over indigenous peoples without their consent or in breach of the terms of any consent given). Depending on the way that the group is identified in the relevant legislation, the starting point in any analysis is to assess the degree of correlation between, on the one hand, indigeneity, membership in an indigenous community or possession of indigenous property rights, and, on the other, the prohibited discriminatory grounds of race, ethnicity, descent and familial status. Approaches taken in Australia, Canada and the United States vary. To summarise the (small) body of comparative law on the correlation between these categories, in Australia distinctions in law between traditional owners and persons who are not traditional owners;[64] holders of native title and other property holders;[65] and Aboriginal and non-Aboriginal persons[66] have been understood as distinctions made on the basis of race. In Canada, distinctions between the members of First Nations and non-members have been found to differentiate on the grounds of race.[67] In the United States, however, differentiation between Indian tribal members and non-Indians is *not* considered to be a distinction based on race.[68] The path to be followed in New Zealand is yet to be determined.

In the New Zealand High Court decision of *Amaltal Fishing Co Ltd v Nelson Polytechnic*, applicants who were ineligible for funded tertiary education placements that were reserved for persons of "Maori or Pacific Island descent" successfully claimed that they had been "refused by reason of, or because of,

---

63 *R v Kapp* above n 34, *Amaltal Fishing Co Ltd v Nelson Polytechnic*, above n 36; *Gerhardy v Brown* above n 35; *Maloney v The Queen* above n 35 and *Morton v Mancari* 417 US 535 (1974).
64 *Gerhardy v Brown* above n 35.
65 *Mabo v Queensland [No. 1]* (1988) 166 CLR 186.
66 *Carr v Boree Aboriginal Corporation* [2003] FMCA 408, [9]. "I am satisfied that the first respondent through its various servants and agents did discriminate against the applicant in her employment and did dismiss her for reasons which were to do with her race or non-Aboriginality."
67 *R v Kapp* above n 34.
68 *Morton v Mancari*, above n 63.

[their] race."[69] However, whether legislation implementing historic Treaty settlements for particular iwi and hapū would be understood to discriminate against non-members or non-beneficiaries depends in the first instance on whether those Māori groups would be characterised in law by reference to their race or ethnicity as Māori collectives, or, whether, in the alternative, the groups would be identified by reference to the distinctive historic wrongs they have experienced, or the distinctive property rights held by the group, its members and its ancestors. Crown legal advice on the BORA implications of Treaty settlement bills has since 2010 included the argument that these do not implicate a prohibited ground of discrimination.[70] However since Treaty settlements benefit descendants of particular ancestors, and this designation is reflected in deeds of settlement and in at least some Treaty settlement statutes, the question engages the complicated relationship between descent criteria and the prohibited grounds of "race",[71] "ethnic or national origins"[72] and "family status" (specifically, being "the relative of a particular person").[73] Either or all prohibited grounds could plausibly be argued, especially in light of the New Zealand Supreme Court's concern that the comparator group or person in BORA cases should not be so narrowly conceived as to "impose too high a threshold" and "artificially rul[e] out discrimination at the first stage of the inquiry."[74] Likewise the existence of other reasons and criteria for the differentiation complained of does not by itself imply that there is no discrimination.[75] The argument that no prohibited ground is implicated is even less likely to succeed where the measure is addressed to "Māori", to the contemporary Treaty claims of "all Māori", or to measures affecting all iwi,[76] especially since in legislative references, Māori

69 *Amaltal Fishing Co Ltd v Nelson Polytechnic*, above n 36 at 35.
70 See for a recent example; Crown Law Office, *Te Awa Tupua (Whanganui River Claims Settlement) Bill: Consistency with the New Zealand Bill of Rights Act 1990* (8 April 2016) at [3]. Identical language is used in Crown Legal advice on at least 21 other Treaty settlement bills. "The Bill does not prima facie limit the right to freedom from discrimination affirmed by s 19 of the Bill of Rights Act through conferring assets or rights on the Whanganui Iwi that are not conferred on other people. Discrimination arises only if there is a difference in treatment on the basis of one of the prohibited grounds of discrimination between those in comparable circumstances. In the context of this settlement, which addresses specified historical claims brought by the Whanganui Iwi, no other persons or groups who are not party to those claims are in comparable circumstances to the recipients of the entitlements under the Bill. No differential treatment for the purposes of s 19 therefore arises by excluding others from the entitlements conferred by the Bill."
71 Human Rights Act 1993, s 21(1)(f).
72 Human Rights Act 1993, s 21(1)(g).
73 Human Rights Act 1993, s 21(1)(l)iv.
74 *CPAG*, above n 15 at [48].
75 *CPAG*, above n 15 at [64] " ... the existence of another criterion which may render the person ineligible for assistance does not of itself mean there may not be discrimination on a prohibited ground."
76 This seems to be the tenor of Crown legal advice on the BORA implications of certain bills

"means a person of the Maori race of New Zealand; and includes a descendant of any such person".[77] It would in any case be open to a court to decide that the measure did not materially disadvantage non-Māori or persons not affiliated to the benefitted iwi. This is the approach taken in Crown legal advice on bills directed to "Māori", and on some Treaty settlement bills, between 2003 and 2012.[78] However, as noted, New Zealand courts have tended to give s 19(1) a wide reading, finding, for example, that a "lack of comparable gain" can constitute material disadvantage.[79] This again suggests that courts are not likely to short-circuit a s 19(1) inquiry in this way unless it is absolutely clear that no prohibited ground is at issue.

What can be said for the time being is that if a measure directed to Māori or iwi is found to be based on a prohibited ground, it must then be asked whether that distinction discriminates against persons who are not the beneficiaries of the measure. In international and comparative law there appear to be two ways to answer this question in the negative, first by showing that the measure is designed to alleviate the disadvantage of members of a particular racial group, and second by showing that the measure is in some other respect a form of "legitimate differentiation". The following section is intended to clarify the ways that the logics of these approaches overlap and diverge in international and domestic jurisprudence as it stands.

In Australia, in the absence of a federal legislative or constitutional bill of rights, if a statute makes a distinction by which "persons of a particular race ... do not enjoy a right that is enjoyed by persons of another race"[80] the only available justification is that the challenged provision is a "special measure" necessary to "secure the adequate advancement" of racial groups disadvantaged

---

    directed to "Māori" or to all iwi, and on provisions of Treaty Settlement bills directed to "Māori" (usually confirming access to cultural sites for "Māori" in addition to the named iwi). See, for example, Crown Law Office *Consistency With the New Zealand Bill Of Rights Act 1990: Maori Fisheries Bill 2003* (10 November 2003) at [8] and [15-18]; Crown Law Office *Consistency with the New Zealand Bill of Rights Act 1990: Te Ture Whenua Māori Bill* (4 April 2016) at [11]; Crown Law Office *Consistency with the New Zealand Bill of Rights Act 1990: Public Works (Prohibition of Compulsory Acquisition of Māori Land) Amendment Bill* (09 February 2016) at [8] and [10]; and Crown Law Office *Te Hiku Claims Settlement Bill – (PCO 15369/6.2) – Consistency with the New Zealand Bill of Rights Act 1990* (11 February 2014) at [5] (substantively similar language appears in advice on at least eight other Treaty Settlement bills).

77 See for example Te Ture Whenua Maori Act 1993, s 2.
78 See for example Crown Law Office *Ngāti Manawa and Ngāti Whare Claims Settlement Bill PCO14148/1.15: Consistency with the New Zealand Bill of Rights Act 1990* (13 September 2010) at [14-17].
79 *CPAG* above n 15 at [72]. This may explain the lack of reference to disadvantage in Crown legal advice on Treaty Settlement bills and other bills affecting Māori interests after 2013.
80 Racial Discrimination Act 1975 (Cth), s 10 "RDA".

in the enjoyment of "human rights and fundamental freedoms".[81] The special measures exemption appears in the federal Racial Discrimination Act (RDA)[82] (cross-referencing the relevant provisions of the International Convention on the Elimination of all forms of Racial Discrimination (ICERD)).[83] It has been used to defend state laws for indigenous communities from challenges brought by non-indigenous applicants,[84] by indigenous non-beneficiaries,[85] and most controversially, by indigenous "beneficiaries" themselves.[86] In Canada substantive equality principles enshrined in s 15(2) of the Canadian Charter of Rights and Freedoms[87] have been used to "save" beneficial laws for indigenous peoples from discrimination-based claims brought by non-indigenous applicants.[88] In New Zealand, in *Amaltal Fishing*, an affirmative-action based defence (HRA s 73)[89] was available to a Polytechnic that was challenged under the Human Rights and Race Relations Acts for limiting enrolment in certain courses to Māori and Pacific Islanders, but the defendant declined to argue the case, so the utility of the defence, and its relation to Treaty rights, remains unclear.[90] To my knowledge, no further jurisprudence engaging the HRA s 73 defence, or the equivalent s 19(2) of the BORA has yet emerged. All of this is to say that in all four CANZUS jurisdictions the liberal concepts of substantive equality, expressed as "special measures" or "affirmative action", can protect some beneficial measures for indigenous peoples, but have been used only occasionally, and never in New Zealand.[91]

81 See *International Convention on the Elimination of All Forms of Racial Discrimination* 660 UNTS 195 (opened for signature 7 March 1966, entered into force 4 January 1969) "ICERD", art 5, as referred to in the RDA, s 10.
82 RDA s 8.
83 ICERD arts 1(4) and 2(2).
84 *Bruch v Commonwealth* [2002] FMCA 29.
85 *Gerhardy v Brown* above n 35.
86 *Bropho v Western Australia* (2008) 169 FCR 59 (FCAFC); *Aurukun Shire Council v Chief Executive Officer of Office of Liquor, Gaming and Racing in the Department of Treasury* (2010) 265 ALR 536 (QCA); *Maloney v The Queen* above n 35.
87 *Canadian Charter of Human Rights and Freedoms. Canada Act 1982* (UK) c 11, sch B pt I, s 15(2): "Subsection (1) does not preclude any law, program or activity that has as its object the amelioration of conditions of disadvantaged individuals or groups including those that are disadvantaged because of race, national or ethnic origin, colour, religion, sex, age or mental or physical disability."
88 *R v Kapp* above n 34.
89 Human Rights Act 1993, s 73 exempting acts or omissions "done or omitted in good faith for the purpose of assisting or advancing persons or groups of persons, being in each case persons against whom discrimination is unlawful . . . " where "those persons or groups need or may reasonably be supposed to need assistance or advancement in order to achieve an equal place with other members of the community."
90 *Amaltal Fishing Co Ltd v Nelson Polytechnic*, above n 36.
91 For a more extensive analysis of the intersection of special measures, specific rights and legitimate differentiation in the Declaration, see Kirsty Gover "Equality and Non-discrimination in the UNDRIP: Articles 2, 6 and 7(1)" in Marc Weller and Jessie Hohmann (eds) *The UN Declaration on the Rights of Indigenous Peoples: A Commentary* (Oxford

The findings of UN human rights treaty bodies offer some insight into the inadequacies of substantive equality measures as vehicles for indigenous claims. As is evident in the jurisprudence and recommendations of the UN Committee on the Elimination of Racial Discrimination (CERD Committee), special measures are carefully circumscribed and narrowly conceived. They must be premised on disadvantage in the enjoyment of human rights and fundamental freedoms (not just any right or interest), and they must "be appropriate to the situation to be remedied, be legitimate, necessary in a democratic society, respect the principles of fairness and proportionality, and be temporary".[92] For this reason, the measures must be brought to an end when substantive equality has been achieved, and "should not lead to the maintenance of separate rights for different racial groups",[93] a requirement that vastly undercuts the utility of special measures as a vehicle for indigenous rights claims. This limitation is one reason why the CERD Committee, in its 2009 General Recommendation 32, drew a distinction between "special measures", and what it calls permanent "specific rights" vested in particular groups. Specific rights include the rights of persons belonging to minorities, the rights of women to "non-identical treatment with men . . . on account of biological differences from men" and the rights of indigenous peoples, "including rights to lands traditionally occupied by them".[94] These rights, the Committee observes, "are permanent rights, recognized as such in human rights instruments, including those adopted in the context of the United Nations and its specialized agencies".[95]

The CERD Committee has not developed a justification for specific rights beyond the brief and rather circular characterisation offered in its General Recommendation. Some further evidence of an underpinning theory is evident, however, in the Committee's 2007 observations on New Zealand's periodic report, in which the Committee discouraged New Zealand from framing its laws and policies on Māori rights under the Treaty of Waitangi as "special measures":[96]

> The Committee is concerned that, in the report of the State party, historical treaty settlements have been categorized as special measures for the adequate development and protection of Maori . . . [and] draws the attention of the State party to the distinction to be drawn between special and temporary measures for the advancement of ethnic groups on the one hand, and permanent rights of indigenous peoples, on the other.

University Press, Oxford, 2017) (forthcoming).
92 Committee on the Elimination of Racial Discrimination *General Recommendation No. 32* CERD/C/GC/32 (2009) at [16].
93 At [26], referring to art 1(4) of ICERD.
94 CERD General Recommendation 32 at [16].
95 CERD General Recommendation 32 at [16].
96 Committee on the Elimination of Racial Discrimination, *Consideration of Reports Submitted by States Parties under Article 9 of the Convention – New Zealand*, 70th sess, UN Doc CERD/C/NZL/CO/17 (15 August 2007), [15].

These comments, made just months before the adoption of the Declaration by the UN General Assembly in 2007, along with the CERD Committee's 2009 General Recommendation 32, show the influence of the Declaration on the development of international human rights law. But what are specific rights, and how could they be deployed in a domestic dispute? Could this concept, or the concept of "legitimate differentiation" to which it is related, provide a methodology for the resolution of a contest between Treaty and non-discrimination rights in New Zealand law?

It is clear that the CERD Committee's concept of "specific rights" bears some resemblance to the more longstanding concept of "legitimate differentiation" developed by the CERD Committee[97] and Human Rights Committee,[98] in which certain forms of differential treatment, while premised on prohibited grounds, are deemed to be non-discriminatory because they are reasonable, objective and directed towards a legitimate aim. As far as I have been able to ascertain, concrete examples of legitimate differentiation in the jurisprudence of the Human Rights Committee and the CERD Committee relate to circumstances where the harm done to the applicant is thought insufficient to trigger an anti-discrimination analysis. None address the interests or rights of indigenous peoples and only one deals directly with racial discrimination (*Sefic v Denmark*: finding that denying Danish car insurance to non-Danish speakers is not discriminatory in terms of the ICERD).[99]

One can imagine how the lack of a prohibited ground, or an approach denying the discriminatory impact of indigenous rights protections on members of an advantaged non-indigenous majority could be used to defend protections of Māori rights if these were subject to a BORA challenge brought by a non-Māori applicant. However, in the 2008 Canadian Supreme Court decision of *R v Kapp*, where a similar scenario was presented on the facts, the court did not take this approach, although such an ex ante defence was available to it. In pivotal Supreme Court cases on s 15 decided prior to *R v Kapp* it has been held that certain forms of differentiation do not constitute discrimination because they do not "create a disadvantage by perpetuating prejudice or stereotyping" the applicant group in a way that impacts on the "human dignity" of its members, an assessment that takes into account, among other matters, a non-exhaustive

---

[97] Committee on the Elimination of Racial Discrimination *General Recommendation 14 – Definition of Racial Discrimination*, 42nd sess, UN Doc A/48/28 (1994), [2]: "... if the criteria for such differentiation, judged against the objectives and purposes of the Convention, are legitimate ...".

[98] Human Rights Committee *General Comment 18 – Non-discrimination* HRI/GEN/1/Rev.1 (1989) at [13]: "... not every differentiation of treatment will constitute discrimination, if the criteria for such differentiation are reasonable and objective and if the aim is to achieve a purpose which is legitimate under the Covenant."

[99] See Committee on the Elimination of Racial Discrimination *Sefic v Denmark* CERD/C/66/D/32/2003 (2005) at [7.2].

set of circumstances including the "pre-existing disadvantage, if any" of the person or group challenging the measure and whether "the law or program has an ameliorative purpose or effect".[100] In *R v Kapp* non-indigenous commercial fishers challenged the issuance of a one-day communal fishing license granted to specified First Nations. While the Court did not hesitate to find that the grant differentiated on the basis of race,[101] the majority was not prepared to engage in a dignity-based test of its discriminatory impact (which would have addressed the claimants' experience, if any, of "historic disadvantage"), preferring instead to emphasise the contribution made by the grant to *substantive* equality, an approach justified by reading s 15(1) and 15(2) together as mutually supportive provisions. According to the Court, if a s 15(2) defence is made out, as it was in this case, the need for a s 15(1) analysis (to decide whether the differentiation is in other respects discriminatory) is obviated altogether.[102]

In this way, rather than operating as an exception to discrimination (as per the Australian High Court's treatment of "special measures" in *Maloney v The Queen*), in *R v Kapp* the s 15(2) substantive equality provision functioned as a threshold test in its own right, limiting the types of differentiation that will be assessed for discriminatory impact, thereby also avoiding the need to rely on any ex post justification provided by the Charter's s 1 (the equivalent of BORA s 5). Could such an approach, whether premised on a broad concept of substantive equality (as per *R v Kapp*), on the "human dignity" and "disadvantage" of the applicant (as per *Law v Canada*) or the "legitimate purpose" of furthering the Crown's Treaty obligations by differentiating between Māori and non-Māori (as per, perhaps, pre-*Maloney* Australian case-law and certain decisions of the CERD Committee and the HRC), assist New Zealand courts to limit those forms of differentiation that fall for analysis under s 19(1) in a way that gives appropriate weight to indigenous historic-collective rights? Such an approach would alleviate the need to rely on a politically-precarious s 5 defence. Paul Rishworth may have had something like this possibility in mind, when he wrote in 2003 that:[103]

> ... there is still a question to explore about the very definition of discrimination (perhaps Treaty-honouring is a legitimate basis for differentiation such that it does not infringe the Bill of Rights at all?).

However, if, as seems likely, at least some measures benefitting Māori or iwi would be found to make a distinction premised on race or ethnicity, the possibility that such measures would then be found to impose no prima facie

---

100 The second factor in the so-called *"Law* test". See *Law v Canada (Minister of Employment and Immigration)* [1999] 1 SCR 497 at [62]-[75].
101 *R v Kapp* above n 34 at [29] and [57].
102 *R v Kapp* above n 34 at [37].
103 Paul Rishworth "Human Rights" (2003) NZ L Rev 261 at 277.

limit on a s 19(1) right is becoming less likely in the face of New Zealand Courts' recent 19(1) jurisprudence. Courts have given the section a very wide reading, effectively characterising most forms of differentiation on prohibited grounds as prima facie discriminatory, and leaving proportionality tests to be actioned through a s 5 inquiry.[104] Whatever the justifications for laws protecting Māori or iwi interests, for the time-being it seems these will have to run the gauntlet of a textually-unqualified and widely-construed s 19(1), or else find purchase in a s 5 justification.

What remains lacking, when indigenous rights are trapped in a human rights framework, be it the BORA or the Declaration, is a compelling theory that explains why certain indigenous rights should be supported by principles other than the inherent-, universal- and equality-based justifications that serve human rights more generally. While international human rights law is groping towards a conceptual framework for indigenous rights, New Zealand's Treaty of Waitangi offers another way out of the impasse. The Treaty is not only foundational, it is constitutive of the state itself. The Treaty expresses a limit on the authority of New Zealand's public government by recording the conditional consent of Māori signatories. In the words of the Privy Council, the Treaty embodies "the obligations which the Crown undertook of protecting and preserving Maori property ... in return for being recognised as the legitimate government of the whole nation by Maori."[105] In my view, constitutive liberalism, supporting protections for Māori collective-historic and Treaty rights as a form of legitimate differentiation, appropriately emphasises the concept of consent that is a cornerstone of liberal political theory.[106]

The Treaty of Waitangi is a palpable and powerful manifestation of New Zealand's "settler social contract", and of the conditions attached to Māori consent to the newly-formed state of Aotearoa New Zealand. It is a pre-condition of the just allocation of rights and resources within and among New Zealand citizens. Efforts to live up to (or at least mitigate failures to live up to) the reciprocity embodied in the Treaty, for instance through the Treaty settlements process and in practices of Crown consultation with Māori, form part of New Zealand's constitutive liberalism. The possibility that classical liberal interpretations of human rights could undermine these reparative and constitutive obligations is a major justification for the omission of Treaty references in the BORA,

---

104 *McAlister*, above n 21 at [51] per Tipping J, following *CPAG* above n 15 at [48]. The New Zealand Supreme Court has, however, mentioned that in BORA discrimination claims "... the choice of the comparator group does provide some inbuilt safeguards against ridiculous claims", noting that "for example, if an able-bodied person complained about the presence of a lift only for disabled persons, the comparator is probably another disabled person rather than the able-bodied person." *Atkinson* above n 16 at [124].

105 *Broadcasting Assets* above n 13.

106 See Steven Curry above n 62.

a sentiment that has found voice again in the recent review of New Zealand's constitutional arrangements. We should carefully consider the consequences of exposing the Treaty relationship, and the Treaty presumption, to the types of anti-discrimination analyses that attend human rights jurisprudence, including where these emanate from the common law presumptions or from the text of the Declaration.

Some scholars with extensive experience of the Declaration drafting process and New Zealand's approach to it (and more general expertise in international and Treaty law) are optimistic about the possible interaction of the Declaration and the Treaty. Matthew Palmer and Matthew Smith, for example, in their chapter in this book, express the view that where international law considerations might be relevant to the interpretation of statutes implicating Māori interests, "courts will turn to the Treaty first",[107] and that the Declaration will likely be deployed to "amplify the Treaty's effect, and fill in the gaps left in its content", because it is "more precisely and specifically worded."[108] Claire Charters has likewise noted that " . . . the Declaration must be read subject to the individual's rights protected in the human rights treaties, which are legally binding, and, again, to the Declaration's art 46(2) limitations provision." In light of this, she says, "[t]he Declaration's focus on collectives simply enables a fairer balancing between indigenous peoples' collective rights and individuals' rights."[109] Palmer, Smith and Charters could very well be right. It is true that Article 37 of the Declaration provides direct support for the Treaty, by specifying that "[i]ndigenous peoples have the right to the recognition, observance and enforcement of Treaties, Agreements and Other Constructive Arrangements concluded with States or their successors and to have States honour and respect such Treaties" and by insisting that "nothing in this Declaration may be interpreted as to diminish or eliminate the rights of Indigenous Peoples contained in Treaties, Agreements and Constructive Arrangements."[110] This provision is not often referenced in debates about the impact of the Declaration in New Zealand, and has not so far appeared in judicial commentary on the scope of Declaration rights. In any case, Article 37 is subject, in some way and form, to the overarching operation of Article 46, allowing "reasonable limits" on Declaration rights in the service of non-discrimination and equality norms. As usual, it really matters which provision is qualified by which. In a sense, then, the connection between Articles 37 and 46 of the Declaration replicates some of the sequencing issues that have animated debates on the interpretation of the BORA (and in Australia, the

---

107 Matthew S R Palmer and Matthew Smith "The Status and Effect in New Zealand Law of the UN Declaration on the Rights of Indigenous Peoples" at 79 in chapter 3 of this book.
108 At 80.
109 Claire Charters "The Rights of Indigenous Peoples" [2006] NZLJ 335.
110 Declaration, above n 1 art 37(2).

Victorian Charter of Human Rights and Responsibilities 2006).[111]

To conclude this section, I note that the current approach of New Zealand courts has been to add common law rights, international law, the Treaty and the BORA to the judicial review mix "to taste", without expressly ranking these influences or being explicit about their impact on outcomes. In the absence of a consensus on the justifications for indigenous historic-collective rights, and given the centrality and symmetry of equality norms in the liberal democracies, indigenous rights are at risk of being considered the most dispensable ingredient in the mix. In the remainder of this chapter I hope to contribute to the conversation by being pessimistic about this possibility.

D. The Treaty Presumption and the Declaration

Here I consider debates about the extent to which the Treaty should be considered in the interpretation of statutes that impact on Māori interests, and the presumption that Parliament intends to legislate consistently with its principles.[112] As a starting point it is worth briefly reviewing the basics. In official discourse the Treaty has been called the Māori Magna Carta,[113] a "major source of the constitution"[114] and "the founding document of the state".[115] It is not, however, enforceable in New Zealand law on its own terms.[116] Instead the Treaty finds its most consistent purchase in New Zealand law in the form of so-called "Treaty clauses" in legislation, requiring decision-makers to have regard to or give effect to the principles of the Treaty of Waitangi when implementing or acting under the relevant statute.[117] The principles of the Treaty, as developed by the Courts, include the following: reasonableness, good faith, the honour of the

---

111 See *Momcilovic v The Queen* (2011) 245 CLR 1.
112 See *New Zealand Maori Council v Attorney-General* above n 12 at 656 per Cooke P. See also *New Zealand Maori Council v Attorney-General* [1989] 2 NZLR 142 (CA).
113 In references dating back to 1841. See David Williams, "The Treaty of Waitangi – The Magna Charta of New Zealand" (paper presented to National Law Librarians Association Conference, Auckland University of Technology, 10–11 September 2015). The analogy also inspired the title of Paul McHugh's very influential book, *The Maori Magna Carta: New Zealand Law and the Treaty of Waitangi* (Oxford University Press, Auckland, 1991). See also Sian Elias "Maori and the New Zealand Legal System" (2002) 76 ALJ 620 at 625: "[The Treaty of Waitangi is] [n]o worthy of veneration or less relevant to New Zealand conditions than *Magna Carta* and the 1689 *Bill of Rights* . . . ".
114 Cabinet Office *Cabinet Manual 2008* at 1. See also at 2, the Treaty is also a "major source of the constitution". See also at [7.60]; Ministers must report on the implications of submitted bills for "(a) the principles of the Treaty of Waitangi; (b) the rights and freedoms contained in the New Zealand Bill of Rights Act 1990 and the Human Rights Act 1993; (c) the principles in the Privacy Act 1993; [and] (d) international obligations . . . ".
115 Robin Cooke "Empowerment and Accountability: The Quest for Administrative Justice" (1992) 18 CLB 1308 at 1328–1329.
116 *Hoani Te Heuheu Tukino v Aotea District Maori Land Board* [1941] AC 308 (PC).
117 See State-Owned Enterprises Act 1986, s 9.

Crown, reasonable cooperation on the part of Māori, and a duty on the Crown to make informed decisions, which will likely include consultation on "truly major issues".[118]

For the purposes of this chapter, I am less interested in these forms of "express reference Treaty review" and much more concerned with what Philip Joseph has called "contextual Treaty review", where there is no express statutory invitation. In his words: "[c]ontextual review arises independently of the statutory language and is avowedly 'constitutional'".[119] In the very small body of jurisprudence where this form of review has occurred, the pivotal case remains the 1987 High Court decision *Huakina Development Trust v Waikato Valley Authority*, in which Justice Chilwell famously stated:[120]

> There can be no doubt that the Treaty is part of the fabric of New Zealand society. It follows that it is part of the context in which legislation which impinges upon its principles is to be interpreted when it is proper, in accordance with the principles of statutory interpretation, to have resort to extrinsic material.

This approach was given further weight a decade later by the second landmark case on contextual Treaty review; the High Court's 1997 decision in *Barton-Prescott v Director-General of Social Welfare*:[121]

> ... since the Treaty of Waitangi was designed to have general application, that general application must colour all matters to which it has relevance ... and for the purposes of interpretation of statutes, it will have a direct bearing whether or not there is a reference to the Treaty in the statute. We also take the view that the familial organisation of one of the peoples party to the Treaty, must be seen as one of the taonga, the preservation of which is contemplated. Accordingly we take the view that all Acts dealing with the status, future and control of children, are to be interpreted as coloured by the principles of the Treaty of Waitangi.

I include this quote in full because I will return later in this chapter to the importance of kinship in Māori political organisation, its status as a taonga in the terms of the Treaty, and its potential conflict with anti-discrimination principles. I conclude here however by noting that there are also traces of the *Huakina* and *Barton-Prescott* approach in the major express reference cases of the 1980s, and many examples of Judges endorsing this approach in their extra-curial writing, including in pieces by Sir Robin Cooke,[122] Dame Sian Elias,[123] and Sir Edmund Thomas.[124]

---

118 *New Zealand Maori Council v Attorney-General* [1989] 2 NZLR 142 at 152.
119 Philip A Joseph "Constitutional Review Now" [1998] NZ L Rev 85 at 93.
120 *Huakina Development Trust v Waikato Valley Authority* [1987] 2 NZLR 188 (HC).
121 *Barton-Prescott v Director-General of Social Welfare* [1997] 3 NZLR 179 (HC) at 184.
122 Sir Robin Cooke "Empowerment and Accountability" above n 115, 1328–1329.
123 Sian Elias "Maori and the New Zealand Legal System" (2002) 76 ALJ 620 at 626.
124 E W Thomas "The Treaty of Waitangi" [2009] NZLJ 277.

New Zealand public law scholars have anticipated the evolution of the Treaty presumption into one that is similar in scope and effect to the principle of legality. Geoffrey Palmer and Matthew Palmer have commented in their 2004 book *Bridled Power* that:[125]

> We even consider that it is increasingly likely that a future New Zealand Court with follow the lead of the House of Lords in the United Kingdom and suggest that the Treaty of Waitangi is such a fundamental document that legislation will not be taken to override it unless such an intention is very explicitly stated.

The small group of New Zealand scholars addressing the Treaty presumption have tended to suggest that it should evolve in line with either the international law presumption, or the principle of legality, usually with an eye on the particular strength and scope in New Zealand of the standard of review in the presumption of consistency with international law,[126] which as it stands, provides that the presumption applies even in the absence of legislative ambiguity.[127] Others have simply embraced the apparent New Zealand confluence of the presumption and the principle[128] and have argued that Treaty review should take the form of either or both of them.[129] They have not, I think, done so with a focus on the content of the bodies of law captured by each of the three presumptions. The right to the equal protection of property rights, for example, did not find its way into the BORA (and efforts to secure an amendment to this effect have not to date been successful),[130] nor into any of the major international human rights instruments

---

125 Geoffrey Palmer and Matthew Palmer *Bridled Power: New Zealand's Constitution and Government* (4th ed, Oxford University Press, Oxford, 2004) at 337, fn 13.
126 See for example Hanna Wilberg "Facing Up to the Original Breach of the Treaty" (2007) NZ L Rev 527 at 549. See also *New Zealand Airline Pilots' Association Inc v Attorney-General* [1997] 3 NZLR 269 at 289, affirming the "presumption of statutory interpretation that so far as its wording allows legislation should be read in a way which is consistent with New Zealand's international obligations".
127 Claudia Geiringer "Tavita and All That: Confronting the Confusion Surrounding Unincorporated Treaties and Administrative Law" (2004) 21 NZULR 66. *Huang v Minister of Immigration* [2009] 2 NZLR 700 (CA); *Takamore v Clarke* [2011] NZCA 587, [2012] 1 NZLR 573; *New Zealand Airline Pilots' Association Inc v Attorney-General* above n 126. See Claudia Geiringer "The Principle of Legality and the Bill of Rights Act: A Critical Examination of *R v Hansen*" (2008) 6 NZJPIL 59 at 77.
128 See Claudia Geiringer "International Law through the Lens of Zaoui: Where is New Zealand at?" (2006) 17 PLR 300 at 317.
129 Jack Oliver-Hood "Ko Ngā Take Ture Māori: Our Significantly Indigenous Administrative Law: The Treaty of Waitangi and Judicial Review" (2013) 19 Auckland U L Rev 53 at 56–57: "Such review, it is suggested, should occur though judicial recognition of a principle of statutory interpretation akin to the principle of legality for human rights and the presumption of consistency for international law."
130 New Zealand Bill of Rights (Private Property Rights) Amendment Bill 2007 (255), discussed in Butler and Butler, above n 22. See also Adcock, above n 36 at 190: "Noticeably absent from debate on inclusion of a property right is robust discussion of the potential benefits for Maori."

enacted after the Universal Declaration of Human Rights,[131] but it is nonetheless considered a fundamental common law right that takes its place alongside those protected by the principle of legality. Its import for indigenous peoples cannot be underestimated. It is this principle that is the basis of the rule that aboriginal title will not be extinguished by executive or legislative action in the absence of evidence of a "clear and plain intention to do so".[132] This was expressly acknowledged in New Zealand as part of the Court of Appeal's reasoning in the famous foreshore and seabed case, *Attorney-General v Ngati Apa* (2003).[133] It should surprise no-one if the rights protected by the Treaty presumption (which include those now recognised as common law aboriginal title rights)[134] extended beyond those currently expressed in our legislation or in the international human rights treaties to which we are a party.

Crucially, then, at least some of the rights and interests protected by the Treaty of Waitangi and its principles are not reflected in standard conceptions of human rights at international law or in the BORA and so far as it is possible to say, they would likely not fall within the "common law bill of rights" protected by the principle of legality.[135] As noted in New Zealand the international law presumption and the principle of legality tend to be read together as mutually supportive principles in cases where human rights are in issue. Both presumptions encompass rights that are not strictly human rights, and so extend beyond the corpus of rights enumerated in the BORA, meaning that both could conceivably provide a basis for considering indigenous and Māori rights where these are implicated in statutory interpretation, even if the BORA does not provide support

---

131 Universal Declaration of Human Rights GA Res 217A (1948), art 17. But see American Convention on Human Rights, 1144 UNTS 123, (opened for signature 22 November 1969, entered into force 18 July 1978) art 21.

132 *Mabo v Queensland* (1988) 166 CLR 186 at 198 per Brennan, Toohey and Gaudron JJ. See also *Mabo v Queensland [No 2]* (1992) 175 CLR 1 at 64 per Brennan J, citing *Te Weehi v Regional Fisheries Officer* [1986] 1 NZLR 680: "It is unnecessary for our purposes to consider the several juristic foundations – proclamation, policy, treaty or occupation – on which native title has been rested in Canada and the United States but reference to the leading cases in each jurisdiction reveals that, whatever the juristic foundation assigned by those courts might be, native title is not extinguished unless there be a clear and plain intention to do so. That approach has been followed in New Zealand. It is patently the right rule." See also *Hamlet of Baker Lake v Minister of Indian Affairs and Northern Development* (1979) 107 DLR (3d) 513 (FCC).

133 *Attorney-General v Ngati Apa* [2003] 3 NZLR 643 at 684. See also *Te Weehi v Regional Fisheries Officer*, above n 132 at 692: "If Parliament's intention is to extinguish such customary or traditional rights it will no doubt do so in clear terms following its exploration of claims by Maori Tribes to specific customary rights."

134 *R v Symonds* [1847] NZPCC 387, at 390 "... in solemnly guaranteeing the Native title, and in securing what is called the Queen's pre-emptive right, the Treaty of Waitangi ... does not assert either in doctrine or in practice anything new and unsettled."

135 See Claudia Geiringer "The Principle of Legality and the Bill of Rights Act" above n 127 at 83. See also Paul Rishworth "Common Law Rights and Navigation Lights" above n 47 at 106.

for those rights (that is, where s 19(2) and s 20 are not applicable). As Claire Charters has pointed out, for the time-being, "[w]hile there is jurisprudence that legislation should be interpreted consistently with the Treaty, there does not appear to be room for Treaty analysis within the prevailing legal tests for discrimination [under the BORA]."[136] If there is, as Claudia Geiringer[137] and Hannah Wilberg[138] have observed in the New Zealand context, a convergence of the presumption of consistency with international law on the one hand and the principle of legality on the other, and this convergence finds expression in the interpretative method deployed under the auspices of the BORA, there are very good reasons to resist a similar confluence that would absorb the Treaty presumption into one or both of the others. I turn now to consider the use that may be made by Māori of the BORA.

E. *The Treaty vs BORA: Back into the Fray with the Declaration?*

In a case involving a BORA discrimination challenge like the one mentioned earlier, would the Treaty come to the rescue to deflect the challenge via the common law, independently of its use in a s 5 "reasonable limitation" defence? As I noted, there seem to be four possibilities. First, the Treaty may enter the equation to neutralise the s 19(1) claim at the outset by tagging the measure as one that does not differentiate on the basis of a prohibited ground because it does not characterise Māori or iwi as racial, ethnic or family groups. Second, it could support a finding that the measure does not impose material disadvantage on persons differentiated against, or is in some other respect a form of "legitimate differentiation" that by definition does not limit s 19(1). Third, the Treaty presumption might support the characterisation of the measure as one falling within the auspices of s 19(2), because it has as its purpose the object of "assisting or advancing" Māori or iwi as "groups of persons disadvantaged because of discrimination", in which case the measure would be deemed to be non-discriminatory.[139] Finally, the presumption may assist a finding that the measure protects the rights of Māori or iwi as an "ethnic minority", entitled by virtue of BORA s 20 to enjoy "the culture ... of that minority".

The s 20 avenue has never been used by Māori to support their claims or protect their interests, although in some recent cases, judges have made passing reference to the provision in matters related to tikanga Māori and cases

---

136 Claire Charters "BORA and Maori: The Fundamental issues" [2003] NZLJ 459 at 459.
137 Geiringer, above n 127 at 85: "More generally it might be said that the strength, if there is one, of the New Zealand approach to value-oriented interpretation is that it conceives of the Bill of Rights Act as inseparable from the rich, textured and multifaceted context provided by the common law and by international law."
138 Hanna Wilberg "Facing Up to the Original Breach of the Treaty" above n 126 at 549.
139 See *CPAG* above n 15 at [31] fn 31. See also *R v Kapp* above n 34.

involving legislative Treaty clauses. The lack of reference by Māori groups to s 20 is particularly striking.[140] Writing in 2003, Paul Rishworth noted that the "impact of s 20 in litigation to date has been minimal" and while the section had been mentioned in several cases, "there was no case in which [it] proved decisive."[141] He noted also that s 20 "had not featured in the reasoning [of cases dealing with the Treaty clause in the State-Owned Enterprises Act] possibly because the Treaty principles are seen as broader and more productive, or because they simply replicate the kind of arguments that s 20 would permit."[142] If it were used to advance a Māori claim, the interpretation of s 20 would likely be informed by the Human Rights Committee's recommendations on Article 27 of the ICCPR, the provision from which its wording is derived. Significantly, the rights protected by Article 27[143] are individual rights, albeit collectively exercised, held by "persons belonging to a minority". They are not rights held by a collective and therefore not "corporate" in the sense that indigenous rights to self-determination, communal property and self-governance are (as these are expressed in the Treaty and the Declaration). The distinction is not clear-cut, however, because as the Human Rights Committee acknowledges, protections for minority members may require protections for minority groups qua groups.[144] This seems to support Māori collective rights, but crucially, according to the Committee, measures necessary to protect Article 27 rights must be consistent with the Covenant's general prohibitions on discrimination, "both as regards the treatment between different minorities and the treatment between the persons belonging to them and the remaining part of the population."[145] Any protections extended to an indigenous minority in furtherance of the rights of its members must not be discriminatory vis-à-vis other (indigenous or non-indigenous) minorities, or indeed, vis-à-vis the majority.[146] Thus s 20 of the BORA may take us back to the place where we began; trying to devise a methodology for the resolution of a conflict between indigenous collective rights and the right to be free from discrimination. In other words, a s 20 right seems likely to be made subject to s 19(1), rather than the other way around.

Some indications of a way forward, however, are evident in the ways the Declaration was discussed by the Court of Appeal and the Supreme Court in the *Takamore v Clarke* decisions, addressing the responsiveness of common

---

140 Butler and Butler above n 22 refer to it as "surprising" at [17.22.1].
141 Paul Rishworth "The Treaty of Waitangi and Human Rights" above n 51 at 402.
142 At 402.
143 *Declaration on the Rights of Persons Belonging to National or Ethnic, Religious and Linguistic Minorities* GA Res 47/135, A/RES/47/135 (1992).
144 Human Rights Committee, *General Comment 23*, 50th sess, UN Doc CCPR/C/21/Rev.1/Add.5 (1989), [6.2].
145 At [6.2].
146 At [6.2].

law to tikanga Māori.¹⁴⁷ In these cases, the Declaration, the Treaty, and the BORA were all considered relevant considerations for the development of New Zealand common law. In the Supreme Court, Chief Justice Elias referred to the Declaration as support for the rights of minorities protected by s 20 of the BORA.¹⁴⁸ Her Honour has also previously (and somewhat tantalisingly) identified s 20 as reflective of a fundamental right protected by the principle of legality,¹⁴⁹ showing, as Claudia Geiringer has pointed out, a striking willingness on the part of New Zealand judges to update the content of the common law bill of rights to accommodate legislative expressions of human rights.¹⁵⁰ Some red flags, however, were raised for me by the Court of Appeal's characterisation (in apparent expression of the presumption in favour of an interpretation consistent with international law obligations) of the relevant provisions of the Declaration. I discuss these in the section that follows.

In brief, *Takamore* arose from competing claims to the authority to determine the burial arrangements of a deceased Māori man, James Takamore. Takamore's Māori family wanted to have him buried in his family's urupā in accordance with tikanga, while his widow sought to enforce her role as executrix to have him buried in Christchurch, where they had lived together for many years. The case was centrally concerned with the extent to which tikanga could and should be accommodated within New Zealand common law to support the claims of Takamore's whānau. All three judges in the Court of Appeal observed that:¹⁵¹

---

147 *Takamore v Clarke* [2011] above n 127; *Takamore v Clarke* [2012] NZSC 116, [2013] 2 NZLR 733.

148 *Takamore v Clarke* [2012] above n 147 at [12] per Elias CJ: "Cultural identification is an aspect of human dignity and always an important consideration where it is raised, as are the preferences and practices which come with such identification, as s 20 of the New Zealand Bill of Rights Act 1990 affirms. In the case of indigenous people, the preference for repatriation of the dead is recognised by the Declaration of the Rights of Indigenous Peoples as a matter of great moment."

149 See *Ngati Apa Ki Te Waipounamu Trust v The Queen*, above n 24 at [82] per Elias CJ: "The question for decision therefore affects Ngati Apa's rights to natural justice, recognised by s27 of the [BORA] and affects the enjoyment of Ngati Apa's cultural rights, recognised by s20 of the [BORA]. Such basic rights cannot be overridden by general or ambiguous words in a statute ... This principle of legality, recognised by the common law, has been expressly enacted by s 6 of the [BORA] 1990."

150 Geiringer, above n 127, at 85. See also *Ngati Apa Ki Te Waipounamu Trust v The Queen*, above n 24 at [82] per Elias CJ.

151 *Takamore v Clarke* [2011] above n 127 at 309 per Chambers J. See also at [250] and fn 259 per Glazebrook and Wild JJ. The judges did not mention the internal qualification of art 34, which provides that "Indigenous peoples have the right to promote, develop and maintain their institutional structures and their distinctive customs, spirituality, traditions, procedures, practices and, in the cases where they exist, juridical systems or customs, *in accordance with international human rights standards*" (emphasis added).

It is noteworthy that the United Nations Declaration on the Rights of Indigenous Peoples, to which New Zealand has subscribed, while recognising the rights of indigenous peoples to develop and maintain "juridical systems or customs" in art 34, also states in art 46(2) that nothing in the exercise of the rights under the Declaration undermines "fundamental freedoms".

On one hand, it is a victory for Māori and indigenous rights advocates to have the Declaration deemed relevant to Māori claims in a New Zealand court. On the other hand, the interpretation given to the Declaration provisions appears to limit those rights in a way that arguably would not be supported by the Treaty itself. The Judges noted, in fact, "the need to develop the common law, so far as is reasonably possible, consistently with the Treaty of Waitangi".[152] This leads me to wonder whether, if the Treaty alone had been brought to bear on the dispute, there would have been a reference to limitations on what is essentially, a claim to the exercise of tino rangatiratanga in a matter of tikanga? In other words, could recourse to the Declaration, via the international law presumption, lead to the reading down of Māori Treaty rights?

A second recent case illustrates the application of the Declaration where there was a legislative direction to decision-makers to consider the principles of the Treaty; a situation where statutory interpretation was directly in issue, rather than (as was the case in *Takamore*), the development of the common law in the absence of legislative direction. In *New Zealand Māori Council v Attorney-General*[153] the Supreme Court noted in passing the resonance between the Declaration's provisions on land and resource rights, and the meaning of the State Owned Enterprises Act's Treaty clause, which provides that "[n]othing in this Act shall permit the Crown to act in a manner that is inconsistent with the principles of the Treaty of Waitangi."[154] The Court in that case did not refer to any qualification on Declaration rights, instead, they said:[155]

> We do not find it necessary to consider the Declaration further. We doubt if the Declaration adds significantly to the principles of the Treaty statutorily recognised under the State-Owned Enterprises Act and Part 5A of the Public Finance Act. We accept, however, that the Declaration provides some support for the view that those principles should be construed broadly. In particular, it supports the claim for commercial redress as part of the right to development there recognised.

---

152 At [16] and [254] per Glazebrook and Wild JJ. See also at [249]: "It requires no leap of faith therefore to suggest that in general the common law of New Zealand should as far as is reasonably possible be applied and developed consistently with the Treaty of Waitangi."
153 *New Zealand Māori Council v Attorney-General* [2013] NZSC 6, [2013] 3 NZLR 31. See also Waitangi Tribunal *Whaia Te Mana Motuhake* (Wai 2417, 2015) at [2.5.4](2).
154 *New Zealand Māori Council v Attorney-General* [2013] above n 153 at [34]; State-Owned Enterprises Act 1986, s 9.
155 *New Zealand Māori Council v Attorney- General* [2013] above n 153 at [92].

To date, then, we have some nascent treatment of the Declaration in New Zealand jurisprudence, using its provisions to bolster Māori interests in the recognition of tikanga and the protection of Māori rights to natural resources. The former includes reference to the Article 46 qualification on the scope of the relevant Declaration rights but the latter seemingly does not.

As noted above, the issue of balancing, proportionality and qualification would be presented in its most acute form if a statutorily recognised Māori interest was thought to have a discriminatory impact on non-Māori. If a comparable issue were to arise again, could reliance on the principle of legality, the presumption of consistency with international law, the Treaty presumption, and the Declaration provide a characterisation of Māori historic-collective and Treaty rights that does not subordinate them at the outset to the rights of others?

F. The Conclusion by Way of an Example

As will now be clear, the relationship between the Treaty of Waitangi and the principle of non-discrimination, established in New Zealand's common law and affirmed in s 19(1) of the BORA, is a complicated one. In one sense, however, it is the single most distinctive and defining question of New Zealand statehood and political theory. I have suggested that the best way to proceed is to give full effect to the Treaty obligations undertaken by the Crown, rather than by confining them to measures that do not infringe the rights of non-Māori to be free from discrimination. To conclude this chapter, then, I offer an example drawn from a set of issues I have written about previously.[156]

Treaty settlements are negotiated by Crown officials and Māori claimants, recorded in Deeds of Settlement, and then implemented in Treaty settlement legislation. Settlement statutes define the beneficiaries of the settlement as the "descendants" of an eponymous ancestor or ancestors. Some Treaty settlement statutes contain an express reference to legally adopted children as descendants of relevant ancestors (and therefore settlement beneficiaries) and some do not. There remains a question then, about whether the "descendant" category includes legal adoptees where they are not otherwise expressly included. The Crown has insisted that the adopted children of settlement beneficiaries are also beneficiaries by descent, following the Adoption Act 1955, which deems adopted children to be "for all purposes" the child of their adoptive parents (with certain exceptions).[157] In internal legal advice and correspondence with iwi and hapū, the Crown has suggested that if a tribe refuses to include a legal adoptee

---

156 Kirsty Gover "The Politics of Descent: Adoption, Discrimination and Legal Pluralism in the Treaty Claims Settlements Process" [2011] NZ L Rev 261.
157 Adoption Act 1955, s 16. For further discussion see Kirsty Gover "The Politics of Descent", above n 156.

as a beneficiary, this could be challenged as a breach of the non-discrimination provisions of the BORA and the HRA.[158] This is significant, because Māori concepts of kinship, or whakapapa, are primarily based on biological genealogical descent. Some tribes have vehemently asserted that they do not admit all legally-adopted children as beneficiaries, because their tikanga confines membership to biological descendants and to whāngai (persons adopted into the whakapapa system in accordance with that tribe's tikanga). The public statements of Ngāi Tahu are illustrative:[159]

> Adopted persons are ... not eligible to enrol as Ngāi Tahu beneficiaries unless they are of Ngāi Tahu descent.

Comparable issues have arisen in recent efforts to amend the Te Ture Whenua Māori Act 1993 (the Māori Land Act), where the amending bill (under consideration by the Māori Affairs Select Committee at the time of writing) empowers the relevant iwi or hapū to decide, in accordance with tikanga, whether or not adopted children are to be admitted to the class of descendants entitled to inherit interests in Māori land.[160] Crown legal advice on the BORA implications of the bill includes the observation that "[the relevant provision] distinguishes lineal descendants (persons of direct genealogical descent) from non-lineal descendants (whāngai or adopted persons). This constitutes a distinction based on family status."[161] The material disadvantage experienced by adopted persons relative to biological descendants meant, in the view of Crown legal counsel, that the provision would limit the s 19(1) rights of those persons. They were further of the view that the limit nonetheless could be justified under s 5 as serving an important objective, consistently with the Treaty and with the Declaration, that was rationally connected to the objective of protecting and enabling tikanga Māori, and imposed a limit that was reasonably necessary for the achievement of that objective, given its importance in the context of the Crown's Treaty obligations.[162]

---

158 Memorandum from Crown Law Office to Ministry of Justice "Treaty Settlements, Succession to Māori land, and adoption" (undated) at [32] (obtained under Official Information Act 1982 request to the Ministry of Justice), and Brief from Office of Treaty Settlements to Minister in Charge of Treaty of Waitangi Negotiations "Consistency of proposed Adoption Act 1955 provisions of Māori Fisheries Bill with Treaty settlements" (19 July 2004) 2004/2005-17 TWP-02-15-07 at [7]-[12] (obtained under Official Information Act 1982 request to the Office of Treaty Settlements).

159 "Registration Information" (1996) Te Rūnanga o Ngāi Tahu – Whakapapa <http://ngaitahu.Iwi.nz/ngai-tahu/whakapapa/registration-information/>.

160 Cl 8(2) Te Ture Whenua Māori Bill: Government Bill 126-1 (introduced 14 April 2016) <http://www/legislation.govt.nz/bill/government/2016/0126/latest/versions.aspx>.

161 Crown Law Office, Consistency with the New Zealand Bill of Rights Act 1990: Te Ture Whenua Māori Bill (4 April 2016) at [20] <https://www.justice.govt.nz/assets/Documents/Publications/te-ture-whenua-maori-bill.pdf>.

162 Crown Law Office, Consistency with the New Zealand Bill of Rights Act 1990: Te Ture Whenua Māori Bill (4 April 2016), [23-31] <https://www.justice.govt.nz/assets/Documents/

A claim arguing that a Treaty settlement statute, or a decision made by an iwi rūnanga empowered by that statute, discriminates against the legally adopted children of beneficiaries on the basis of familial status, might result in a reading of the Act that includes legal adoptees in the class of "descendants" where they are not expressly included in the definition, even if they are not descendants in accordance with tikanga. Reading the statute in this way, on the basis that Parliament could not have intended to exclude legal adoptees from the category of descendants deemed to be beneficiaries, would result in an interpretation that intrudes on Māori law, as well as, depending on the terms of the Deed of Settlement, on the deal struck by the Crown and Māori claimants in Treaty settlement negotiations. Settlement legislation typically requires an interpretation "that best furthers the agreements expressed in the deed of settlement".[163] To my way of thinking, in keeping with recent BORA jurisprudence, a court taking this approach would take a wide reading of s 19(1), and defer consideration of competing claims to the s 5 "demonstrable justification" test (unless s 19(2) or s 20 are called on to render the measure non-discriminatory at the outset). A justification offered under s 5 test would be expected to refer to the obligations of the Crown under the Treaty including the obligation to take "active and positive steps to redress past breaches",[164] the legitimate goal of protecting and enabling tikanga in the preservation, management and inheritance of Māori land and taonga and the necessity of supporting tribal economic self-sufficiency and tino rangatiratanga. Applying a Treaty presumption to the Treaty settlement statute ahead of the s 5 justification however, would favour a reading protective of whakapapa or "family structure" as a taonga, following *Barton-Prescott*. Finally, adding the Declaration to the mix could support whakapapa as tikanga, as in the Court of Appeal's judgment in *Takamore*. This may, however, at least in the case of matters involving customary law, lead a court to limit the Treaty right indirectly, by qualifying the relevant provision of the Declaration, probably by reference to Art 46(2), just as the Court of Appeal did in *Takamore*. In this scenario, the Declaration would weaken the already limited protection offered by the Treaty presumption.

Some indication that New Zealand judges understand the import of maintaining whakapapa ties notwithstanding the legal effect of adoption in public law (of a non-Māori child by Māori parents, or of a Māori child by non-Māori parents) is evident in obiter comments made by Young J in the 2005 High Court

Publications/te-ture-whenua-maori-bill.pdf>.
163 See, for example, Ngāi Tahu Claims Settlement Act 1998, s 7. "It is the intention of Parliament that the provisions of this Act are interpreted in a manner that best furthers the agreements expressed in the deed of settlement." For identical wording, see for example the Ngaa Rauru Kiitahi Claims Settlement Act 2005, s 11; and the Tūhoe Claims Settlement Act 2014, s 11.
164 *New Zealand Maori Council v Attorney-General* [1992] 2 NZLR 576. Also *Lands*, above n 12 at 664, 674, 693, 702, and 716–718.

case of *Hemmes v Young*.[165] Young J was of the view that there are circumstances where "a blood relationship may continue to have legal significance despite an adoption order" and went on to say that:[166]

> ... blood relationships may be relevant to membership of descent-based Maori groups (i.e. Iwi or hapu). It must be open for such groups, if they choose, to grant and withhold membership and associated benefits based on actual blood relationships rather than legal fictions.

More recently, outside of the Treaty settlements process and in a matter not implicating the BORA, in 2013 Judge Isaac of the Māori Land Court relied on tikanga to give the word "descendant" a meaning consistent with whakapapa when interpreting regulations governing access to Māori land and the exercise of harvesting rights on the Tītī Islands. Emphasising that the views expressed in the judgment were "not a ruling or an opinion", the Judge noted that:[167]

> [w]hile Māori embraced customary adoption my reading suggests that the child adopted was invariably of the bloodline and that were [sic] an outsider was involved the adoption was either not recognised as a customary adoption or did not confer on the adopted child rights to land.

Accordingly, the word "descendant" in the relevant regulations was a provision that limited the otherwise comprehensive effect of an adoption order, because it was in the terms of 16(2) of the Adoption Act 1955 "[an] enactment which distinguishes in any way between adopted children and children other than adopted children".[168] In the view of the Judge:[169]

> The use of the word descendant which has a particular legal meaning requiring a person to be of the bloodline creates a distinction between a natural child any [sic] adopted child who is from outside of the bloodline. I therefore take the view that s 16(2)(a) does not enable an adopted person from outside the bloodline to qualify as a descendant in the terms of the Titi (Muttonbird) Islands Regulations 1978.

This further highlights the potential conflict between Treaty-based measures designed to accommodate and protect tikanga and taonga, and the non-discrimination principles animating the BORA.

As I have written elsewhere, where the relevant provision forms part of Treaty settlement legislation, I think the solution to this conflict is better progressed as an extension of the original Treaty settlement negotiations, with the aim of concluding an agreement between the Crown and tribes to the effect that legal adoptees will be afforded, in tikanga, the status of beneficiaries and members, even

---

165 *Hemmes v Young* [2005] 2 NZLR 755 (CA).
166 At [136] and [138]; see also [55] per Hammond J.
167 *Re Coote* [2013] CJ 1018 (MLC) at 17.
168 At 21–24.
169 At 23.

if they lack whakapapa connections. This would establish a meeting of tikanga and public law, both recognised as valid sources of New Zealand law, on terms broadly resembling rules of comity that already structure inter-jurisdictional relations in private international law and some forms of federalism. If the matter found its way to court as a BORA challenge, however, I would prefer to see the Treaty presumption utilised by Courts to interpret ambiguous legislation, that on its face may engage s 19(1), in line with the Crown's Treaty obligations, at the first stage of an BORA inquiry, and in so doing mitigate the extent to which Treaty obligations and rights are read down in deference to s 19(1) rights, or in deference to limits expressed in the text of the Declaration.

II
The Declaration's Application

3
The Status and Effect in New Zealand Law of the UN Declaration on the Rights of Indigenous Peoples

Matthew S R Palmer* and Matthew S Smith**

A. Introduction

The Declaration is clearly a signal event in the struggle of indigenous peoples internationally. But the topic of this paper is more prosaic: to explore the status and effect of the Declaration in New Zealand domestic law. We do this from the perspective of constitutional realists – who seek to probe beneath the impressively swirling robes of justice to see with clear eyes the hard reality of what lies beneath.

B. Conventional Legal Status

The starting point is that the Declaration does not, itself, have binding legal force in New Zealand's legal system. It would not have such force even if it were a Treaty, given New Zealand's dualist approach to international law. As a declaration, it certainly does not have legal force. It has not been incorporated into domestic law in New Zealand, as it has been in Bolivia. It is soft law, not hard law. And that is said with respect and admiration for the norm-shifting dynamic force of soft international law.

C. Indirect Legal Effect

Are there other, less direct, means of the Declaration being reflected in law? In searching for these, we note Melissa Water's label of "creeping monism". She said there is a cross-national trend of courts finding indirect ways to give legal

---

*   Judge of the High Court of New Zealand (appointed after this chapter was written).
** Thorndon Chambers.

leverage to international obligations, even where they are not incorporated into domestic law.[1]

And we are conscious of the example of exactly this by the Supreme Court of Belize in 2007 in *Aurelio Cal*, which gave force to a provision of the Declaration because it "embodied general principles of international law".[2] But, as noted below, we expect the New Zealand courts would be more conservative.

We identify four ways by which New Zealand courts could give legal leverage to the Declaration.

1. Administrative Law

A court could determine that the Declaration constitutes a mandatory relevant consideration that the Crown or other public law decision-maker must consider in making a decision. Given the right set of facts, this is entirely plausible.

But we expect that, in practice before doing this, a New Zealand court would be more likely to find that the Treaty of Waitangi is a mandatory relevant consideration. The Treaty is directly reflected in a range of legislation. It is simply more salient in the New Zealand legal and constitutional landscape. Use of the Declaration in this way would be likely to support that use of the Treaty.

2. Statutory Interpretation

Statutory interpretation tends to shade into adminstrative law in some ways. But statutory interpretation is more ubiquitous, and more routine, as a judicial task.

New Zealand courts are used to thinking of international obligations as relevant to statutory interpretation.[3] But our observation is that they are not inclined to do so unless it supports an interpretation they wish to reach anyway. And, of course, the same point applies about the Treaty as applies to administrative law: courts will turn to the Treaty first.

3. Customary International Law

In theory, customary international law is part of common law in New Zealand's legal system. And there is an argument that the Declaration is declaratory, or at least evidence, of the current state of customary international law, though we are aware that opinions on this are divided in the literature.[4]

1   Melissa Waters "Creeping Monism: The Judicial Trend Toward Interpretive Incorporation of Human Rights Treaties" (2007) 107 *Colombia Law Review* 628.
2   *Aurelio Cal and the Maya Village of Santa Cruz v Attorney-General of Belize; and Manuel Coy and Maya Village of Conejo v Attorney-General of Belize* (Consolidated) Claim Nos 171 & 172, 2007, Supreme Court of Belize (18 October 2007).
3   *Ye v Minister of Immigration* [2009] NZSC 76, [2010] 1 NZLR 104.
4   Emmanuel Voyiakis "Voting in the General Assembly as evidence of Customary International

So, an argument might be mounted that executive action that is contrary to the Declaration is contrary to customary international law and therefore contrary to the common law of New Zealand. And it might have legs, depending on the context. But in practice we would expect that the justice of the particular complaint would be crucial in convincing a New Zealand court to take such a step.

4. Principle of Legality

The principle of legality is the European principle of statutory interpretation, adopted in the United Kingdom. It maintains that Parliament could not possibly have intended to override fundamental human rights without saying so very, very clearly. The New Zealand Supreme Court has effectively adopted the principle of legality in *Cropp* in 2008,[5] though it adopted the principle without, it seems deliberately, adopting the label.

Again, this could be useful in giving legal leverage to the Declaration. But, in practice, we would expect such an argument in relation to the Declaration to have most effect in reinforcing other arguments, perhaps based on the Treaty of Waitangi.

D. Relationship with the Treaty

We have mentioned the Treaty several times in traversing these indirect means of giving legal bite to the Declaration. That is because we think the Treaty is a more powerful instrument in New Zealand domestic law, in the sense that the Courts are more accustomed to have regard to it having legal effect. Of course, the Treaty is not fully part of New Zealand law for all purposes. Matthew Palmer has described the Treaty elsewhere as half in and half out of the legal system.[6] It follows that we see the Declaration as living, in New Zealand domestic law, in the half shadow of the Treaty.

E. But an Advantage in Specificity

This is not to say the Declaration is unimportant. There is one particular advantage the Declaration has over the Treaty – one respect in which the Declaration may well prove to amplify the Treaty's effect, and fill in the gaps left in its content. That is, the Declaration is more precisely and more specifically worded.

Law?" in Stephen Allen and Alexandra Xanthaki (eds) *Reflections on the UN Declaration on the Rights of Indigenous Peoples* (Hart Publishing, Oxford; Portland, 2011).
5   *Cropp v A Judicial Committee* [2008] NZSC 46, [2008] 3 NZLR 774.
6   Matthew S R Palmer *The Treaty of Waitangi in New Zealand's Law and Constitution* (Victoria University Press, Wellington, 2008).

Unlike the Treaty, the Declaration, deliberately, is specifically worded as a formal legal instrument. For a lawyer looking for support for a legal argument, often under time pressure, such precision is very helpful, if it is apposite. Instead of fossicking amongst Treaty principles to identify a vibe, you can cite a specific article with a reassuringly (to judges) numerical identity.

Indeed, the Waitangi Tribunal has recognised the value of this. It did so particularly in the 2015 Whaia te Mana Motuhake Report, which described the Declaration "as a tool, where possible, to understand the Crown's obligations in specific circumstances, in a way that assists [the] assessment of Crown actions against the principles of the Treaty".[7]

In this regard we note a certain irony in the New Zealand government's positions on the Declaration. New Zealand initially opposed the Declaration in the General Assembly on 13 September 2007. New Zealand rejected the argument that the Declaration was merely aspirational, "intended to inspire rather than to have legal effect". New Zealand said it did "not accept that a State could responsibly take such a stance towards a document that purported to declare on the contents of the rights of indigenous peoples". Once New Zealand belatedly endorsed the Declaration in April 2010, that might suggest it is rather difficult for the Crown to argue the Declaration is simply aspirational. But Prime Minister Key did so in Parliament on 20 April 2010. As did the official New Zealand Statement, though, interestingly, in relation to specific articles.

Those utterances might appear to be a roadblock to giving the Declaration legal teeth. But that need not be the case if the Declaration is seen through the prism of the Treaty. Recognising that, the Tribunal reasoned in its Whaia te Mana Motuhake Report that official statements on the Declaration, read in context, envisage:[8]

> ... that the New Zealand government, including its officials, will respect the rights of Maori under the Treaty of Waitangi and that it will strive to act consistently with its principles, as further elucidated by any relevant articles of [the UN Declaration on the Rights of Indigenous Peoples], subject to any lawful limitations.

We have found that the legal specificity of the drafting of the Declaration is useful in argument in the High Court and Waitangi Tribunal. On behalf of the New Zealand Māori Council, Matthew Palmer has invoked articles 4 and 39 of the Declaration to support an argument before the High Court about the importance in trust law of facilitating tribal groups' own procedures with respect to their

---

7   Waitangi Tribunal *Whaia te Mana Motuhake: In Pursuit of Mana Motuhake* (Wai 2417, 2015), at 55–56. See similarly at 505 (relying on "the guidance provided by article 19 [of the Declaration] to define in more precise terms the Treaty principle of collaborative agreement").
8   At 54 (emphasis added).

internal affairs, rather than interfering with them.⁹ The Declaration was not mentioned in the judgment.

Matthew Smith has done the same on behalf of the New Zealand Māori Council, relying on expert evidence from Dr Claire Charters, in the Whaia te Mana Motuhake claim to the Waitangi Tribunal. That claim was a challenge to the Crown's administration of Māori Wardens and its consultation over proposals to reform the legislation establishing the Māori Council system. It can be noted for the Tribunal's in-depth consideration of the status of the Declaration and its relationship to the Treaty.[10] The Tribunal's report is also notable for the fact that it makes findings of breaches of articles 4, 18 and 19.[11]

Nevertheless, we think, for the foreseeable future, that the Treaty will be the more important source of legal rights for Māori in New Zealand.

F. The Courts So Far

What of the practice of the New Zealand Courts and Tribunals to date. First, we note that the Waitangi Tribunal has, naturally, considered the Declaration on several occasions. It did so particularly in the 2011 Ko Aotearoa Tēnei Report, which described the Declaration as "groundbreaking",[12] and referred to its potential to become customary international law.[13] That analysis was affirmed and expanded on by the Tribunal in its Whaia te Mana Motuhake Report, which, as noted, also found breaches of articles 4, 18 and 19. The Tribunal also invoked the Declaration in the 2011 Petroleum Report, the 2012 Freshwater and Geothermal Report,[14] and the 2013 Kōhanga Reo Report.[15]

We see these Tribunal reports as providing a good first port of call for policy-makers, lawyers and judges looking at how the Declaration might impact on issues before them.

Indeed, officials arguably have been put on notice by the Tribunal that it expects to see the Declaration factored into what they are doing. As the Tribunal notes in its Whaia te Mana Motuhake Report:[16]

---

9   *New Zealand Maori Council v Foulkes* [2014] NZHC 1777.
10 Waitangi Tribunal *Whaia te Mana Motuhake* (Wai 2417), at 47–63
11 Refer for instance to 463 (Crown funding regime for Māori Wardens not consistent with article 18), 502 (Crown approach to the (re)appointment of Māori Wardens was a breach of articles 4 and 18) and 517 (Crown-led review of Māori Community Development Act was inconsistent with the declaration as a whole and in particular with articles 18 and 19).
12 Waitangi Tribunal, *Ko Aotearoa Tenei: A Report Into Claims Concerning New Zealand Law and Policy Affecting Maori Culture and Identity* (Wai 262, 2011) at 673.
13 At 669.
14 Waitangi Tribunal *The Stage 1 Report on the National Freshwater and Geothermal Resources Claim* (Wai 2358, 2012).
15 Waitangi Tribunal *Matua Rautia – Report on the Kōhanga Reo Claim* (Wai 2336, 2012).
16 Waitangi Tribunal *Whaia te Mana Motuhake* (Wai 2417, 2015), at 432.

We note, too, that the exclusion of Maori communities – as organised and represented under the 1962 [Maori Community Development] Act or otherwise – from any role in guiding, leading, or overseeing a project involving such an important Maori institution [as Maori Wardens] is not consistent with the rights affirmed in the UNDRIP. . . . [W]e are surprised to find that the total exclusion of Maori from decisions relating to one of their own institutions could happen in the second decade of the twenty-first century. An advisory group or governance board of some kind is now standard. The rights of indigenous peoples to the autonomous management of their own affairs and institutions, through their own chosen representatives, are affirmed in the Declaration. The [Crown's Maori Wardens Project], as it has been governed since early 2011, is inconsistent with those rights.

With more legal effect, there are also examples of the Courts citing the Declaration. Indeed, in *Barton-Prescott* in 1997 the High Court cited the Draft Declaration.[17]

The most extensive consideration of the Declaration by the New Zealand courts is by the Court of Appeal in *Takamore* in 2011.[18] There Glazebrook J, on behalf of a majority of the Court of Appeal, made some downright adventurous comments about the Declaration. These have been somewhat lost sight of, given that the case then went on to the Supreme Court (as did Glazebrook J herself). Specifically, the Court noted that the Declaration "recognises the need to safeguard both the individual and the collective rights of indigenous peoples" in rebutting the notion that there is "one law for all".[19] The Court quotes one international commentator's view that simply the Declaration "restates, in one systematic text, human rights contained in previously adopted international instruments and confirmed through the case law of international bodies".[20] The Court also cites the Declaration as support for the need to develop the common law consistently with the importance of recognising the collective nature of the culture of indigenous peoples and the value of their diversity.[21]

The most authoritative treatment by a Court to date was by the Supreme Court in its Water judgment in 2013.[22] That judgment is more subtle and more affirmative of previous Treaty jurisprudence than first appears in relation to the Treaty of Waitangi. The Supreme Court's unanimous judgment mentioned the Declaration and its affirmation by New Zealand in 2010. The Court quoted article 28(1). It doubted that the Declaration "adds significantly to the principles of the

17 *Barton-Prescott v Director-General of Social Welfare* [1997] 3 NZLR 179 (HC).
18 *Takamore v Clarke* [2011] NZCA 587, [2012] 1 NZLR 573.
19 At [251]-[254].
20 At [253] per Professor Elsa Stamatopoulou.
21 At [254].
22 *New Zealand Maori Council v Attorney-General ("Water Case")* [2013] NZSC 6, [2013], 3 NZLR 31.

Treaty statutorily recognised".[23] But the Court also accepted:[24]

> ... that the Declaration provides some support for the view that those principles should be construed broadly. In particular, it supports the claim for commercial redress as part of the right to development there recognised.

The Supreme Court returned to the Declaration in its *Paki* (No 2) judgment in 2014.[25] There, the Chief Justice indicated that article 28 might support a claim by Māori that the Crown in acquiring Māori land had breached legally enforceable duties it owed to Māori so as to justify the grant of restitutionary remedies.[26] On the facts, those issues did not need to be finally resolved by the Supreme Court, and they were not. Nevertheless, the suggestion that the Declaration might inform the scope and application of common law (fiduciary) principles, including questions of relief, should be noted for the future.

G. Conclusion

So, in conclusion, there are legal avenues by which the Declaration could be given indirect legal effect. However, we doubt the Declaration will be an effective lever for legal action in its own right in the short to medium term. Instead, we expect that the New Zealand courts are likely to mention the Declaration to bolster findings the courts would be prepared to make anyway. At least, in terms of legal force and effect, it is, and will remain, overshadowed by the Treaty of Waitangi which, itself, is struggling for coherent recognition in New Zealand law. This suggests that, at least for now, the Declaration is likely to play a supporting role in New Zealand law. It is probably more important politically and morally, in easing New Zealand into recognition of indigenous rights on the international stage and opening up international law avenues of pressure on the Crown. And, in the longer term, perhaps the Declaration will come to influence the development of the law in New Zealand.

---

23 At [92].
24 At [92].
25 *Paki v Attorney-General (No 2)* [2014] NZSC 118, [2015] 1 NZLR 67.
26 At [158]-[159] and [164]. See also [317] of Glazebrook J's separate judgment.

4
The Declaration and the Implementation of the Rights of the Indigenous Child in Aotearoa New Zealand

*Claire Breen**

A. Introduction

The rights of Māori children, both collective and individual, are protected by a range of international legal instruments. This chapter will focus on two of those instruments, namely, the Declaration on the Rights of Indigenous Peoples (the Declaration),[1] and the Convention on the Rights of the Child (CRC).[2] Ratification of the CRC and endorsement of the Declaration serve, "as a blueprint for the protection and promotion of the rights of indigenous peoples and provide a solid basis for accelerated implementation of the rights of indigenous children."[3] This chapter will consider this "blueprint" with a particular emphasis on the rights to health and education for two reasons. First, health and education outcomes of Māori children lag behind those of the rest of the New Zealand population. Secondly, such negative outcomes have short-term, long-term and intergenerational effects upon Māori children. The chapter will explore the extent to which the indigenous child's rights to health and education can be more effectively realised under the guiding role of the Declaration.

B. The Rights of the Indigenous Child: The International Legal Framework

The international legal framework of human rights protection applies to everyone, including the indigenous child. Although this framework is largely

---

* Associate Professor, Te Piringa Faculty of Law, University of Waikato.
1 *United Nations Declaration on the Rights of Indigenous Peoples* GA Res 61/295, A/RES/61/295 (2007) [The Declaration].
2 Convention on the Rights of the Child 1577 UNTS 3 (opened for signature 20 November 1989, entry into force 2 September 1990) ["Convention on the Rights of the Child"].
3 *Status of the Convention on the Rights of the Child Report of the Secretary-General* A/67/225 (2012) at [67].

aimed at securing individual rights, there have been efforts to protect group rights. Article 27 of the International Covenant on Civil and Political Rights (ICCPR) makes provision for the cultural rights of minorities.[4] Although the ICCPR's monitoring body, the UN Human Rights Committee, has interpreted this right as adhering to the individual rather than being a collective right,[5] the Committee has, elsewhere, expressed the opinion that the collective element of Article 27 is crucial.[6] Thus, the "practical application" of Article 27 results in the protection of group rights.[7] More recently, the Committee monitoring state compliance with the International Covenant on Economic Social and Cultural Rights has stated that "indigenous peoples have the right to the full enjoyment, as a collective or as individuals, of all human rights and fundamental freedoms."[8] As members of indigenous groups, indigenous children's collective freedoms are also guaranteed by the International Labour Organization (ILO) Convention (No 169) concerning Indigenous and Tribal Peoples in Independent Countries; and ILO Convention (No 107) concerning the Protection and Integration of Indigenous and Other Tribal and Semi-Tribal Populations in Independent Countries.[9]

However, the Declaration and the CRC are the most notable international legal instruments that make provision for the collective rights of indigenous children. The CRC is a legally binding international human rights treaty that sets out the basic rights of children and places concomitant legally binding obligations upon states to fulfill these rights. The CRC was ratified by Aotearoa New Zealand in 1993 and thus the state is legally bound by its provisions, which make specific reference to the rights of indigenous children.[10] In fact, the CRC was one of the first international human rights instruments to make specific provision for the

4   *International Covenant on Civil and Political Rights* 999 UNTS 171 (opened for signature 16 December 1966, entered into force 23 March 1976), art 27.
5   UN Human Rights Committee *CCPR General Comment No. 23: Article 27 (Rights of Minorities)* CCPR/C/21/Rev.1/Add.5 (8 April 1994) at [6.2] ("Although the rights protected under article 27 are individual rights, they depend in turn on the ability of the minority group to maintain its culture, language or religion.").
6   See *Lubicon Lake Band v Canada*, HRC Communication No. 167/1984 (26 March 1990), in *Report of the Human Rights Committee (Volume II)* Supp No 40 (A/45/40) Annex IX (4 October 1990) at [32.2]; *Angela Poma Poma v Peru*, HRC Communication No 1457/2006 (27 March 2009) CCPR/C/95/D/1457/2006 (24 April 2009) at [7.3] and [7.4].
7   James Anaya *Indigenous Peoples in International Law* (2nd ed, Oxford University Press, Oxford, 2004) at 135. See also, *CERD Committee General Recommendation No. 23: Indigenous Peoples* A/52/18 (18 August 1997) at Annex V.
8   Committee on Economic, Social and Cultural Rights *General Comment No 21: Right of Everyone to Take Part in Cultural Life* E/C.12/GC/21 (21 December 2009) at [7]; see also, [36].
9   International Labour Organization *Convention concerning Indigenous and Tribal Peoples in Independent Countries, C169* (entered into force 5 Sep 1991) (27 June 1989); and Convention (No. 107) concerning the Protection and Integration of Indigenous and Other Tribal and Semi-Tribal Populations in Independent Countries, 26 June 1957, 328 UNTS 247 (entered into force 2 June 1959).
10 Convention on the Rights of the Child, above n 2, arts 17 and 30.

rights of indigenous children, and significantly with reference to their cultural background.[11] The Preamble to the CRC calls on State parties to take "due account of the importance and cultural values of *each people* for the protection and harmonious development of the child".[12] More significant, however, is the impact of Article 30 of the CRC which states that:[13]

> In those States where minorities or persons of indigenous origin exist, a child belonging to such a minority or who is indigenous shall not be denied the right, in community with other members of his or her group, to enjoy his or her own culture, to profess and practise his or her own religion or to use his or her own language.

Although, like Article 27 of the ICCPR, Article 30 refers to the individual person, it clearly signals that the rights of indigenous children are to be applied in the context of their unique cultures and histories.[14] Also, in its General Comment on Indigenous Children, the Committee has noted that the child's right to culture is to be exercised collectively.[15]

The Declaration has been described as an important guide for the proper implementation (or fulfillment) of other human rights agreements or conventions affecting indigenous peoples, such as the CRC.[16] The preamble to the Declaration specifically recognises "the rights of indigenous families and communities to retain shared responsibility for the upbringing, training, education and well-being of their children, *consistent with the rights of the child*" (emphasis added).[17] A number of the Declaration's substantive rights make reference to the rights of indigenous children, including the indigenous child's right to education,[18] and the right to be free from economic exploitation.[19] In relation to the right to improved economic and social conditions, the needs of indigenous children are to be given particular attention.[20] More generally, children are identified as a group to whom

---

11 UNICEF "Ensuring the Rights of Indigenous Children" (2004) Innocenti Digest no 11 at 3 and 6.
12 Convention on the Rights of the Child, above n 2, Preamble.
13 Convention on the Rights of the Child, above n 2, art 30.
14 See also, Convention on the Rights of the Child, above n 2, art 17 which requires states to ensure that all children have access to information that is relevant and important to their well-being and directing States to "encourage the mass media to provide this information in indigenous languages."
15 See Committee on the Rights of the Child *General Comment No 11: Indigenous Children and their Rights under the Convention* CRC/C/GC/11 (12 February 2009) at [16].
16 UNICEF *Know Your Rights! United Nations Declaration on the Rights of Indigenous Peoples for Indigenous Adolescents* (UNICEF, New York, 2013) at 10.
17 The Declaration, above n 1, at Preamble.
18 Article 14.
19 Article 17.
20 Article 21(2).

particular attention is to be given in the implementation of the Declaration,[21] while states are put under an obligation to protect children (and women) from all forms of violence and discrimination.[22] The CRC, with its recognition of the rights of the indigenous child, together with the Declaration, provide a comprehensive package of rights protection for Māori children in Aotearoa New Zealand, and indigenous children generally.

The fundamental principles underpinning the Declaration can inform the manner in which the CRC promotes and protects the rights of indigenous children by elaborating on how children's rights can be interpreted according to indigenous values. The article 3 right to self-determination and article 4 right to self-government in the Declaration are key in this regard, along with the key role of free, prior and informed consent (FPIC) in relation to policy making, the setting of priorities and the delivery of (education and health) services to indigenous peoples.[23] Further depth to the relationship between the Declaration and the CRC can be added if we look at certain articles in the CRC, which contain general principles that are to inform the interpretation of the substantive rights in the convention. Article 2 of the CRC prohibits discrimination "of any kind".[24] On this basis, according to the Committee on the Rights of the Child, "indigenous children have an inalienable right to be free from discrimination".[25] Article 2 creates negative and positive obligations and, in that regard, the Committee has noted that:[26]

> [I]ndigenous children are among those children who require positive measures in order to eliminate conditions that cause discrimination and to ensure their enjoyment of the rights of the Convention on equal level with other children. In particular, States parties are urged to consider the application of special measures in order to ensure that indigenous children have access to culturally appropriate services in the areas of health, nutrition, education, recreation and sports, social services, housing, sanitation and juvenile justice.

Article 3 of CRC refers to the "best interests of the child" as being a primary consideration.[27] The focus is on the interests of the individual child even though that decision may not be in the best interests of the indigenous collective that the child belongs to. However, the individualism inherent in article 3 can be

---

21 Article 21(1).
22 Article 21(2).
23 See for example, Expert Mechanism on the Rights of Indigenous Peoples, Study on the Right to Health and Indigenous Peoples with a Focus on Children and Youth A/HRC/33/57 (10 August 2016) [21].
24 Convention on the Rights of the Child, above n 2, art 2.
25 *General Comment No 11: Indigenous Children and their Rights under the Convention*, above n 15, at [23].
26 At [25].
27 Convention on the Rights of the Child, above n 2, art 3.

tempered by the fact that what is in the best interests of the individual indigenous child may be a decision that can only be made with reference to collective cultural rights as guaranteed by article 30 of CRC. This construction is supported by the Committee on the Rights of the Child, which has noted "the application of [article 3] to indigenous children as a group requires consideration of how the right relates to collective cultural rights."[28]

The final general principle is the right of the child to have his or her voice heard in all proceedings affecting him or her under Article 12 of the CRC. This principle straddles the individual right of the child to express his or her opinion and the collective right of children to be heard in such proceedings. It also facilitates children as a group to be involved in consultations on matters involving them in an environment that encourages the free opinion of the child. The school is one environment in which States parties must ensure the application of this principle.[29] However, the Declaration's statement that indigenous peoples have the right to take part in decision-making in all matters affecting them, along with the principle of FPIC, strengthens the voice of the indigenous child provided for in article 12 of the CRC.

In essence, the general principles underpinning the CRC require states to ensure that the best interests and opinions of the children are taken into account in decision-making affecting them. They also require states to ensure that all children are given equal opportunities with other children to survive and develop. Through these general principles the CRC and the Declaration are able to straddle individual and collective rights within a human rights framework. These principles also work in conjunction with Article 30 of the CRC which acts as a means to address the often insufficient attention that is given by states to indigenous children, as it obliges states to better protect indigenous children through legislative and policy measures compiled in consultation with indigenous children and their communities. The significance of these and other measures contained in the CRC is amplified by the fact that it is the most widely ratified international human rights treaty.

C. Realising the Rights to Health and Education of Māori Children: The Role of the Declaration and the CRC

It is against this backdrop that the specific rights to health and education of Māori children can be considered. Such an analysis is warranted, given that Māori children are overrepresented in poor outcomes in health and education, outcomes

---

28 *General Comment No 11: Indigenous Children and their Rights under the Convention* above n 15, at [30].
29 At [39].

that have been linked to poverty rates.[30] On average from 2012 to 2014, around 16% of European/Pākehā children lived in poor households, while 33% of Māori children lived in poor households.[31] The higher poverty rate for Māori children is consistent with the relatively high proportion of Māori children living in sole-parent beneficiary families and households.[32] Such statistics are of concern, not only for children currently living in poverty but because of the inter-generational effect of poverty. High rates of poverty are a cause for concern, as low family income is associated with a range of negative outcomes including low birth weight, infant mortality, poorer mental health and cognitive development, and a higher rate of hospital admissions.[33] Low family income during childhood and early adolescence may increase the risk of leaving school without qualifications, economic inactivity, early parenthood and contact with the justice system.[34] The Committee on the Rights of the Child has continued to be concerned at ongoing manifestations of discrimination against Māori children and has called upon Aotearoa New Zealand to take, "urgent measures to address disparities in access to education, health services and a minimum standard of living by Maori (and Pasifika) children and their families."[35]

1. *The Right to Health*

Article 24 of the CRC obliges States parties to ensure that all children, which includes indigenous children, enjoy the highest attainable standard of health and have access to health-care services. Article 24 also requires states to secure the child's right to health by combatting disease and malnutrition, including within the framework of primary health care.[36] States can meet their obligations stemming from the child's right to health with initiatives such as provision of adequate nutritious foods and clean drinking-water; and appropriate pre-natal and post-natal health care for mothers. Not only that, in securing the right to health for indigenous children, the State must ensure that everyone has access to education and is supported in the use of basic knowledge of child health

---

30 *Consideration of Reports Submitted by States Parties under Article 44 of the Convention, Concluding Observations: New Zealand*, Advance Unedited Version CRC/C/NZL/CO/5 (30 September 2016), at [35].
31 Bryan Perry *Household Incomes in New Zealand: Trends in Indicators of Inequality and Hardship 1982 to 2015* (Ministry of Social Development, Wellington, 2016), at 135.
32 At 135.
33 Jean Simpson "Child Poverty Monitor 2015 Technical Report" (NZ Child and Youth Epidemiology Service, University of Otago, 2015), at 16.
34 At 16.
35 *Consideration of Reports Submitted by States Parties under Article 44 of the Convention, Concluding Observations: New Zealand*, Advance Unedited Version CRC/C/NZL/CO/5 (30 September 2016), at [15(a)].
36 Convention on the Rights of the Child, above n 2, art 24.

and nutrition, the advantages of breastfeeding, hygiene and environmental sanitation, and the prevention of accidents.

Article 24 of the Declaration states that indigenous peoples have the right to use health practices that they find suitable and they also have the right to access health care and social services without discrimination. In particular, under Article 24 indigenous peoples have the right to their traditional medicines and to maintain their health practices. Article 23 of the Declaration provides that indigenous people have the right to be actively involved in developing and determining health programmes affecting them and, as far as possible, to administer such programmes through their own institutions.[37] This right is to be understood within the context of indigenous peoples' concept of health, "which extends beyond the physical and mental well-being of an individual to the spiritual balance and well-being of the community as a whole."[38] Although the role of the right to self-determination regarding the right to health is not explicit, any lack of explicitness can be countered by Articles 3 and 4 of the Declaration, as well as the right to FPIC. On this basis, indigenous peoples should have increased autonomy in relation to the design and delivery of health services.

The Committee on the Rights of the Child has repeatedly expressed concerns about the profoundly significant barriers that indigenous children face in the realisation of their right to health. Amongst the barriers faced by indigenous children are expressions of racism and other forms of discrimination, and physical, economic, and information inaccessibility, as well as barriers within the context of the acceptability and the quality of health services.[39] The Committee has urged states to consider applying special measures in order to ensure that children have access to culturally appropriate health services.[40] The Committee has further stated that health services for indigenous peoples should to the extent possible be community based, and planned and administered in co-operation with the indigenous peoples concerned[41] who also have the right to their traditional medicines.[42]

In many ways, each of these aspects of the right to health are indicative of the failings in Aotearoa New Zealand that seem to perpetuate poor health outcomes for Māori children. Statistics on the health status of Māori children reflect those

---

37 See also, *Convention concerning Indigenous and Tribal Peoples in Independent Countries, C169*, above n 9, art 25.
38 Myrna Cunningham "Chapter 5: Health" in Department of Economic and Social Affairs *State of the World's Indigenous Peoples* ST/ESA/328 (2009) at 156.
39 At 173.
40 *General Comment No 11: Indigenous Children and their Rights under the Convention*, above n 15, at [25].
41 At [51].
42 At [53].

of indigenous children generally.[43] Outcomes in health are generally poorer for Māori children in comparison with the rest of the child population. For example, the rate of Sudden Unexplained Death in Infancy (SUDI) among Māori infants are nearly five times as high as that among non-Māori infants, and Sudden Infant Death Syndrome (SIDS) is nearly five times that of non-Māori infants.[44] In 2016/2017, 11% of Maori children were obese and 21% were overweight.[45] Māori children are more likely to be hospitalised for Type II diabetes.[46] Māori children also experience higher rates of asthma[47] and rheumatic fever.[48] The data on young people are also cause for concern as they show suicide rates amongst Māori teenagers that have reached epidemic proportions.[49] The effects of these negative outcomes for Māori children are concerning because a child's early life experiences have a critical effect on his or her health in later life so that a child's exposure to overwhelming stress, emotional neglect and violence has a profound influence on the incidence of a number of diseases in later life and future mental health problems.[50] As the New Zealand Medical Association (NZMA) has observed, "the length of time that Māori have lagged behind non-Māori in terms of the social determinants of health has led to the creation of intergenerational problems, as children born into poverty and with one or more parents on a benefit are increasingly found to have followed in the same cycle."[51]

The Committee on the Rights of the Child has previously expressed concern that inequalities continue to exist in Aotearoa New Zealand, manifested by, among other matters, the disparities in infant mortality rates between the Māori

43 Jean Simpson and others *Te Ohonga Ake: The Determinants of Health for Māori Children and Young People in New Zealand* (New Zealand Child and Youth Epidemiology Service – University of Otago, March 2015) at 19; Compare, *State of the World's Indigenous Peoples*, above n 38, at 22.
44 Ministry of Health "Infant Health" (8 October 2015) Ministry of Health NZ <http://www.health.govt.nz/our-work/populations/maori-health/tatau-kahukura-maori-health-statistics/nga-mana-hauora-tutohu-health-status-indicators/infant-health>.
45 Ministry of Health "Obesity Statistics" (June 2017) Ministry of Health NZ <http://www.health.govt.nz/nz-health-statistics/health-statistics-and-data-sets/obesity-statistics>.
46 Elizabeth Craig and others. *The Health of Māori Children and Young People with Chronic Conditions and Disabilities in New Zealand: Series Two* (New Zealand Child and Youth Epidemiology Service – University of Otago, February 2014), at 32.
47 Ministry of Health "Annual Update of Key Results 2015/16: New Zealand Health Survey" (Ministry of Health, 15 December 2016), at 59.
48 Ministry of Health "Progress on the Better Public Services rheumatic fever target" (15 March 2015) Ministry of Health NZ <http://www.health.govt.nz/about-ministry/what-we-do/strategicdirection/better-public-services/progress-better-public-services-rheumatic-fever-target>.
49 Jean Simpson and others, above n 43, at 33.
50 New Zealand Medical Association *Inquiry into the Determinants of Wellbeing for Māori Children* (New Zealand Medical Association, March 2012) at [11].
51 At [24].

population and the rest of the population and in immunisation rates, which tend to be lower among Māori children.[52] In 2016, the Committee recommended that Aotearoa New Zealand: [53]

> Promptly take the necessary measures to ensure adequate access to health services to all children, including age-appropriate mental health services, with particular attention to Māori and Pasifika children;
> Take immediate action to reduce the prevalence of preventable and infectious diseases, including by improving housing conditions, especially for Māori, Pasifika and children living in poverty.

Such views have been echoed by the New Zealand Medical Association which has stated:[54]

> The approach for improving the social determinants of health for Māori children needs to be a multi-sectorial, whānau-centred and support development that is by Māori, for Māori.

It has been observed that, in order to improve the health situation of indigenous peoples, it is essential that a "fundamental shift" take place "in the concept of health so that it incorporates the cultures and world views of indigenous peoples as central to the design and management of State health systems".[55]

2. The Right to Education.

Several international instruments protect the right to education as an essential means of achieving the recognition and implementation of other human rights, such as the right of indigenous peoples to self-determination. Article 28 of the CRC sets out the child's right to education, which obliges states in particular to:

- Make primary education compulsory and available free to all;
- Encourage the development of different forms of secondary education, including general and vocational education, make them available and accessible to every child, and take appropriate measures such as the introduction of free education and offering financial assistance in case of need;

---

52 *Consideration of Reports Submitted by States Parties under Article 44 of the Convention, Concluding Observations: New Zealand*, CRC/C/NZL/CO/3-4 (11 April 2011) at [37]. See also, *Report of the Special Rapporteur on the Rights of Indigenous Peoples, James Anaya, Addendum, The situation of Maori people in New Zealand* A/HRC/18/35/Add.4 (2011) at [61].
53 *Consideration of Reports Submitted by States Parties under Article 44 of the Convention, Concluding Observations: New Zealand*, Advance Unedited Version CRC/C/NZL/CO/5 (30 September 2016), at [31 (a) and (b)].
54 *Inquiry into the Determinants of Wellbeing for Māori Children*, above n 50; see, Social Service Taskforce *Ngāi Tūhoe Service Management Plan* (November 2012).
55 *State of the World's Indigenous Peoples*, above n 38, at 156.

- Make higher education accessible to all on the basis of capacity by every appropriate means;
- Make educational and vocational information and guidance available and accessible to all children;
- Take measures to encourage regular attendance at schools and the reduction of drop-out rates.

In sum, Article 28 provides that every child has the right to education on the basis of equality of opportunity. In this regard, the Committee on the Rights of the Child has stated that states should allocate targeted financial, material and human resources in order to implement policies and programmes which specifically seek to improve the access to education for indigenous children. Education programmes and services should be developed and implemented in co-operation with the peoples concerned to address their specific needs. Furthermore, governments should recognise the right of indigenous peoples to establish their own educational institutions and facilities, provided that such institutions meet minimum standards established by the competent authority in consultation with these peoples.[56] Article 28 must also be read in conjunction with Article 30 which establishes the right of the indigenous child to use his or her own language. Consequently, "education in the child's own language is essential."[57] In this way, the Committee on the Rights of the Child has stressed the urgent need to adopt special measures to ensure that indigenous children are able to exercise their right to education under the same conditions as all other children, and urges States to establish culturally appropriate education services and to improve access to schools in areas where indigenous children live.

The provisions of Article 28 must also take into account the aim of education, which, according to Article 29(1)(c) of the CRC, is to direct all children towards objectives such as, "the development of respect for the child's ... cultural identity, language and values ... and for civilizations different from his or her own".[58] In addition, Article 29(1)(d) provides that:

[E]ducation of the child shall be directed to the preparation of the child for responsible life in a free society, in the spirit of understanding, peace, tolerance, equality of sexes, and friendship among all peoples, ethnic, national and religious groups and persons of indigenous origin.

The Committee on Economic, Social and Cultural Rights has elaborated on

---

56 *General Comment No 11: Indigenous Children and their Rights under the Convention,* above n 15, at [60].
57 At [62].
58 See also, Convention concerning Indigenous and Tribal Peoples in Independent Countries, C169, above n 9, arts 28 and 29.

children and their right to education. It has stated that one of the fundamental aims of education is the transmission and enrichment of common cultural and moral values in which the individual and society find their identity and worth. Thus, education must be culturally appropriate, include human rights education, and enable children to develop their personality and cultural identity and to learn and understand cultural values and practices of the communities to which they belong, as well as those of other communities and societies.[59] Similarly, the Expert Mechanism on the Rights of Indigenous Peoples (EMRIP) has noted that the implementation of the right to education is of crucial importance to indigenous children and indigenous peoples as a whole, as it is an essential means by which they can achieve individual empowerment and self-determination.[60] The EMRIP has also noted, in particular, that traditional education is a lifelong pedagogic process and encompasses an intergenerational transfer of knowledge aimed at maintaining a flourishing and harmonious society or community.[61]

Article 14 of the Declaration expands the right to education contained in the CRC.[62] Article 14(1) provides that indigenous peoples have the right to establish and control their educational systems and institutions providing education in their own languages, in a manner appropriate to their cultural methods of teaching and learning.[63] Article 14(2) provides that every indigenous child has the right to all levels and forms of education of the State without discrimination.[64] Article 14 also means that governments must ensure that indigenous children in particular benefit from the education as much as non-indigenous children but that they do so in ways that respect indigenous cultures, languages and rights.[65] The language of Article 14 provides a clear role for the exercise of the right to self-determination. Article 15 states that indigenous peoples have the right to have their cultures and traditions correctly reflected in education and public information. It requires governments to work with indigenous peoples to educate non-indigenous peoples in ways that respect indigenous peoples' rights and promote a harmonious society. Article 15 resonates with article 29 of the CRC with the latter's stipulation that states ensure that the child's right to education should include the provision of opportunities for indigenous and non-indigenous children to learn, appreciate and respect each other's culture. The

---

59   *General Comment No 21: Right of Everyone to Take Part in Cultural Life,* above n 8, at [27].
60   See Expert Mechanism on the Rights of Indigenous Peoples *Study on Lessons Learned and Challenges to Achieve the Implementation of the Right of Indigenous Peoples to Education* A/HRC/EMRIP/2009/2 (26 June 2009) at [6].
61   At [43]. See also, Peter Bille Larsen *Indigenous and Tribal Children: Assessing Child Labour and Education Challenges* (International Labour Office, Geneva, 2003).
62   The Declaration, above n 1, art 14.
63   Article 14(1).
64   Article 14(2).
65   Article 14(3).

rights contained in Articles 12 and 13 of the Declaration provide further context for understanding the content of the right to education. To that end, Article 12 (1) provides that indigenous peoples have the right to manifest, practise, develop and teach their spiritual and religious traditions, customs and ceremonies. Article 13(1) recognises that indigenous peoples have the right to revitalise, use, develop and transmit to future generations their histories, languages, oral traditions, philosophies, writing systems and literatures.

Indigenous children face significant challenges in exercising their right to education, which results in their having, in most countries throughout the world, low school enrolments, poor school performance, low literacy rates, high dropout rates, and disparities in academic achievements nationally.[66] The UN Special Rapporteur on the Right to Education has expressed concerns about indigenous peoples having markedly fewer years of schooling when compared with non-indigenous populations (particularly at the secondary level).[67] Such concerns are reflected in the statistics regarding educational outcomes for Māori. Despite improving rates of achievement by Māori, their secondary school results are poorer in comparison with other ethnic groups.[68] A clear positive correlation can be seen between the socio-economic mix of the school and the level of student achievement; students from schools in "higher decile" secondary schools with wealthier students had higher rates of achievement[69] or University Entrance.[70] Māori currently participate in tertiary education at a much higher rate than non-Māori, but when broken down by level of study, Māori currently have substantially higher rates at non-degree level, while non-Māori participation rates are highest at degree level and above.[71] Another way of looking at educational achievements is to look at retention of students in secondary school. In 2014, Māori students had the lowest proportion of students remaining at school to age 17 (69.1%),[72]

66 *State of the World's Indigenous Peoples*, above n 38, at 132.
67 See, *Report of the Special Rapporteur on the Right to Education, Vernor Muñoz Villalobos, addendum, Mission to Paraguay* A/HRC/14/25/Add.2 (16 March 2010) [56].
68 Ministry of Education "School leavers with NCEA Level 1 or above" Education Counts (August 2016) <https://www.educationcounts.govt.nz/indicators/main/education-and-learning-outcomes/28788>; Ministry of Education "School leavers with NCEA Level 2 or above" Education Counts (August 2016) <https://www.educationcounts.govt.nz/indicators/main/education-and-learning-outcomes/1781>; Ministry of Education "School leavers with NCEA Level 3 or above" Education Counts (August 2016) <https://www.educationcounts.govt.nz/indicators/main/education-and-learning-outcomes/1891>.
69 "School leavers with NCEA Level 1 or above", above n 68; "School leavers with NCEA Level 2 or above", above n 68; "School leavers with NCEA Level 3 or above", above n 68.
70 "School leavers with NCEA Level 3 or above", above n 68.
71 Ministry of Education "Participation rates in tertiary education" Education Counts (October 2014) <http://www.educationcounts.govt.nz/indicators/main/student-engagement-participation/1963>.
72 Ministry of Education "Retention of students in senior secondary schools" Education Counts (August 2016) <https://www.educationcounts.govt.nz/indicators/main/student-

with the highest rate of stand-downs, suspensions, exclusions and expulsions being amongst Māori.[73] Again, these figures correlate with socio-economic factors, as students from decile 9 and 10 schools were, on average, more likely to remain at school until the age of 17 than students from lower decile schools.[74] However, (the limited and historic) data on students at immersion and bilingual schools shows that the majority of candidates at immersion and bilingual schools gain secondary school qualifications and that Year 13 students at immersion and bilingual schools were more likely to gain University Entrance.[75]

A right to education that draws from the CRC and the Declaration should result in a right to education for Māori children where cost is not a barrier to going to school and where the schools themselves cater for different forms of educational environments that reflect and support traditional values, as well as the types of education that provide better outcomes for children such as schools using Ngā Whanaketanga Rumaki Māori (national standards for Māori medium education) or immersion or bilingual schools.

D. Conclusion

This chapter indicates just some of the challenges faced by Māori children and echoes the observation by the UN General Assembly Secretary-General that, "Indigenous children suffer extreme forms of exclusion and discrimination, which result in a denial or curtailment of their access to, inter alia, education [and] health."[76] Thus, while the Declaration is a distinctive instrument in the overall framework of human rights with its recognition of the individual rights of indigenous women, men and children and the collective rights of indigenous societies, nations and communities, it also builds on the example set by the CRC as a treaty that recognises both individual human rights and the collective cultural rights of the child. In this way, the Declaration is a means to give effect to the rights contained in other human rights instruments, such as the CRC. Working together, proper application of the rights contained in these two international legal instruments can further the realisation of the rights of Māori children in Aotearoa New Zealand.

engagement-participation/1955>.
73 Ministry of Education "Stand-downs, suspensions, exclusions and expulsions from school" Education Counts (August 2016)
<http://www.educationcounts.govt.nz/indicators/main/student-engagement-participation/Stand-downs-suspensions-exclusions-expulsions>.
74 Ministry of Education "Retention of students in senior secondary schools" above n 72.
75 Ministry of Education "Achievement at Māori Immersion and Bilingual Schools 2005" Education Counts (April 2007).
<http://www.educationcounts.govt.nz/publications/schooling/11240/maori_immersion_2005>.
76 *Status of the Convention on the Rights of the Child Report of the Secretary-General,* above n 3, at [9].

5
The "False Generosity" of Treaty Settlements: Innovation and Contortion

Linda Te Aho[*]

A. Introduction

In Aotearoa New Zealand the ways in which indigenous claims to lands and waters are addressed are often looked to as good, or even best, practice by indigenous peoples around the world. While things are far from perfect, in recent decades Māori have succeeded in changing perceptions about the Treaty of Waitangi as the foundation of the nation, and work steadily continues on settling outstanding Treaty claims. The resulting Treaty of Waitangi settlements are negotiated arrangements which aim to remove a sense of historical grievance and achieve significant rebuilding of the Māori economy. They are seen by some as dynamic and powerful steps towards economic independence, as a means of recognising special relationships to lands and waters, and a necessary prerequisite to improved relationships between the state and the indigenous Māori in the future.[1] Critics see the settlements and the processes followed to reach them as too heavily weighted in the government's favour.[2] They argue that the settlements do not sufficiently compensate for actual losses. They are said to pit Māori against Māori. Diverse claimant groups are effectively forced to negotiate within standardised and fixed parameters. For these and other reasons, the settlement agreements, policies and processes have been labelled as divisive and compromising self-determination.[3]

---

[*] Associate Professor, Te Piringa Faculty of Law, University of Waikato.
[1] Joe Williams, High Court Judge "Truth and Reconciliation in Aotearoa and Canada" (Transcript of presentation to Te Piringa Faculty of Law, University of Waikato, September 2009). See also Linda Te Aho "Ngā Whakataunga Waimāori: Freshwater Settlements" in Nicola R Wheen and Janine Hayward (eds) *Treaty of Waitangi Settlements* (Bridget Williams Books, Wellington, 2012) at 102, 112–113.
[2] For an excellent critique of the settlement process, see Ani Mikaere "Settlement of Treaty Claims: Full and Final or Fatally Flawed?" (1997) 17 NZULR 425 at 452–455.
[3] Ani Mikaere, above n 2, at 34.

This chapter reflects upon recent developments in the area of Treaty of Waitangi settlements in order to assess whether iwi have paid too high a price for what might be described as innovative and pragmatic agreements. As the Chapter title suggests, what some see as innovation, others see as contortion. Part II sets out a brief background to Treaty settlements and offers insights into how negotiations are conducted.[4] It also highlights interesting developments regarding lands returned to iwi and the involvement of claimant groups in the governance and management of natural resources. New Zealand's recent endorsement of the United Nations Declaration on the Rights of Indigenous Peoples (Declaration) provides a new dimension within which to consider Treaty settlements. Part III of the chapter concludes with some observations as to how the Declaration might assist Treaty settlement negotiators in the future.

B. Treaty Settlements

1. Background

Māori are tangata whenua (people of the land) who descend from Papatūānuku, the Earth Mother, and Ranginui, the Sky Father. As a response to British settlement, rangatira (chiefs) signed Te Tiriti o Waitangi (the English version of which is known as the Treaty of Waitangi) which guaranteed the continuation of tino rangatiratanga – authority and control over their lands, waters and other treasures. The inconsistencies between the English and Māori texts of Articles 1 and 2 have spawned many different interpretations of the Treaty, and ongoing debate.[5] Setting aside the principle of contra proferentum (ambiguity will be construed against the party that drafted an agreement), the way around the debate has been to invent the concept of 'the principles' of the Treaty, the meaning of which was the subject of the landmark *Lands Case*.[6] There, Māori opposed the proposed transfer of Crown lands to newly established state owned enterprises as a breach of section 9 of the State Owned Enterprises Act 1986, which provides: "Nothing in this Act shall permit the Crown to act in a manner inconsistent with the principles of the Treaty of Waitangi."[7] With no definition or explanation of what was meant by "the principles of the Treaty of Waitangi" it was effectively left to the courts to distil these principles and what they might require in particular contexts. In the now famous words of Court of Appeal

---

4   The author has served as a specialist advisor to negotiation teams and as Treaty negotiator for the Ngāti Koroki Kahukura settlement. See, Ngāti Koroki Kahukura Claims Settlement Act 2014. Many of the examples in this chapter come from those negotiations.
5   For example, the Waitangi Tribunal recently concluded that Māori did not cede sovereignty: Waitangi Tribunal *Report on Stage 1 of the Te Paparahi o Te Raki Inquiry* (Wai 1040) at ch 10 [*Te Paparahi o Te Raki Inquiry*].
6   *New Zealand Māori Council v Attorney General* [1987] 1 NZLR 641 at 651.
7   State Owned Enterprises Act 1986, s 9.

president, Sir Robin Cooke (as he was then) the Treaty principles: "require the Pakeha and Māori Treaty partners to act towards each other reasonably and with the utmost good faith. That duty is no light one. It is infinitely more than a formality".[8]

Rangatira consented to the Treaty on the basis that they and the representatives of the British Crown who also signed, were to be equals, though they were to have different roles and different spheres of influence. The detail of how this relationship would work in practice, especially where the Māori and European populations intermingled, remained to be negotiated over time on a case-by-case basis.[9]

Over time, the combined impact of land confiscation, public works takings and the operations of institutions like the Native Land Court has been to strip from Māori the lands and waters necessary to sustain their people. The development of European farming practices which involved draining wetlands and led to the gradual silting of rivers, compounded the effect by destroying traditional food sources. Later decisions of the government to use their rivers to generate hydro-electricity worsened their plight. What had once been prosperous and flourishing communities became remnants.[10] Struggles for restorative justice and redress have been part of a larger set of goals and aspirations, at the heart of which is rangatiratanga.[11]

The Waitangi Tribunal was established in 1975 against a backdrop of increasing pressure from Māori to have such grievances addressed by the Crown. Under its establishing statute, the Treaty of Waitangi Act 1975, any Māori person who claims to be prejudicially affected by the actions, policies or omissions of the Crown in breach of the Treaty of Waitangi may make a claim to the Tribunal.[12] The Tribunal then has the power to inquire into the claim. On 21 September 1992, Cabinet agreed on general principles for settling Treaty of Waitangi claims. This date then became the cut-off date for historical claims, so that consistent comparisons could be made between the redress provided to different claimant groups. Historical claims are those arising out of Crown acts or omissions before 21 September 1992. Contemporary claims arise out of Crown actions or omissions after that date.[13] A recent example of a contemporary claim

---

8 *New Zealand Māori Council v Attorney General*, above n 6, at 667.
9 *Te Paparahi o Te Raki Inquiry*, above n 5, at 528.
10 These are the conclusions of Erik Olsen, a historian who peer reviewed the historical account for the Ngāti Koroki Kahukura Deed of Settlement 2012.
11 Roger Maaka and Augie Fleras *The Politics of Indigeneity* (1st ed, Otago University Press, Dunedin, 2005) at 26–63.
12 Treaty of Waitangi Act 1975, s 6(1).
13 Office of Treaty Settlements *Ka Tika a Muri, Ka Tika a Mua: Healing the Past and Building a Future* (2nd ed, Office of Treaty Settlements, Wellington, 2015) at 23, www.govt.nz/assets/Documents/Red-Book-Healing-the-past-building-a-future.pdf accessed 4 October 2016 [The

is the National Freshwater and Geothermal Resources Claim (Wai 2358) lodged in response to the Government's proposed plan to offer for sale up to 49% of the shares in state owned enterprises that generate power from water.[14] The Tribunal was asked to address the key question of what rights and interests (if any) in water and geothermal resources were guaranteed and protected by the Treaty of Waitangi and whether the proposed sale amounted to a Treaty breach. This was lodged as a contemporary claim on the basis that the proposed sale was the Treaty breach, rather than the historical 'taking' of water bodies by government regulation. Oral histories form a significant part of claimants' cases and are intended to inform the Waitangi Tribunal as to how a claimant group established their customary interests in a particular area and how those interests were maintained. In order for a claim to be successful claimants must demonstrate that they suffered harmful consequences as a result of a Crown Treaty breach. The Tribunal decides whether, on the balance of probabilities, the claim is "well-founded". The Tribunal publishes its findings and recommendations in a report. Except in very limited circumstances, Waitangi Tribunal recommendations are not binding on the Crown.[15] In order to achieve a settlement, an inquiry by the Waitangi Tribunal will need to be followed by negotiations between the claimant group and the Crown. This results in a Deed of Settlement, which is then enshrined in a Settlement Bill that is adopted by Parliament.[16]

The other way to achieve a settlement is to enter into direct negotiations with the Crown, bypassing the Waitangi Tribunal. Claimant groups may be eligible to enter direct negotiations where, usually after having lodged a Tribunal claim, they can satisfy the Crown that they are the correct claimant group. Direct negotiations are generally quicker and less expensive for claimants who must decide whether the therapeutic value of taking time to go through the Tribunal outweighs the opportunity costs from likely delays in receiving redress. Settlements are intended to "heal the past and build a future" with the Crown acknowledging the grievance and then providing a "fair, comprehensive, final and durable settlement"; as well as establishing an ongoing relationship between the Crown and the claimant group based on the principles of the Treaty of Waitangi.[17]

Red Book].
14   Waitangi Tribunal, *The Stage 1 Report on the National Freshwater and Geothermal Resources Claim* (Wai 2358, 2012).
15   The Tribunal has the power to make binding recommendations for the return of land that is subject to a Crown forestry licence and certain lands owned, or formerly owned, by a state-owned enterprise or a tertiary institution, or former New Zealand Railways lands, that have a memorial (or notation) on their certificate of title advising that the Waitangi Tribunal may recommend that the land be returned to Māori ownership (see <http://www.justice.govt.nz/tribunals/waitangi-tribunal/about/frequently-asked-questions>).
16   Copies of the deeds are available at <https://www.govt.nz/organisations/office-of-treaty-settlements/>.
17   The Red Book, above n 13, at 77.

In moving that the Ngāti Koroki Kahukura Claims Settlement Bill be enacted, Hon Christopher Finlayson, Minister for Treaty of Waitangi Negotiations, chose these introductory words:[18]

> [w]e gather in this House to consider, to debate, and to address matters of State and matters of Government—matters that often define us as a nation. Very few things can be more defining than the occasion of a third reading of Treaty settlement legislation. This is an occasion that brings the Crown and iwi together for a common purpose: to reconcile past differences and to seal our shared commitment to a more enlightened and rewarding future together.

Justice Joe Williams, Māori scholar and High Court judge, has described Treaty settlements as fusing two pathways to justice – that of aboriginal title claims (which are based on residual common law rights), and Waitangi Tribunal processes which render Māori as victims blaming the state for the consequences of colonisation and "modern imbalances".[19] Justice Williams has further described the process of negotiating Treaty settlements as "the most dynamic and powerful process in the transitional justice game, a politically realistic approach to the results the Government is prepared to put up with".[20]

2. The Parameters of Treaty Settlement Negotiations

Justice Joe Williams provides a fitting description. The Crown defines the parameters for negotiation and redress, and claimants are expected to negotiate within those parameters if they want their claims resolved. For example, in 1997, Cabinet adopted specific principles for natural resource redress relating to rivers, lakes, minerals and forests.[21] In 2010, Cabinet approved a number of further guidelines for involving iwi in natural resource management in Treaty settlements to be considered as Crown "bottom lines".[22] The Resource Management Act 1991 (RMA) sets out a comprehensive regime for the sustainable management of natural resources.[23] While central government retains some responsibility to influence this regime through mechanisms such as national

---

18 (9 December 2014) 702 NZPD 1277 <http://www.parliament.nz/en-nz/pb/debates/debates/speeches/51HansS_20141212_00000009/finlayson-christopher-ng%C4%81ti-koroki-kahukura-claims-settlement>.
19 Joe Williams, above n 1, at 3. It is well documented that Māori occupy the bottom rung of social and economic strata, see generally the work of Dr Tahu Kukutai, such as Tahu Kukutai "Making Visible the Big C: Colonisation and Indigenous Health and Wellbeing" (paper presented to The Australian Sociological Association (TASA) Conference: Reflections, Intersections and Aspirations: 50 years of Australian Sociology, Melbourne, 2013).
20 At 10.
21 Cabinet Minute, "natural resource redress", 1997, CAB (97) 46/16A; Cabinet Minute, "natural resource redress", 1997, CAB Min (97) 46/35.
22 Cabinet Minute, "natural resource redress", 2010, CAB Min (10) 24/3 Rev 1.
23 Section 5 defines "sustainable management".

environmental standards and national policy statements,[24] day-to-day control is devolved to local government. Regional councils and local authorities (local government) prepare plans that regulate the use of land, air and water within their jurisdiction and specify when and where proposed activities may require consents to permit certain use.[25] Collectively the Crown's Treaty settlement principles for natural resource redress specify, among other things, that redress should not intrude on the powers and functions of local government who should retain final decision making rights over natural resource management.[26] Although the RMA requires local government to take iwi resource management plans into account when making certain decisions relating to the making and changing of plans,[27] the RMA is clear that there is no duty for local government to consult on resource consents.[28] Cabinet has prescribed that two "standard arrangements" be available in Treaty settlements for facilitating dialogue between iwi and local authorities on RMA matters: a Māori advisory board and a joint council committee.[29] These arrangements provide opportunities for iwi to have input into both planning and consenting processes under the RMA. As noted below, the tribal-specific agreements negotiated with Waikato-Tainui and Whanganui tribes in relation to the Waikato and Whanganui rivers also contain measures intended to facilitate tribal engagement with RMA processes associated with the rivers.[30]

Negotiations on behalf of the Crown are carried out by the Office of Treaty Settlements in conjunction with other Ministries and Government Departments whose staff religiously operate within these parameters. Any significant deviation from these standard arrangements would require Cabinet approval. This "rule by administrative fiat" has never been formalised by statute and consequently claimant groups are left with no remedy when the Crown itself does not obey them or unilaterally changes them.[31] The courts frequently refuse to review Treaty settlement policy or agreements given their political, non-justiciable nature.[32]

24 Resource Management Act 1991, ss 43-58A.
25 At sections 30 and 31.
26 Cabinet Minute, "natural resource redress", 2010, Cab Min (10) 24/3 Rev 1.
27 Resource Management Act 1991, s 61.
28 Section 36A.
29 Cabinet Minute, "natural resource redress", 1997, CAB (97) 46/16A; Cabinet Minute, "natural resource redress", 1997, CAB Min (97) 46/35; Cabinet Minute, "natural resource redress", 1997, CAB Min (10) 24/3 Rev 1. See also, RMA, sections 36B-36E.
30 See also the discussion of co-management agreements in Chapter 6 of this volume, Erueti and Down "International Indigenous Rights and Mining in Aotearoa New Zealand".
31 Ani Mikaere, above n 2. See also Linda Te Aho "Contemporary Issues in Māori Law and Society: The Tangled Web of Treaty Settlements, Emissions Trading, Central North Island Forests, and the Waikato River" (2008) 16 Wai Law Rev 229 and the references cited therein.
32 See generally *Milroy v Attorney General* [2005] NZAR 562. For a general discussion of legal

Despite these constraints, skilled negotiators have operated on behalf of claimant groups to achieve innovative settlements. But the impact of Treaty settlements upon Māori must also be seen as a form of contortion – with claimant groups feeling forced to work within a framework not of their making, and that goes nowhere near fully compensating them for their actual loss: politically, economically, culturally, environmentally or spiritually.

3. Relativity and Actual Loss

Perhaps the best example of the tensions Māori face in achieving these settlements lies in the task of creating value when constrained by the Crown's relativity policy of 1994. The policy fixed the total fiscal value of all Treaty claims at $1 billion. In 1995 negotiators for two powerful tribal groups, Waikato-Tainui and Ngāi Tahu, persuaded the Crown to agree to ratchet clauses in their settlements in return for taking the leap of faith to be the first to settle comprehensively their historical claims. In essence, the clauses allow for these two groups to each receive an additional 17% of the final fiscal sum spent on settlements in the event the total exceeds $1 billion.[33] As a result, all later settlements that have been reached have been benchmarked against these two settlements. Relativity clauses have not been made available for claimant groups that settled later. Although this 'fiscal envelope' policy was officially rescinded in 1996, it continues to have a major impact on the relativities of settlements. Waikato-Tainui and Ngāi Tahu have already triggered their relativity clauses. Waikato-Tainui has received additional cash sums. Current evidence suggests that the total value of all claims may exceed $2 billion. With no recourse to a relativity clause, it is not surprising that there are some claimant groups who feel that they have not been treated equitably. The relativity policy may well be the subject of contemporary Treaty claims arising out of the settlement process itself.[34]

A major criticism of Treaty settlements, even for the larger groups who settled early, is that they do not compensate for actual loss. The Crown's fiscal envelope policy has meant that claimants "settle" for some 1–2% of actual loss. In clause 2.3 of the Waikato-Tainui deed of settlement, the Crown acknowledges that the contribution of the confiscated land to the development of New Zealand is estimated to have a value as at 1995 of $12 billion.[35] Yet, the cash quantum

---

challenges to Treaty settlements, see Baden Vertongen "Legal Challenges to the Treaty Settlement Process" in Nicola R Wheen and Janine Hayward (eds) *Treaty of Waitangi Settlements* (Bridget Williams Books, Wellington, 2012) at 65.

33 Alan Ward *An Unsettled History: Treaty Claims in New Zealand Today* (Bridget Williams Books, Wellington, 1999) at 55, 57.

34 Jeremy Gardiner "Achieving enduring settlements" Post Treaty Settlements <http://posttreatysettlements.org.nz/achieving-enduring-settlements>.

35 Waikato-Tainui Deed of Settlement 1995, cl 2.3.

of the settlement was $170 million. In order to achieve settlements, claimant groups are compelled to agree to standard clauses acknowledging that it is "not possible to fully compensate" them for all loss and prejudice suffered and that they "intend their foregoing full compensation to contribute to New Zealand's development".

This point is often highlighted in parliamentary debates by members of New Zealand's Green Party. Member of Parliament, Denise Roche, explained her party's position in relation to the Ngāti Koroki Kahukura Claims Settlement Bill:[36]

> This bill addresses just a tiny fraction of what Ngāti Koroki Kahukura have endured ... and yet there are some New Zealanders who have no understanding of the history and who will declare this Treaty settlement, and all Treaty settlements, a gravy train. My response to that is to remind those people that in 2010 this Government bailed out South Canterbury Finance to the tune of $1.7 billion. This settlement is a drop in the bucket—and those people did not lose their land ... [We] do not believe that it is full compensation, and we must acknowledge the generosity of this iwi, who will accept this settlement ... and all the people of New Zealand benefit from that generosity.

Innovation has occurred where skilled claimant negotiators have added value to settlement packages over and above the relative cash quantum without breaching the Crown's (now unofficial) relativity policy. Structuring sale and lease back arrangements of Crown-owned commercial properties and mechanisms such as a "single purchaser discount" have enabled some claimant groups to increase the number of properties acquired with their fixed Treaty credits.[37]

4. Returning Ancestral or Traditional or Tribal Lands

I riro whenua atu, me hoki whenua mai
Land was taken, land must be returned

Land is central to indigenous identity. Te Ture Whenua Māori (Māori Land Act) 1993 recognises that land is a "taonga tuku iho of special significance to Māori", an inheritance from the past to be protected and enhanced for future generations.[38] Land was confiscated and alienated in other ways that have

---

36 (9 December 2014) 702 NZPD 1289 <http://www.parliament.nz/en-nz/pb/debates/debates/speeches/51HansS_20141212_00000044/roche-denise-ng%C4%81ti-koroki-kahukura-claims-settlement>.

37 Claimants may "purchase" redress properties with the cash quantum allocated to their settlement. Claimant negotiators have successfully argued that the fact that a claimant group is a single purchaser saves the Crown transaction costs. This translates into an overall "discount" in the price of the redress properties, thus enabling claimants to purchase more properties with their settlement cash.

38 Te Ture Whenua Māori 1993, Preamble and s 2.

been acknowledged by the Crown in many settlements as Treaty breaches.[39] A fundamental premise of many Treaty settlements is that land should be returned as an important part of an overall redress package. Often, as a result of having been dispossessed of certain significant lands for over a century, many claimant groups seek that the lands returned be inalienable and/or vested in the names of important ancestors. This has resulted in new forms of title being created such as that created in the Waikato-Tainui lands settlement of 1995.[40] By that settlement certain lands were vested in the name of the first Māori King, Pōtatau Te Wherowhero (1770–1860), an ancestor representative of the Waikato-Tainui peoples. The inalienable status comes with constraints to developing the lands.[41]

There are two key examples of government policy that contorts land redress. First, lands returned to claimant groups are likely to be subject to public access and conservation conditions. For example, Ōkahu Bay, a prime piece of beachfront property in central Auckland was returned to Ngāti Whātua o Ōrākei under its Treaty settlement in 2012. The Ngāti Whātua settlement states that Ōkahu Bay will be a new form of title, whenua rangatira (chiefly land), which is deemed a Māori reservation under the Reserves Act 1977 and set apart for the common use and benefit of Ngāti Whātua o Ōrākei *and the citizens of Auckland* (emphasis added).[42] These provisions ensure public access and continue reserve protections for prime Auckland real estate, while symbolically overlaying the land with a deemed Māori reservation status. Notably, the Ngāti Whātua settlement in relation to Okahu Bay reaffirms and continues an arrangement made in 1991, which is an early example of co-management regimes between iwi and government established under Treaty settlements.[43] Under this arrangement, the fee simple title to the returned lands is registered in favour of Ngāti Whātua's Trust Board, but the reservation is jointly administered by Ngāti Whātua and the Auckland City Council through a Reserves Board which comprises three representatives of Ngāti Whātua and three representatives from the Council.[44] By statute, the land is managed, financed and developed at the expense of the Council in view of the land, including foreshore, being kept for the public as well as the enjoyment of Ngāti Whātua. The chairperson (and the casting vote) is reserved for a Ngāti Whātua representative in recognition of title and territorial authority.[45]

This arrangement did not come about easily.[46] Like many other settlements

---

39 Waitangi Tribunal *The Taranaki Report – Kaupapa Tuatahi* (Wai 143, 1996).
40 Waikato-Tainui Deed of Settlement 1995.
41 Deed of Settlement between Her Majesty in right of New Zealand and Waikato 1995, cls 4.1 and 4.4. See also Deed Creating Waikato Raupatu Lands Trust 1995, cl 7.
42 Ngāti Whatua o Ōrākei Claims Settlement Act 2012, s 60.
43 Orakei Act 1991.
44 Ngāti Whatua o Ōrākei Claims Settlement Act 2012, s 66 and Sch 4.
45 Schedule 4.
46 Sections 6 and 7.

of this kind it was born of conflict and collision. Following a government announcement of a housing development destined for their ancestral lands, tribal members and supporters of the Ngāti Whātua occupied and refused to leave those lands for 506 days – the longest and perhaps most famous of protest actions in New Zealand history. On 25 May 1978, the government sent in a massive force of police and army personnel to evict them. Hundreds of protesters were arrested and their temporary buildings and gardens were demolished. A young tribal member lost her life during the ordeal. Ten years later the Waitangi Tribunal supported the hapū's claims to the land.[47] In the words of the late Sir Hugh Kawharu, the inaugural chairperson of the Reserves Board:[48]

> ... from the trauma and the ashes the Crown restored title to Orakei's 150 acre 'Whenua Rangatira' ... The arrangement has worked successfully and without untoward incident since its inception in 1992 ... It is a benign but efficient regime; and here at least the mana of Ngati Whatua stands tall, intact and protected ... [P]ublic access to the foreshore of Okahu Bay has been unrestricted from the day title returned to Ngati Whatua.

5. *Mountain Ownership and Management*

Mountain ownership and management is an important part of Treaty settlements in Aotearoa. However, the return of whole mountains and mountain ranges is rendered unachievable given relativity constraints – their value would eclipse the fiscal envelope. Instead, settlements have included the return of significant mountains, the title to which are then "gifted to the nation";[49] or the return of mountain peaks only, fragments of the whole.[50] A recent departure from established patterns in Treaty settlements is seen in the case of the Ngāti Koroki Kahukura settlement and provisions for Maungatautari, the ancestral mountain of the Ngāti Koroki Kahukura iwi. Maungatautari is deemed to be a "reserve" under the Treaty settlement. Traditionally the mountain and its forests offered shelter and provided physical sustenance for Ngāti Koroki Kahukura. They have kept their fires of occupation alight through the turbulence of inter-tribal conflict and colonisation, and have continued to live close to the mountain ever since. While the mountain has a rich human history, the Crown acknowledges that Ngāti

---

47 Waitangi Tribunal *Report of The Waitangi Tribunal on The Orakei Claim* (Wai 9, 1987) at 149–152.
48 As quoted in Pat Sneddon "Rangatiratanga and Generosity: Making the Connections" (Paper presented to the Philanthropy New Zealand Conference, 2004). This settlement predates the amendments made in 2005 to the Resource Management Act 1991 that included new sections to explicitly provide for joint management agreements between and councils and iwi authorities – sections 36B, D and E.
49 Ngāi Tahu Claims Settlement Act 1998, ss 15, 16.
50 See, for example, Affiliate Te Arawa Iwi and Hapu Claims Settlement Act 2008, s 105.

Koroki Kahukura are the iwi with "dominant mana whenua" rights and interests in respect of Maungatautari.[51] With iwi and local government support, a major restoration project was initiated by the members of the community to remove introduced pests and predators from the mountain, and restore to the forest a healthy diversity of indigenous plants and animals on the brink of extinction, including 47 kilometres of predator-proof fence enclosing 3400 hectares.[52] However, Ngāti Koroki Kahukura were not to know that their agreement to support the restoration project years prior to their Treaty settlement negotiations would result in them being denied the return of the Crown lands within the mountain reserve lest the return prejudice "the community endeavor" in establishing the project. Claimants sought to change the name of Queen Elizabeth II on the title of Maungatautari but were told by Crown negotiators they would have to accept that title be vested in a new construct called "Te Hapori o Maungatautari" (the community of Maungatautari) with non-indigenous peoples being represented by the Waipā district's mayor.[53] Ngāti Koroki Kahukura would not enjoy even the symbolic reality of the mountain being "returned" to them for a moment in time. Nor would title to the mountain be vested in the name of an appropriate ancestor with inalienable status. The politics of volatile reaction from non-indigenous peoples in the rural community meant that such options were denied to them.[54] Te Hapori o Maungatautari is not a legal entity, nor a co-governance body. Not only was it incomprehensible that the Crown would allow such public reaction to influence decisions that denied their ancestral rights, Ngāti Koroki Kahukura is left to grapple with the implementation of these new concepts. The iwi will at least, have more say in how the reserve will be administered in the future, another example of the growing trend towards co-management. Experienced politician, Hon Nanaia Mahuta, recognised that:[55]

> There has been a very gracious acknowledgment made by Ngāti Koroki Kahukura to the people of the Waipā District and, in fact, to New Zealand for the future management of the Maungatautari maunga. I want to put on the record that that is huge and significant.

Public access is guaranteed. Reserve restrictions in favour of conservation values are imposed as per other settlements. Such restrictions make sense in terms of this particular settlement. However, they may be too onerous where

---

51 Ngāti Koroki Kahukura Claims Settlement Act 2014, s 70.
52 <http://www.sanctuarymountain.co.nz/the_project>.
53 Ngāti Koroki Kahukura Claims Settlement Act 2014, s 82.
54 Nikki Preston "Critic Slams Iwi 'Pirates'" *Waikato Times* (online ed, New Zealand, 21 November 2010); Bruce Holloway "Maungatautari Landowner Backs Maori" *Waikato Times* (online ed, New Zealand, 10 March 2011) [accessed 29 February 2016].
55 (9 December 2014) 702 NZPD 1279 <http://www.parliament.nz/en-nz/pb/debates/debates/speeches/51HansS_20141212_00000016>.

reserve lands are in urban areas and suitable for development. Negotiating for the removal of reserve status is difficult for claimant groups and often comes at a significant cost to other aspects of settlement packages.

6. Settling Freshwater – Co-Management and Co-Governance

Twists and turns of a legal nature also appear in settlements involving lakes and rivers. There is a diverse range of views amongst Māori about who might own water. Many iwi and hapū assert ownership of water largely because ownership is the strongest tool possible for the purpose of restoring and protecting waterways, but also to support rights of accessing water for their own commercial purposes. Others are of the view that one cannot own an ancestor and would express their rights in different ways.[56] Freshwater settlements avoid the issue of water ownership on the basis of the Crown's policy that "no-one owns water". The Te Arawa Lakes Settlement Act 2006 follows a history of challenge by the iwi in relation to the ownership, governance and management of water bodies in their territory. However, instead of the thirteen freshwater lakes the settlement vests the fee simple estate of the lake *beds* in the iwi. The Te Arawa example is of particular note because it creates a disturbing form of title that certainly fits the dual descriptors of legal innovation and contortion. The Crown is deemed the owner of a new construct, the "Crown stratum", which is defined as the space occupied by water and the space occupied by air above each lake bed, thus precluding the ability of the iwi to claim ownership to the water or the airspace.[57] In addition to the vesting of lakebeds the settlement establishes a co-management entity comprised of the iwi and regional and district councils.[58] The vision of this entity is for the lakes and their catchments to be preserved and protected for the use and enjoyment of present and future generations.[59] The vision recognises and provides for the iwi's traditional relationship with their ancestral lakes, and the iwi provide cultural advice on all aspects pertaining to the lakes.

The growing number of these freshwater co-management regimes provide more freedom for Māori to carry out customary activities, and have led to more collaborative planning processes, joint projects, and generally more effective relationships between local government and Māori.[60] The settlements have

---

56 For a summary of the debate, see IC Solutions Ltd, "Report to the Iwi Advisory Group from the Freshwater Iwi Leadership Regional Hui, Whiringa a Rangi" 2014 at 11 <http://iwichairs.maori.nz/our-kaupapa/fresh-water/>.
57 Te Arawa Lakes Settlement Act 2006, s 23.
58 Section 48.
59 Section 49.
60 For example, the Waikato Regional Council Healthy Rivers Plan Change project and process: http://www.waikatoregion.govt.nz/healthyrivers/.

provided funding for restoration projects and have paved the way for an increase in the use of traditional knowledge indicators to monitor and assess the health and well-being of waterways.

The Waikato-Tainui River settlement is considered as the high water mark of these types of co-management arrangements.[61] This settlement requires a joint management arrangement between iwi and local government[62] (prior settlements simply encourage local government to build relationships with claimant groups), effectively forcing local government to negotiate new ways of conducting planning and consenting processes under the RMA in order to achieve the overarching principle of the settlement: to restore and protect the health and wellbeing of the Waikato River for future generations.[63] The settlement also included a scoping study and substantial clean-up fund to improve the health and wellbeing of the Waikato River. This was provided alongside the settlement;[64] in other words, it was not intended to be redress and was outside of quantum. Cabinet has determined that scoping studies and clean-up funds should not be included in settlement negotiations generally[65] and this means that Crown negotiators will only progress remediation activities alongside settlements in what they consider to be exceptional circumstances.[66]

The Waikato-Tainui River settlement is also notable for a provision that explicitly defers any conversation about ownership of water.[67] The Crown and Waikato-Tainui acknowledge that they have different concepts and views regarding relationships with the Waikato River (which the Crown would seek to describe as including "ownership") and that the settlement is not intended to resolve those differences. If the Crown or a Crown entity proposes to create or dispose of a property right or interest in the Waikato River the Crown must first engage with Waikato-Tainui in accordance with the principles described in the settlement.[68]

---

61 Waikato-Tainui Raupatu Claims (Waikato River) Settlement Act 2010. See also, Linda Te Aho "Indigenous Challenges to Enhance Freshwater Governance and Management in Aotearoa New Zealand – The Waikato River Settlement" (2009) 20 Journal of Water Law 285. See below for a discussion about the Whanganui River settlement which provides an opportunity for more effective recognition of the rights and interests of the River through affording the River legal personality.
62 Waikato-Tainui Raupatu Claims (Waikato River) Settlement Act 2010, s 41.
63 Section 3.
64 Waikato-Tainui Raupatu Deed of Settlement 2010, cl 15 provides for co-management funding and an education endowment fund.
65 CAB Min (09) 12/11.
66 In later settlements, other iwi have succeeded in negotiating for clean-up funds, but no other iwi has achieved the same level of funding, $210 million. For example, Whanganui iwi secured $30 million: Ruruku Whakatupua 2014 (the Deed of Settlement for the Whanganui River) cls 7.1 and 7.2.
67 Waikato-Tainui Raupatu Claims (Waikato River) Settlement Act 2010, ss 64 and 90.
68 Section 64(3).

Like the relativity clauses, these water clauses have only been made available to select claimant groups.[69] Even so, in light of the Waitangi Tribunal's findings in relation to rights and interests, the absence of these clauses should not jeopardise other claimant groups from asserting claims to water.

In its Interim report on the National Freshwater and Geothermal Resources Claim, the Waitangi Tribunal addressed the key question of what rights and interests (if any) in water and geothermal resources were guaranteed and protected by the Treaty of Waitangi? It reached a bold conclusion:[70]

> Maori had rights and interests in their water bodies for which the closest English equivalent in 1840 was ownership. Those rights were then confirmed, guaranteed, and protected by the Treaty of Waitangi, save to the extent that the Treaty bargain provided for some sharing of the waters with incoming settlers . . . The nature and extent of the proprietary right was the exclusive right of hapu and iwi to control access to and use of the water while it was in their rohe.

In the context of the current discussions between the Crown and Māori about how to give effect to rights and interests in freshwater,[71] the Crown is seeking detailed information about mechanisms to appropriately recognise such rights and interests from indigenous perspectives. It is generally accepted by Māori that the various co-management arrangements referred to above deal primarily with the restoration and protection of the health and wellbeing of the waterways, not the issue of recognising their rights and interests in their water bodies.[72]

7. Legal-Personality

A recent development that has stirred interest in the Treaty settlements arena for its innovative nature is an agreement signed between the Crown and Whanganui iwi.[73] Settlements such as those that relate to the Waikato,[74]

---

69 For example, Whanganui negotiated a "water" clause, Ruruku Whakatupua, above n 51, cl 9, but a request from Ngāti Koroki Kahukura for such a clause was denied.
70 Waitangi Tribunal, *The Stage 1 Report on the National Freshwater and Geothermal Resources Claim* (Wai 2358, 2012) at 110.
71 In *The New Zealand Māori Council v Attorney General* [2013] NZSC 6, the Supreme Court noted the Crown's acceptance that some hapū will have interests in particular waters and their interests are protected by Article 2 of the Treaty of Waitangi.
72 IC Solutions Ltd, "Report to the Iwi Advisory Group from the Freshwater Iwi Leadership Regional Hui, Whiringa a Rangi" 2014, at 11.
73 See Te Awa Tupua (Whanganui River Claims Settlement) Act 2017. See also, Linda Te Aho "Ruruku Whakatupua Te Mana o te Awa Tupua – Upholding the Mana of the Whanganui River" (2014) 5 Māori Law Review <http://maorilawreview.co.nz/2014/05/>.
74 Waikato-Tainui Raupatu Claims (Waikato River) Settlement Act 2010.

Waipā[75] and Kaituna Rivers,[76] and the Te Arawa Lakes settlement,[77] have established co-management regimes, and have recognised to varying degrees Māori conceptions of the environment.[78] For example, the Waikato-Tainui River settlement recognises that to Waikato-Tainui the river is an ancestor, which has a prestige, authority and a life force of its own.[79] The Whanganui River settlement recognises the river as an indivisible and living whole comprising the Whanganui River from the mountains to the sea, incorporating its tributaries and all its physical and metaphysical elements.[80] However, the settlement goes a step further. In recognising the profound relationships that Whanganui iwi have with their ancestral river, the settlement accords legal personality to the Whanganui River, providing an opportunity for more effective recognition of the rights and interests of the river.[81] The Whanganui settlement, like that in relation to the Waikato River, provides for a clean-up fund, and compels local government relationship agreements. Part 5 of the settlement establishes a co-governance group ("Te Kōpuka") comprising iwi, local and central government, commercial and recreational users and environmental groups. The purpose of the group is to act collaboratively to advance the environmental, social, cultural and economic health and wellbeing of the Whanganui River. While the RMA provides legislative rights to ensure Māori interests are recognised to varying degrees in decision making,[82] case law illustrates that these rights remain vulnerable when weighed against other priorities.[83] This is why Māori have turned to Treaty settlement processes. The Whanganui River settlement states that the post-settlement governance entity has an interest in the river greater than the public generally when balancing the competing interests outlined in the RMA, and should therefore have an increased ability to influence decision making in the day-to-day management of the river.[84] There is innovation too, in the redress included in relation to protecting the river's rapids, which may well assist iwi and the river in any future proposals to dam the river for water storage, given climate change challenges.[85]

75 Nga Wai o Maniapoto (Waipa River) Act 2012.
76 Tapuika Claims Settlement Act 2014, s 114.
77 Te Arawa Lakes Settlement Act 2006.
78 Linda Te Aho "Ngā Whakataunga Waimāori: Freshwater Settlements" in Nicola R Wheen and Janine Hayward (eds) *Treaty of Waitangi Settlements* (Bridget Williams Books, Wellington, 2012) at 102.
79 Waikato-Tainui Raupatu Claims (Waikato River) Settlement Act 2010, Preamble.
80 Te Awa Tupua (Whanganui River Claims Settlement) Act 2017, s 12.
81 Te Awa Tupua (Whanganui River Claims Settlement) Act 2017, s 14.
82 Resource Management Act 1991, ss 6, 7 and 8.
83 Jacinta Ruru "Undefined and Unresolved: Exploring Indigenous Rights in Aotearoa New Zealand's Freshwater Legal Regime" (2009) 20 Journal of Water Law 236.
84 Te Awa Tupua (Whanganui River Claims Settlement) Act 2017, s 72(d).
85 Drought is a common feature of New Zealand's climate. In 2013, New Zealand experienced

In the context of current debates about how the Crown might recognise Māori proprietary rights and interests in freshwater,[86] there are other notable features of the Whanganui settlement. Firstly, the Deed of Settlement makes elaborate statements about ownership of water, not seen in other settlements. The Crown confirms its position that no one, including the Crown, owns water.[87] While Whanganui iwi do not view their relationship with water in terms of ownership in a strict sense, they also assert that its rights and responsibilities in relation to the Whanganui river (an indivisible and living whole being) are of a proprietary nature.[88] The parties agree that this settlement is not intended to derogate from a freshwater policy review process being carried out simultaneously by the Government, which, among other things, addresses the issue of Māori proprietary rights and interests in water.[89] To avoid doubt, the Deed of Settlement confirms that the vesting of the riverbed does not create proprietary interests in water.[90] That being said, the Te Awa Tupua (Whanganui River Claims Settlement) Act 2017 gives effect to the Whanganui River Deed of Settlement. Of particular interest is the definition of the "bed": the space of land that the waters of the Whanganui River cover at its fullest flow without overtopping its banks.[91] It includes the subsoil, the plants attached to the bed, *the space occupied by the water and the airspace above the water* (emphasis added).[92] This approach differs to that discussed above in relation to the Te Arawa Lakes Settlement.[93]

Yet for all of its innovation, the settlement still falls short of the recommendations made by the Waitangi Tribunal in its substantial report on the Whanganui River in 1999.[94] There, the Tribunal found that as at 1840 the Whanganui River and its tributaries were possessed and controlled by the iwi and that the extinguishments of Māori river interests in the particular context

---

the worst drought in history. On average, every year or two somewhere in New Zealand experiences a drought. It is foreseeable that there will be more need to store water beyond what can be naturally sourced at any one time and stopping the natural flow of a river, particularly at the site of rapids, has proven to be an effective and popular way to do this in New Zealand (see <https://www.niwa.co.nz/climate/information-and-resources/drought>). This redress should provide the iwi with a stronger voice in decision-making over any proposals to dam the Whanganui River.

86 Ruruku Whakatupua Te Mana o te Awa Tupua 2014, clause 9.2
87 Ruruku Whakatupua Te Mana o te Awa Tupua 2014, clause 9.3.
88 Ruruku Whakatupua Te Mana o te Awa Tupua 2014, clause 9.3.
89 Ruruku Whakatupua Te Mana o te Awa Tupua 2014, clause 9.4.
90 Ruruku Whakatupua Te Mana o te Awa Tupua 2014, clause 9.5. See also Te Awa Tupua (Whanganui River Claims Settlement) Act 2017, s 46(1)(a).
91 Te Awa Tupua (Whanganui River Claims Settlement) Act 2017, s 7.
92 Te Awa Tupua (Whanganui River Claims Settlement) Act 2017, s 7.
93 See text above relating to the Te Arawa Lakes Settlement Act 2016. The Waikato River Settlement did not involve the return of riverbeds.
94 The Waitangi Tribunal *Whanganui River Report* (Wai 167, 1999) at 343–345.

were inconsistent with Treaty principles.[95] The Tribunal recommended that the Crown negotiate with the iwi having regard to two forward looking proposals. First, that the river *in its entirety* be vested in an ancestor or ancestors of the iwi (emphasis added).[96] Secondly, any resource consent application in respect of the river would either require the approval of the iwi governance entity, or that entity could be added as a "consent authority" in terms of the RMA to act with the current consenting authority.[97] Both would need to consent to any resource consent application.[98] Under the settlement while, as noted above, the iwi interest has additional weight in RMA planning and consent processes, the iwi's consent is not required for the use of water, though the parties acknowledge that this may change in the future following the freshwater review process.

While it is too early to assess the effectiveness of the innovation in this settlement, it appears to provide the strongest opportunity for more effective participation by Māori in planning processes of all freshwater settlements to date.

C. Future Implications – United Nations Declaration on the Rights of Indigenous Peoples

> Notwithstanding the progress made through all the tribunal reports and court cases from the 1980s, and the consequential changes in legislation and official policy, I would still rank the day that New Zealand gave support to the declaration as the most significant day, in advancing Maori rights, since 6th February 1840.
>
> *Sir Edward Taihākurei Durie, 2010*[99]

Māori, like many other indigenous peoples around the world have sought to affirm indigenous rights via international institutions, and have long been part of the Declaration negotiations. The self-determination framework, and in particular Article 3, is at the heart of the Declaration.

> Indigenous peoples have the right to self-determination. By virtue of that right they freely determine their political status and freely pursue their economic, social and cultural development.

Article 3 equates most with tino rangatiratanga. The issue for all claims relating to lands and resources is control over use. There are other powerful articles in the Declaration, such as Article 25, which provides that:

---

95 The Waitangi Tribunal *Whanganui River Report* (Wai 167, 1999) at 261.
96 The Waitangi Tribunal *Whanganui River Report* (Wai 167, 1999) at 343
97 The Waitangi Tribunal *Whanganui River Report* (Wai 167, 1999) at 343–344.
98 The Waitangi Tribunal *Whanganui River Report* (Wai 167, 1999) at 343–344.
99 Tracy Watkins "Judge hails big advance for Maori" stuff.co.nz (online ed, New Zealand, 22 April 2010).

> Indigenous Peoples have the right to maintain and strengthen their distinctive spiritual relationship with their traditionally owned or otherwise occupied or used lands, territories, waters and coastal seas and other resources and to uphold their responsibilities to future generations in this regard.

Article 26 goes further to provide that States shall give legal recognition and protection to these lands, territories and resources and such recognition shall be conducted with due respect to the customs and traditions of the indigenous peoples concerned.

The Declaration also contains a number of articles that require free, prior and informed consent. According to Article 32:

> States shall consult and cooperate in good faith with the indigenous peoples concerned ... in order to obtain their free and informed consent prior to the approval of any project affecting their lands or territories and other resources, particularly in connection with the development, utilization or exploitation of mineral, water or other resources.

One way of viewing the Declaration is that it fleshes out and provides more clarity and certainty around the meaning of the short articles that make up the Treaty of Waitangi (as expressed by Sir Edward Taihākurei Durie). On this view, the rights expressed in the Declaration may be of assistance to claimant negotiators in addressing the power imbalance and further expanding the parameters of Treaty settlement negotiations. It is of some concern that the New Zealand Government plays down the importance of the Declaration, stressing its non-binding nature, noting "[i]t is an expression of aspiration; it will have no impact on New Zealand law and no impact on the constitutional framework."[100] New Zealand's formal endorsement of the Declaration was also diluted with numerous references to New Zealand's "existing frameworks", "own distinct approach" and "existing legal regimes" which would "define the bounds of New Zealand's engagement with the aspirational elements of the Declaration."[101]

These attitudes will change in time.[102] With respect, there is a strong argument that the articles of the Declaration more appropriately reflect the "principles of the Treaty" than those espoused by the Courts. The approach of the Courts has been the subject of academic critique on the basis that while the *Wi Parata v The*

---

100 Pita Sharples, Minister of Maori Affairs "UNPFII Opening Ceremony New Zealand Statement" (speech to United Nations Permanent Forum on Indigenous Issues, New York, 19 April 2010).
101 NZ *Hansard* Ministerial Statements: UN Declaration on the Rights of Indigenous Peoples—Government Support (20 April 2010) 662 NZPD 10229.
102 There was once a time when the Chief Justice of this country dismissed the Treaty of Waitangi as a "simple nullity": *Wi Parata v The Bishop of Wellington* (1877) 3 NZ Jur (NS) SC 72. The Treaty is now widely regarded as the founding document of the nation: *Ngati Apa v Attorney-General* [2003] 3 NZLR 643 (CA).

Bishop of Wellington position no longer enjoys widespread popularity:[103]

> ... it has largely been replaced by a range of views that are, in reality, no less oppressive, despite being conveyed in the soothing language of partnership, mutual respect, or aboriginal rights. While Prendergast's overt racism has for the most part been spurned in favour of greater cultural sensitivity, any concessions that are made to Māori aspirations of tino rangatiratanga ... are nevertheless envisaged as occurring within the framework of Crown sovereignty. As such they represent the false generosity of the oppressor ...

This critique resounds strongly here. Treaty settlements may well be seen as concessions made within an oppressive Crown framework while conveyed in the soothing language of healing the past, of recognising rights and providing redress. They will certainly be seen by some as a further example of the false generosity of the Crown. Despite the Government's current view of the Declaration, there remains an enthusiasm amongst Māori to further explore and promote greater understanding of the implications of New Zealand's endorsement of the Declaration for New Zealand law and policy on Māori rights and interests, and it is increasingly cited in legal submissions to the courts and parliamentary select committees, and to the Waitangi Tribunal.

D. Conclusion

Māori claims to lands and waters in Aotearoa New Zealand are mainly historical and date back to breaches of the 1840 Treaty of Waitangi. Crown breaches of the Treaty guarantees have resulted in the loss of ancestral lands by way of early Crown purchases, the impacts of the "New Zealand Wars" and the major land confiscations that followed, early Native Land Court transactions and public works takings. The degradation of waterbodies and the extinguishment of indigenous rights and interests in water have also been the subject of Treaty claims. Māori continue in their struggle for reconciliation and justice, and have come a long way. But there is a way to go. While the negotiated settlements that are aimed at settling grievances that arise from the Crown's Treaty breaches are creative, offer economic opportunities and go some way to recognising special relationships between Māori and their lands and waters, they are tainted with inequity and constrain the ability of Māori as indigenous peoples to be free and self-determining. They are therefore inconsistent with the United Nations Declaration on the Rights of Indigenous Peoples, now endorsed by the New Zealand Government. The Declaration is a valuable tool that ought to be called upon to assist both the Crown and Māori in future Treaty settlement negotiations and in the complex debate around indigenous rights and interests in water.

---

103 Ani Mikaere above note 2, at 330. See also Jane Kelsey *A Question of Honour: Labour and the Treaty 1984–1989* (Allen & Unwin, Auckland, 1990) at 217.

6
International Indigenous Rights and Mining in Aotearoa New Zealand

Sarah Down[*] and Andrew Erueti[**]

A. Introduction

Many mining and petroleum activities (mining activities) are conducted in areas occupied or used by indigenous peoples.[1] Such activities often negatively impact on indigenous peoples' rights to self-determination, land and economic development.[2] However, recent years have seen a number of developments in international law aimed at protecting the rights of indigenous peoples, in particular the adoption in 2007 of the United Nations Declaration on the Rights of Indigenous Peoples (the Declaration) and the United Nations Guiding Principles on Business and Human Rights (Guiding Principles).[3] Yet, despite these developments, indigenous peoples continue to struggle to have their interests in natural resources recognised. This chapter considers: (a) the regulation of mining activities in New Zealand and provisions for Māori interests; and (b) the potential for recognising Māori interests in natural resources, including models

---

[*] Doctoral Candidate, Australia National University.
[**] Senior Lecturer, Faculty of Law, University of Auckland.
[1] For example, in Australia it is estimated that more than 60 per cent of mineral operations neighbour indigenous communities. Minerals Council of Australia website: <http://www.minerals.org.au/policy_focus/indigenous_economic_development>.
[2] There is a vast amount of literature on mining and indigenous peoples in different countries. See, for example, Jon Altman and David Martin *Power Culture Economy: Indigenous Australians and Mining* (ANU E-Press, Canberra, 2009); Saleem H Ali *Mining the Environment and Indigenous Development Conflicts* (University of Arizona Press, Tuscon, 2004); Ciaran O'Faircheallaigh and Saleem H Ali (eds) *Earth Matters: Indigenous Peoples, the Extractive Industries and Corporate Social Responsibility* (Greenleaf Publishing, Sheffield, 2008); Chris Ballard and Glenn Banks "Resource Wars: the Anthropology of Mining" (2003) 32 Annual Review of Anthropology 287.
[3] United Nations Declaration on the Rights of Indigenous Peoples, GA Res 61/295, UNGAOR, 61st Sess, Supp No 49, UN Doc A/RES/61/295 (2007).

that have emerged for ownership or the co-management of natural resources. Our argument is that in New Zealand there needs to be reform, including the recognition of iwi proprietary interests in minerals and the right to control their use. The best means to achieve this is likely to be through iwi–government negotiated agreements – which New Zealand has much experience with through Treaty settlements, by which historical grievances investigated by the Waitangi Tribunal are settled through negotiated agreements. Part B of this chapter outlines international law relating to indigenous rights in natural resources, with a focus on the Declaration and the Guiding Principles. Business and human rights – the notion that companies must respect human rights – is a relatively new field in international law and there has been very little written about it in the New Zealand context.[4] However, it has generated a great deal of interest for indigenous peoples globally given the proliferation of mining activities, forestry and hydropower projects within their traditional territories. Part C provides an overview of New Zealand's regulation of mining activities and evaluates this regulatory environment in light of New Zealand's obligations under the Declaration and the Guiding Principles. In Part D, we outline suggestions for reform.

B. International Law

1. The UN Declaration on the Rights of Indigenous Peoples

The Declaration stands as a significant achievement in setting standards for the protection of indigenous peoples' rights, including their interests in natural resources and protection against displacement and despoliation caused by mining activities. In this regard, the most powerful suite of norms in the Declaration are the rights to self-determination;[5] and self-government;[6] free, prior and informed consent (FPIC);[7] and the obligation of states to recognise traditional land rights (that is, demarcate and issue a formal title to lands).[8] Of all the rights in the Declaration, so far FPIC has generated the most interest. The right to FPIC is cited several times, but Article 32 specifically addresses the requirement to obtain indigenous peoples' FPIC with respect to mining activities within their traditional lands:[9]

---

4 But see, Andrew Erueti and Joshua Pietras "Extractive Industry, Human Rights and Indigenous Rights in New Zealand's Exclusive Economic Zone" (2013) 11 NZYIL 37; Henry Clayton "Business and Human Rights: Businesses Doing More Than Domestic Law Requires" [2011] Human Rights Research Journal 2.
5 At art 3.
6 At art 4.
7 At art 10, art 11(2), art 19, art 28, art 29, art 32.
8 At art 26, 27 and 28.
9 Art 32.

States shall consult and cooperate in good faith with the indigenous peoples concerned through their own representative institutions in order to obtain their free and informed consent prior to the approval of any project affecting their lands or territories and other resources, particularly in connection with the development, utilization or exploitation of mineral, water or other resources.

States were generally opposed to the inclusion of FPIC in the Declaration, arguing that it provided indigenous peoples with a right of veto.[10] However, a body of policy, scholarship and jurisprudence has provided greater clarity about the content of the right to FPIC. The right to FPIC has been affirmed in several UN human rights treaty body decisions, including the UN Human Rights Committee,[11] the UN Committee on the Elimination of Racial Discrimination,[12] and the African Commission on Human and Peoples' Rights.[13] In particular, the Inter-American Court of Human Rights has given perhaps the most comprehensive authoritative guidance on the content of FPIC. In the decision of the *Saramaka People v Suriname*,[14] the Court ruled that, regarding large-scale development or investment projects that would have a major impact within Saramaka territory, the State has a duty, not only to consult with the Saramaka, but also to obtain their FPIC, according to their customs and traditions. The former UN Special Rapporteur on the Rights of Indigenous Peoples, James Anaya, has stressed the need to focus not only on consent, but on establishing a process that will result in indigenous peoples' full engagement with a proposed development. The key is ensuring that indigenous peoples are involved early in the process including in the preparation of regulatory frameworks on relevant areas such as the environment, and natural resource allocation and strategic planning for resource extraction.[15]

In addition to FPIC is the issue of indigenous peoples' rights to lands and natural resources. Often states do not recognise indigenous peoples' ownership of their traditional lands – assuming them to be "state-owned" – despite the fact that many indigenous peoples have occupied and used the lands for many

---

10 Rosemary Banks "Explanation of Vote by HE Rosemary Banks, New Zealand Permanent Representative to the United Nations" (13 September 2007).
11 Human Rights Committee *Angela Poma Poma v Peru Comm No 1457/2006* CCPR/C/95/D/1457/2006 (2009) at [7.6].
12 See CERD General Recommendation XXIII: Indigenous Peoples A/52/18 (1997) at [5].
13 *Centre for Minority Rights Development (Kenya) and Minority Rights Group International on Behalf of Endorois Welfare Council v Kenya (Judgment)* African Commission on Human and Peoples Rights 276/03, November 2009 at [291].
14 *Saramaka People v Suriname (Judgment – Preliminary Objections, Merits, Reparations, and Costs)* Inter-American Court of Human Rights Ser C No 172, 28 November 2007 [*Saramaka*] at [20], [129]-[134].
15 James Anaya *Report of the Special Rapporteur on the Rights of Indigenous Peoples: Extractive Industries and Indigenous Peoples* A/HRC/24/41 (2013) at [59].

generations.[16] While land rights may not have received formal recognition domestically (for example, through some grant of title), the Declaration requires that states demarcate and recognise those rights.[17] The Declaration does not however have a strong position on ownership of minerals, noting only that indigenous peoples have rights to their traditional lands.[18] This no doubt is due to states' concern about indigenous peoples seeking control over minerals and petroleum.

However, there are larger questions of political authority over natural resources not addressed by the indigenous right to lands and only hinted at by FPIC. The Declaration states: "Indigenous peoples have the right to self-determination"[19] and indigenous peoples, "as a specific form of exercising their right to self-determination, have the right to autonomy or self-government in matters relating to their internal and local affairs."[20] The right to self-determination is contentious in international law given its close association with the UN sponsored decolonisation movement.[21] This was the reason why indigenous advocates sought its inclusion in the Declaration – it indicated that indigenous peoples might possess the right of independence.[22] There remains disagreement about the meaning of self-determination in the Declaration especially given the express reference to the need to maintain territorial integrity in article 46.[23] However, at the very least, the right to self-determination indicates that indigenous peoples should have control over matters of concern to them, including the use of natural resources in their traditional lands. In the context of mining activities, self-determination could find expression in the types of ownership models and co-management agreements negotiated in New Zealand in Treaty settlements. We address the implications of the right to self-determination and mining activities in the New Zealand context below in Part D.

---

16 *Awas Tingni Mayagna (Sumo) Indigenous Community v Nicaragua (Judgment – Merits, Reparations and Costs)* Inter-American Court of Human Rights Series C (No 79), 31 August 2001 [*Awas Tingni*].
17 Art 26. See also *Awas Tingni* above n 16.
18 See also, Convention (No. 169) concerning Indigenous and Iwi Peoples in Independent Countries, Geneva, adopted by the International Labour Conference on 27 June 1989, in force 5 September 1991, 28 ILM 1382. [Convention (No. 169)].
19 Article 3.
20 Article 4.
21 Karen Engle *The Elusive Promise of Indigenous Development: Rights, Culture, Strategy* (Duke University Press, Durham (NC), 2010).
22 Andrew Erueti "UN Declaration on the Rights of Indigenous Peoples: A Mixed-Model Interpretative Approach" (SJD thesis, University of Toronto, 2016).
23 Karen Engle "On Fragile Architecture: The UN Declaration on the Rights of Indigenous Peoples in the Context of Human Rights" (2011) 22(1) Eur J Int Law 141.

2. Business and Human Rights

During the early 1990s, the international community began to focus its attention on whether human rights might extend to businesses. This was a marked departure from the orthodox approach of seeing human rights as obligations owed by the state to its citizens. However, it was clear that many businesses were now encroaching into areas formally administered by governments and that specific business practices, including mining activities, were violating human rights. The UN responded in 2011 when the UN Human Rights Council unanimously endorsed the United Nations Guiding Principles on Business and Human Rights (Guiding Principles).[24] These principles set out a three-pronged "Protect, Respect and Remedy" framework. First, states have a duty to protect against human rights abuses by third parties, including businesses. States are not per se responsible for the human rights abuses of private actors however they may breach their human rights obligations where such abuses are attributable to them, or where they fail to take the appropriate steps to prevent, investigate, punish and redress business-related human rights abuses. Secondly, businesses have a responsibility to respect (as opposed to a State duty to protect) human rights and must take active steps to avoid violating human rights and address such impacts when they do occur. Thus, businesses must "show and tell" how they are meeting their responsibilities, including how they become aware of, prevent and address any adverse human rights impacts.[25] Thirdly, states have a duty to provide effective remedies through judicial, administrative, and legislative means; and businesses have the responsibility to address and remedy any adverse human rights impacts that they contribute to. The Guiding Principles were never intended to create new binding international law or impose additional obligations on companies.[26] According to John Ruggie, the architect of the Guiding Principles:[27]

> ... its normative contribution lies in elaborating on existing standards and practices of States and businesses; integrating them within a single framework; and identifying where the current regime falls short and how it could be improved.

---

24 See Human Rights Council *Report of the Special Representative of the Secretary-General on the issue of human rights and transnational corporations and other business enterprises, John Ruggie: Guiding Principles on Business and Human Rights: Implementing the United Nations "Protect, Respect and Remedy" Framework* UN doc. A/HRC/17/31 (2011).

25 United Nations Office of the High Commissioner for Human Rights "The Corporate Responsibility to Respect Human Rights: An Interpretative Guide" (United Nations, Geneva, 2012) at 32.

26 Robert C Blitt "Beyond Ruggie's Guiding Principles on Business and Human Rights: Charting an Embracive Approach to Corporate Human Rights Compliance" (2012) 48 Texas Journal of International Law 33 at 43.

27 John G Ruggie, Special Representative for the Secretary General for Business and Human Rights "Presentation of Report to United Nations Human Rights Council" (Geneva, 30 May 2011).

In this sense, the Guiding Principles provide governments, businesses and international organisations with a normative framework to guide business practice and policy. Several states have already established plans of action outlining how they intend to give effect to the Guiding Principles and many businesses, including mining and petroleum companies, have established policies on corporate accountability for communities affected by their activities. The New Zealand government has not been particularly responsive to the Guiding Principles. It has, for example, no national strategic plan on business and human rights.[28] However, the New Zealand Human Rights Commission has recently prioritised business and human rights including through developing resources for businesses and by hosting forums to discuss business and human rights.[29]

C. Overview of New Zealand Legislation Relating to Mining Activities

1. Permitting for Crown Owned Minerals and Protection of Māori Interests

New Zealand has reasonable mineral wealth, most prominently petroleum, iron sands, coal, gold and silver. The Crown Minerals Act 1991 (CMA) governs the promotion, exploration and mining of "Crown owned minerals" through a permitting regime.[30] Under the CMA all petroleum, gold, silver, and uranium is deemed to be "the property of the Crown."[31] Other minerals may be owned by the Crown if a specific reservation has been made.[32] Privately owned minerals do not require a permit under the CMA, but generally require a resource consent under the Resource Management Act 1991 (RMA), which regulates the environmental effects of mining and other activities.

The CMA contains several measures to protect Māori interests. Section 4 provides that all persons exercising powers and functions under the Act "shall have regard" to the principles of the Treaty of Waitangi. Details of how to give effect to this section is provided for in minerals and petroleum "programmes"

---

28 This can be compared with Switzerland, for example, which has published an action plan on the Guiding Principles. See Government Offices of Sweden, *Action Plan for Business and Human Rights* (24 August 2015).
29 For more information, see the New Zealand Human Rights Commission website: <https://www.hrc.co.nz/your-rights/business-and-work/new-zealand-business-and-human-rights-forum/>.
30 Section 1A. As a general rule, prospecting, exploration or mining for Crown-owned minerals requires a permit under the CMA. For the range of exceptions to the rule, see Jacinta Ruru and A Suzoko "Chapter Three: Te Ture-Mineral Law and Māori" in Katarina Ruckstuhl and others (eds) *Māori and Mining* (Te Poutama Māori, University of Otago, Dunedin, 2013) at 31.
31 Section 10.
32 Section 11.

which set out government obligations to Māori in relation to consultation, exclusion of land from mining, requirements for company engagement with iwi, and access to land.[33] In relation to consultation, before permits are awarded affected iwi must be provided with the details of the proposed permit.[34] They must also be notified that they may request that certain areas – or the whole area – within the permit area be excluded on the basis that it is of special significance to local iwi (for example the area is a wāhi tapu (sacred site)).[35] The programmes provide that the form of consultation is flexible and if iwi and the Crown think it is appropriate there may be kanohi ki te kanohi (face-to-face) consultation or a hui held.[36] The CMA states that as part of the process for amending the programmes all iwi must be notified of the draft programme and be provided with information about submissions and how they are to be made.[37] Additionally, a number of iwi also hold protocols regarding consultation with the Crown as part of their Treaty settlement.

For mining companies, the CMA does not require that they consult Māori before undertaking any activities under a mineral permit. However, the CMA imposes requirements on "tier 1"-mining companies (that is, all complex, large scale mining operations) to prepare "annual engagement reports" with tribes whose rohe (territory) includes some or all of the permit area or who otherwise may be directly affected by the permit.[38] However, there is no requirement that the tribe be involved in the drafting and review of the reports, nor are reports independently commissioned or reviewed.[39] Government commissioned research which evaluated these reports found that very few permit holders explained if and how they sought the views of Māori stakeholders and took their views into account in their projects.[40] However, in 2016 the Government released a document entitled "Permit Holder Guidance for iwi engagement reporting".[41] This document sets out what is expected from iwi engagement reports, including

---

33 Minerals Programme for Minerals 2013 s2 (MPM); Minerals Programme for Petroleum 2013 s2 (MPP). Roger Perkins "Maori Participation in the Management of Petroleum" (2004) 7 Yearbook of New Zealand Jurisprudence 80 at 81.
34 MPM s2.5(1) and s2.6(1), MPP s2.4 and s2.5.
35 MPM s2.5(1) and s2.6(1), MPP s2.4 and s2.5.
36 MPM s2.12; MPP s2.10.
37 Section 17.
38 Section 33C.
39 The MMP provides, "[p]ermit holders are *encouraged* to consult with relevant iwi and hapū before submitting their report and, where possible and appropriate, to include in the report the views of those iwi and hapū on the content of the report" (emphasis added). MPP s 2.11(3). See also MPM s2.13(3) which has an identical provision.
40 Tuia Group *Permit Holder Reporting on Iwi Engagement* (New Zealand Petroleum and Minerals, Wellington, July 2015) at 2.
41 Ministry of Business, Innovation and Employment "Permit Holder Guidance for iwi engagement reporting" (Wellington, February 2016).

detailing what engagement occurred, if and how that engagement affected decision making and whether iwi had been consulted on the report.[42] This clarification from the government is to be welcomed and may result in better processes of engagement as between tribes and companies.

As for land access, the granting of a permit under the CMA does not give the permit holder an automatic right to access land. The general rule is that the permit holder must negotiate an agreement with the landowner (and occupier) before undertaking any activity (apart from minimum impact activities) on their land.[43] This gives landowners strong rights to decide whether mining may proceed and gives them the opportunity to negotiate a benefit-sharing agreement.[44] However, the law regarding access to petroleum is different due to its national significance. For "minimum impact activities," Māori have a right to withhold access to "Māori land" – a special category of land now comprising five per cent of New Zealand's land mass[45] – if the land is a sacred site.[46] However, for more intrusive activities on Māori land, compulsory arbitrated access arrangements can be imposed on the owners.[47] If the matter goes to arbitration, the arbitrator must grant access on reasonable conditions. In other words, the arbitrator cannot prohibit the permit holder from obtaining access to the land, apart from when the land falls into a number of very restricted categories.[48]

2. Environmental Regulation of Mining and Protection of Māori Interests

The principal legislation for regulating the use of New Zealand's physical environment is the Resource Management Act 1991 (RMA).[49] Much of the responsibility for maintaining sustainable management is delegated to local governments (called "consent authorities" under the RMA), who must prepare, publicise and monitor compliance with resource planning documents.[50] The

---

42 At 3.
43 CMA s 49.
44 On benefit-sharing in the context of mining and indigenous peoples, see Rachel Wynberg, Doris Schroeder, Roger Chennells (eds), *Indigenous Peoples, Consent and Benefit Sharing: Lessons from the San-Hoodia Case* (Springer, Australia, 2009).
45 Te Ture Whenua Maori Act (the Maori Land Act) 1993.
46 CMA s 51.
47 CMA s 53. Section 63 of the CMA allows the permit holder to serve a notice on each owner and occupier asking them to agree to the appointment of an arbitrator to determine an access arrangement on reasonable terms. Section 64 provides for an arbitrator to be appointed by the Chief Executive of the Ministry of Business, Innovation and Employment at the request of either party, if agreement cannot be reached to appoint an arbitrator.
48 CMA s 55(2).
49 There is also legislation governing the exclusive economic zone (EEZ). See Exclusive Economic Zone and Continental Shelf (Environmental Effects) Act 2012.
50 Under the Act, regional councils are required to prepare and regularly review a regional policy

planning documents set out whether local government consent is required for a proposed resource use or development in their area, including mining activities. Given the potential impact of many mining activities, often a resource consent will be required before exploration or extraction.

Like the CMA, the RMA contains several measures to protect Māori interests. Tribes must be consulted in the preparation of national and regional planning documents and are encouraged to prepare "iwi [tribal] management plans", detailing the general resource management priorities of tribes and special interests which local governments must take into account when amending or creating planning documents. Further, all decision makers under the RMA must "take into account the principles of the Treaty of Waitangi,"[51] and have "particular regard" to "kaitiakitanga" [guardianship],[52] and "recognise and provide for ... the relationship of Māori and their culture and traditions with their ancestral lands, water, sites, waahi tapu [sacred sites], and other taonga [treasures]."[53] As a result of these provisions, when a local council draws up development plans or grants resource consents to carry out some activity, it must first, for example, consider the implications of the plan and consent to the kaitiakitanga of relevant iwi.

However, these measures do not appear to be advancing the interests of Māori. As the Waitangi Tribunal has said many times, iwi feel sidelined by the RMA consent process.[54] In particular, the Tribunal has found that this framework has prevented Māori, particularly iwi and hapū from controlling the management of their own taonga or natural resources. Part of the challenge lies with the weak statutory directions to "take into account" the principles of the Treaty and the fact that the Māori interests are one of several other competing interests including the overall commitment to sustainable development. Additionally, section 36A of the RMA states that neither an applicant nor a local authority have a duty to consult any person (including Māori) about a resource consent application unless this is required under other legislation. Furthermore, Māori communities struggle to keep up with the paperwork associated with resource consent applications and planning.[55] There are mechanisms that may help to

>statement and a regional coastal plan for each region. Regional councils may also formulate regional plans to address specific resource issues for which they have responsibility, namely those relating to water, air and any land uses of regional significance. Additionally, district and city councils must also prepare, regularly review and administer a district plan detailing the effects of land use for which they are responsible. See RMA s 60–68 and s 72–76.

51 Section 8.
52 Section 7.
53 Section 6.
54 See Waitangi Tribunal *Ko Aotearoa Tenei: A Report Into Claims Concerning New Zealand Law and Policy Affecting Maori Culture and Identity* (Wai 262, 2011) [*Ko Aotearoa Tenei* Report].
55 See, Waitangi Tribunal *The Report on the Management of the Petroleum Resource* (Wai

address Māori lack of political control over natural resources. The devolution of power from local governments to tribes is possible under the RMA, however to date the provision has not been used to transfer powers to tribes.[56] It is also possible under the RMA to establish joint management agreements.[57] However, these have only been used on a few occasions due to barriers that exist under the legislation and resistance from local councils.[58] We also discuss below how co-management agreements may improve iwi participation in RMA processes.

D. Suggestions for Reform Consistent with the Declaration and the Guiding Principles

1. The Ownership of Natural Resources Model

As noted above, the Declaration recognises the right of indigenous peoples to their traditional lands and the right to redress for lands that have been taken from them. There is no express reference to minerals and petroleum in this context. However, arguably rights to these resources can be inferred from the right to self-determination. In addition to international indigenous rights, indigenous peoples in common law countries can also seek recognition of aboriginal title and rights to land, including mineral rights.[59] The Canadian Supreme Court for example, has recognised that aboriginal title includes rights to sub-surface minerals.[60]

In New Zealand, Māori have been successful in asserting a right of ownership over specific natural resources. There are now a host of negotiated agreements based on the notion of tribes possessing existing de facto property rights in natural

---

796, 2011) at 94 (noting "how time consuming – and protracted – the processes can be. Indeed, they show that for some claimant groups, and for those members who shoulder the responsibility, the task of staying abreast of petroleum activities so that taonga can be protected is relentless. . . . All the claimants we heard from were volunteers for their hapu. The sheer size of the files that they had assembled about particular projects to which they had objected provided some indication of the extent of the work required of them, which was done in their own time").

56 *Ko Aotearoa Tenei*, above n 54 at 258. See also Caren Fox and Chris Bretton "Maori Participation, Rights and Interests" (paper presented to the RMLA Conference, Dunedin, 26 September 2014).

57 RMA s 2 and s 36B.

58 See, for example, the agreement between Taupo District Council and Ngāti Tūwharetoa at <http://www.taupodc.govt.nz/our-council/policies-plans-and-bylaws/joint-management-agreements/Documents/Joint-Management-Agreement.pdf>. Ngāti Porou has also recently entered into such an agreement with the Gisborne District Council in relation to the Waiapu River. Gisborne Herald "Historic Waiapu River agreement signed" *Gisborne Herald* (online ed, Gisborne, 10 November 2015). For analysis on the barriers to joint management agreements, see Natalie Coates "Joint-Management Agreements in New Zealand: Simply Empty Promises?" (2009) 13(1) JSPL 32.

59 PG McHugh *Aboriginal Title* (Oxford University Press, Oxford, 2011).

60 *Delgamuukw v British Columbia*, [1997] 3 S.C.R. 1010.

resources. In other words, prior to the agreements there were no established legal rights in the resource in question, though there was an arguable case for legal rights on the basis of aboriginal title, for example. This includes deals relating to the rights to commercial and customary fisheries,[61] lakebeds,[62] forests,[63] lands,[64] aquaculture[65] and the coastal marine area.[66] For Māori, "ownership" is about as good as it gets, since typically owners have the right to use and occupy the natural resource to the exclusion of others, including the right to alienate the resource and charge for its use. And as private property the natural resource ordinarily cannot be subjected to a resource consent application by a developer under the RMA without the iwi's consent.

However, successive governments have refused to engage with Māori on petroleum ownership and other precious minerals, which as noted are declared under the CMA to be Crown owned. Before the Waitangi Tribunal, iwi argued that Crown nationalisation of petroleum under the Petroleum Act 1937 and the Crown's continued claim to own petroleum violated the principles of the Treaty. The Tribunal in its Petroleum Report found that prior to 1937 Māori had legal title to the petroleum in their land and that expropriation in 1937, without compensation, was a breach of the Treaty.[67] The Tribunal also found that Māori had a "Treaty interest"[68] in petroleum which entitled Māori to a remedy for its wrongful loss.[69] The government refused to accept the Waitangi Tribunal recommendations stating that the nationalisation of petroleum was, and continues to be, in the public interest.[70] The government, so far, is only willing to recognise a Māori right to own minerals in those cases where the minerals are of relatively lesser value and there is evidence of traditional use –

61 Treaty of Waitangi (Fisheries Claims) Settlement Act 1992.
62 Te Arawa Lakes Settlement Act 2006 (section 23(1) provides that the fee simple estate in each Te Arawa lakebed is vested in the Trustees of the Te Arawa Lakes Trust.
63 The proposed sale of forest lands resulted in objection by Māori, who claimed an interest in the forests. A Treaty settlement was reached which led to the creation of the Crown Forestry Rental Trust to manage rental gained from the selling of cutting rights and leasing of forest lands while the Tribunal investigated ownership rights to forestry lands. Alan Ward *An Unsettled History: Treaty Claims in New Zealand Today* (Bridget Williams Books, Wellington, 1999), at 39.
64 See for example: Waitangi Tribunal *Waiheke Report* (Wai 10, 1987); Waitangi Tribunal *Orakei Report* (Wai 9, 1987); Waitangi Tribunal, *Muriwhenua Land Report* (Wai 45, 1997).
65 Maori Commercial Aquaculture Claims Settlement Act 2004.
66 See *Attorney-General v Ngati Apa* [2003] 3 NZLR 643; and Marine and Coastal Area (Takutai Moana) Act 2011.
67 Waitangi Tribunal *The Petroleum Report* (Wai 796, 2003) at 79.
68 At 79. For a discussion of the idea of a "treaty interest", see Huia Woods *The Treaty Interest: A New Concept in Indigenous Rights?* (Working Paper, University of Waikato, 2006).
69 At 40. See also, Craig Coxhead "Māori Title to Petroleum: The Waitangi Tribunal Petroleum Report" (2004) 7 *Yearbook of New Zealand Jurisprudence*, 66, at 71-72.
70 See Richard Boast and Deborah Edmunds "Māori Claims to Petroleum" (2001) AMPLA Yearbook 425 at 434-435.

for example Ngāi Tahu ownership of pounamu (greenstone).[71] It may be possible to seek an aboriginal right to petroleum (and other precious minerals) in the courts, although the result of such an action is uncertain. Not only would Māori need to establish an aboriginal right in petroleum, they would also need to prove that it has not been extinguished by the declaration in the CMA that all precious minerals are "the property of the Crown."[72] The government has also rejected claims of ownership to the foreshore and seabed (despite significant potential aboriginal title interests in the area)[73] and freshwater bodies (lakes and rivers),[74] given their significance to public and national interests.[75]

2. Models Aimed at Promoting Māori Effective Participation in Decision Making

The right to self-determination and FPIC point to the need for indigenous peoples to be involved in decisions that may affect their communities and interests in their territories. In New Zealand, while Māori can participate in the preparation of national environmental planning documents under the RMA, the regulation of mining activities does not in our view do enough to include Māori in higher-decision making. For the permitting regime under the CMA, there are few

---

71 Ngāi Tahu (Pounamu Vesting) Act 1997. M Gibbs "The Ngāi Tahu (Pounamu Vesting) Act 1997" (2000) 4 NZJEL 257. See also Crown policy regarding minerals and Treaty settlements, Office of Treaty Settlements *Ka tika ā muri, ka tika ā mua: Healing the past, building a future: Guide to Treaty of Waitangi Claims and Negotiations with the Crown* (March 2015, Wellington) at 111.

72 Section 10. Arguably this property is confined to the Crown's radical title, not the proprietary interest in the minerals. For the distinction between the two, see *Attorney-General v Ngati Apa* [2003] 3 NZLR 643; and *Mabo v Queensland No.2* (1992) 175 C.L.R. 1.

73 See *Attorney-General v Ngati Apa* [2003] 3 NZLR 643 where the New Zealand Court of Appeal recognised potential customary rights in the foreshore and seabed including the possibility of freehold titles. However, the decision has been overridden by legislation that declares that no one including the Crown owns the foreshore and seabed. Instead of proprietary rights in the foreshore and seabed, Māori can seek the right to engage in customary activities and seek a reserve should they provide evidence of continuous occupation of the area; see, Marine and Coastal Area (Takutai Moana) Act 2011.

74 The government position is that water is not capable of ownership and that the government has the right to regulate its use. Recently, the Waitangi Tribunal found that Māori did have a proprietary interest and indeed that the iwi interest was more than proprietary, that is that the iwi interest included some form of political authority over the river. See, Waitangi Tribunal *The Stage 1 Report on the National Freshwater and Claim* (Wai 2358, 2012). See also, Waitangi Tribunal *The Ika Whenua Rivers Report* (Wai 212, 1998); Waitangi Tribunal *The Wanganui River Report* (Wai 167, 1999); Waitangi Tribunal *The Ngawha Geothermal Resource Report* (Wai 304, 1993); Waitangi Tribunal, He *Maunga Rongo: Report on Central North Island Claims* (Wai 1200, 2008).

75 Dean Nathan "Māori Council Scrutinises Water Ownership", 19 April 2016, Māori Television; Mihingarangi Forbes "Iwi Closely Watches Govt Moves on Water Ownership", 22 March 2016, Radio New Zealand.

means of influencing the minerals programme. The role of Māori is restricted to consultation.

The Waitangi Tribunal in its Petroleum Report called for more mechanisms of engagement between Māori and central and local government to enable their full participation in decision making regarding minerals.[76] For example, the Tribunal recommended the establishment of a "ministerial advisory committee" to provide the Minister of Energy and the Minister of Māori Affairs with advice on Māori perspectives on petroleum issues and related matters on a regular and formal basis;[77] and the re-establishment of representative bodies for iwi at a district and regional level.[78] In other reports, the Waitangi Tribunal has called for statutory reform that calls for more robust forms of iwi management plans.[79] However, a fundamental issue is the lack of resourcing for Māori participation. In order to address this, the Waitangi Tribunal has recommended that a proportion of petroleum royalties should be put into a fund to which Māori tribes can apply to enable their participation in RMA processes. However, no measures have been adopted by government. The Waitangi Tribunal also advocated that there should be increased application of user-pays principles, with companies paying for the cost of engagement, including for the provision of cultural impact assessments.[80]

In April 2017, the Government introduced a new mechanism, called a Mana Whakahono ā Rohe or iwi participation arrangement, into the RMA whereby iwi and local government negotiate an agreement about iwi participation in resource management decision making under the RMA.[81] In particular, the arrangements are initiated by iwi and the RMA specifies what needs to be included in the agreements, including a dispute resolution process. There is, however, considerable resistance to "special measures" such as these in the RMA from some sections of the New Zealand public.[82]

---

76 Waitangi Tribunal *The Report on the Management of the Petroleum Resource* (Wai 796, 2011) at 184–185.
77 At 179–181.
78 At 178–179.
79 The proposal for IPAs has some commonalities with the Tribunal's recommendation for "enhanced iwi management plans". See *Ko Aotearoa Tenei,* above n 55, at 280–283 (Critiquing the RMA and noting the "lynchpin" of a Treaty-compliant RMA system would be enhanced iwi management plans, called iwi resource management plans, at 281).
80 At 182.
81 Resource Management Act 1991, s 58L-58U.
82 For example, the NZ First political party leader Winston Peters has labelled the Resource Management Act reforms as "separatist" and "racist". Jo Muir "Winston Peters Says the National Party's Handling of Water Rights and RMA is 'Racist'" *Stuff* (online ed, 2 June 2016).

3. Alternatives to the Ownership Model – Negotiated Iwi-specific Co-management Models

Despite the government's rejection of Māori ownership of freshwater bodies, it has negotiated alternatives to ownership in the form of co-management agreements. The agreements have been negotiated as iwi-specific Treaty settlements, but also as iwi-specific "joint committee agreements" under the RMA. For example, in relation to the largest river in the North Island, the Waikato river, Waikato-Tainui tribes negotiated an agreement given effect in the Waikato-Tainui Raupatu Claims (Waikato River) Settlement Act 2010. This Act establishes the Waikato River Authority (the Authority), which is made up of roughly equal numbers of iwi and government representatives.[83] The Authority is responsible for establishing the "vision and strategy to achieve the restoration and protection of the health and wellbeing of the Waikato River for future generations."[84] Following the confiscation of Waikato-Tainui iwi lands in the late 1800s, the Crown assumed control of the river and the river suffered from pollution from farm run-off, coal mining and sewage.[85] This "clean up" is to be assisted by a series of agreements with the local council that seek to better integrate Waikato-Tainui tribes into the RMA planning processes, including the preparation of an "integrated river management plan" and an "environmental plan" that local councils must consider when preparing planning documents; and the inclusion of iwi-appointed commissioners to participate in the granting of consents relating to the Waikato River – for example, requests to "take, use, dam, or divert water in the Waikato River".[86] However, the issue of ownership of the river remains unresolved. As noted by Linda Te Aho, "[the Treaty settlement] is not about ownership of water. The overarching purpose is to restore and protect the health and wellbeing of the [river] for future generations."[87]

More recently, the government negotiated a novel co-management agreement with iwi associated with the Whanganui River. The agreement vests the Whanganui River, Te Awa Tupua, with legal personality and establishes a trust, Te Pou Tupua, constituted equally of iwi and government members to co-manage the river.[88] Recognition of the independent autonomy of the river roughly accords with the customary view that rivers possess their own mauri (life force). Like

---

83   Section 22 and schedule 6.
84   Section 22.
85   Linda Te Aho "Indigenous Challenges to Enhance Freshwater Governance and Management in Aotearoa NZ – The Waikato River Settlement" (2010) 20 The Journal of Water Law 285.
86   Sections 25–31.
87   See chapter by Linda Te Aho in this book.
88   Te Awa Tupua (Whanganui River Claims Settlement) Bill (section 14 Te Awa Tupua declared to be legal person). The Bill gives effect to the Whanganui River Deed of Settlement signed on 5 August 2014, which settles the historical claims of Whanganui iwi as they relate to the Whanganui River.

the Waikato agreement, the focus is on the future health and well-being of the river and its people with measures to facilitate iwi engagement in the RMA planning and consent making processes associated with the river.[89] However, by vesting the river with legal personality, the government has effectively sidestepped the issue of ownership.[90] The iwi thus cannot gain any benefit from use of the resource. Furthermore, while Whanganui River and Waikato River tribes have a greater say in RMA decisions, they cannot, for example, stop the issuing of natural resources consents over the river to extract, or divert water or build dams on them.[91] This outcome is a far cry from the recommendation made by the Waitangi Tribunal that the river in its entirety be vested in the tribes, which would mean that any resource consent application would require the tribe's approval. And, as noted above, the right to FPIC and self-determination in the Declaration indicate that iwi should have much more robust rights of control over natural resources in their rohe.

A question that arises is whether the co-management model has potential application to mining given the government's rejection of Māori ownership of mining and petroleum. What is clear is that, like co-government deals made to date, this will need to be conducted on a case-by-case basis with iwi. This makes sense in the mining and petroleum context in that, for example, Ngāi Tahu would claim rights to gold in their territory while Taranaki tribes would claim rights to petroleum in theirs. In short, tribes would claim an interest in the resources in their territory above or below the ground, so claims to mining and petroleum would be akin to those made to land, waterbodies (lakes and rivers) or forests. To date, the co-management deals have been directed at restoring the health and vitality of natural resources and have sidestepped the issue of proprietary rights. They nonetheless do seek to facilitate consultation and iwi participation in RMA processes. Their strength would lie in the ability of iwi and local and central government to negotiate specific agreements that address the concerns that iwi have with their lack of engagement in the regulation of mining activities. In this respect, as noted above, the RMA allows for "joint committees" made up of iwi and local government members to share decision making under the RMA, including the grant of resource consents. Now iwi can initiate Mana Whakahono ā Rohe with local government. Moreover, it is possible to delegate local government decisions on resource management to iwi. What all these measures point to is the potential for tribes to negotiate specific deals on a case-by-case basis to work

---

89 Sections 8 and 63.
90 See also the Tūhoe deal where the Crown rejected ownership of conservation land and offered instead to vest the park with legal personality to be co-chaired by Māori and the Crown. Te Urewera Act 2014. See also the Marine and Coastal Area (Takutai Moana) Act 2011, which simply declares that no one owns the foreshore and seabed.
91 However, the consent of Te Pou Tupua may be required in relation to the use of the bed of the Whanganui River. See section 41.

towards an arrangement that recognises iwi self-determination over natural resources in their territory.[92] These models, however, do not answer the question of how indigenous peoples may benefit from the resource's use.

4. Corporate Responsibility

As noted above, the Guiding Principles set out a three-pronged "Protect, Respect and Remedy" framework. However, from our experience, few mining and petroleum companies are aware of the Guiding Principles or even have a coherent internal policy on how to effectively engage with tribes. Iwi engagement reports prepared under the CMA provide a vehicle for companies to actively address human right obligations. While these reports are not required to be made public under legislation, companies should of their own accord put their reports into the public domain so that the record of their human rights conduct is transparent. Legislative reform should also require that the past relationship that companies have had with Māori and/or other indigenous peoples in other countries or a company's plans and processes for engagement with Māori should be an express consideration by the Minister in awarding permits. This would give companies a meaningful interest in engagement with iwi and would set out clearly the government's expectations. Government has been slow to prompt a shift in the culture of mining activities in New Zealand. The Ministry of Business, Innovation and Employment has a link on its website to a section on the Treaty and this sets out a list of principles to consider during engagement with Māori, including the recommendation to engage with tribes "before a permit application is lodged but most certainly once an application has been accepted and granted."[93] The only detailed advice is contained in a "Best practice guideline for engagement with Maori" commissioned partly by the Ministry and prepared by Taranaki tribe Ngāti Ruanui, but not adopted as a government policy.[94] This is an area in which the New Zealand government should be showing leadership.

E. Conclusion

New Zealand's regulatory framework for mining includes important distinctive protections for Māori, yet in several important respects it falls short of

---

92 See also Carwyn Jones (2010) J Maori L W 59 (arguing for an environmental law regime that "would provide for recognition of the rights and obligations contained in the Treaty of Waitangi", including tino rangatiratanga or "Maori authority over Maori resources". At 66).

93 New Zealand Petroleum and Minerals "Permit holder engagement with Māori: Principles to consider during engagement with Māori" <http://www.nzpam.govt.nz/cms/doing-business/maori-waitangi/permit-holder-engagement/?searchterm=well>.

94 Te Runanga o Ngāti Ruanui Trust *Best Practice Guidelines for Engagement with Māori* (August, 2014).

international standards. In particular, the government has thus far failed to engage with tribes over the question of ownership of petroleum and other mineral resources, which represents a continuing grievance for iwi. Tribes have little say in the management of minerals in their traditionally owned areas. There is a lack of clear direction by the government towards companies to respect the indigenous rights of tribes. In our view, the international indigenous rights outlined above and recent innovations in co-management offer some guidance to a more equitable model for New Zealand's mineral wealth.

III

The Declaration and Indigenous Rights Advocacy in New Zealand

7
Use It or Lose It: The Value of Using the Declaration on the Rights Of Indigenous Peoples in Māori Legal and Political Claims

*Claire Charters**

A. Introduction

One of the most effective ways to increase the legal and political impact of the Declaration on the Rights of Indigenous Peoples (the Declaration) is for indigenous peoples to use it in their legal and political advocacy. In doing so, indigenous advocates can compel states to interact with the Declaration in ways that may lead, in the longer term, to better cognizance and conformity with it, even in cases where the state rejects or qualifies those norms and the norms are strictly speaking non-binding. The legal and political value of the Declaration is thus increased through "using it". Part B of this chapter outlines relevant legal and political theory explaining how advocacy can enhance state interaction and, ultimately, compliance with international norms. Part C then focuses on a case study – the Waitangi Tribunal hearing and decision in its report 'Whaia te Mana Motuhake, In Pursuit of Mana Motuhake: Report on the Māori Community Development Act Claim' (Wai 2417), relating to Māori rights to self-determination – as a concrete example of the Declaration being used in a legal forum to promote state interaction with the Declaration's norms.[1] I summarise the claim and detail the way I sought to prove the relevance of the Declaration in my expert evidence. Part D then details how the Declaration was used by the Waitangi Tribunal in its reasoning.

I argue that use of the Declaration in arguments before the Waitangi Tribunal in the Wai 2417 hearing and the Tribunal's reliance on it in its report, will compel the New Zealand government – from politicians, to the Ministry of Māori

---

* Associate Professor, Faculty of Law, University of Auckland. Ngāti Whakaue, Ngā Puhi, Tainui and Ngāti Tūwharetoa.
1 Waitangi Tribunal *Whaia te Mana Motuhake: In Pursuit of Mana Motuhake:* (Wai 2417, 2015) [*Whaia te Mana Motuhake*].

Development/Te Puni Kōkiri to Crown Law – to engage with the Declaration. Together with the many other references to the Declaration in the Waitangi Tribunal and the courts, especially New Zealand's Supreme Court,[2] such activity can over time lead to greater state conformity with the Declaration. To that end, I hope that advocates for Māori claims will continue to use the Declaration in their arguments for Māori claimants in various fora and that they can use my expert evidence as a form of precedent for such arguments.

B. *The Value of "Using It"*

The value of using international norms as a means to increase their compliance pull on states over time, even when they may be resistant to the norms or the norms are not binding, is supported by theories on constructivism, transnational legal process theory and social movement theory. At heart, these theories share the proposition that there are methods to embed norms in the domestic political and legal landscape in such a way that states view conformity with them as ordinary and rationally-appropriate behaviour or, conversely, contravention as politically and legally illegitimate. The theories stem from the idea that norm conformity can be achieved not only through legal sanctions or compulsion but also through the gradual normalisation and acceptance of the legitimacy of norms by the state especially and also the public at large.

Constructivist theories maintain that states' interests can be socially influenced – or constructed – by exogenous factors in such a way that norm conformity comes to be considered consistent with state interests. It is a process of socialisation.[3] Under transnational legal process theory states' interaction with norms leads states to engage with them and then internalise them.[4] Harold Koh writes:[5]

> One or more transnational actors provokes an interaction (or series of interactions) with another, which forces an interpretation or enunciation of the global norm applicable to the situation. By doing so, the moving party seeks not simply to coerce the other party, but to internalise the new interpretation of the international norm into the other party's internal normative system . . . The transaction generates a legal rule which will guide future transnational interactions between the parties;

---

2   See, *Takamore v Clarke* [2012] NZSC 116; *New Zealand Maori Council v Attorney General* [2013] NZSC 6; *Paki v Attorney General* [2014] NZSC 118; *Proprietors of Wakatū & Rore Stafford v Attorney General* [2017] NZSC 17.
3   Ryan Goodman and Derek Jenks "How to Influence States: Socialization and International Human Rights Law" (2005) 54(3) Duke L J 621 and Martha Finnemore *National Interests in International Society* (Cornell University Press, Ithaca, 1996).
4   Harold H Koh "Bringing International Law Home" (1998) 35 Houston L Rev 623; Harold H Koh "Internalization Through Socialization" (2005) 52 Duke L J 975; and Harold H Koh "Why Do Nations Obey International Law?" (1997) 106 Yale L J 2599.
5   Koh "Why Do Nations Obey International Law?" above n 4, at 2646.

future transactions will further internalise the norms, and eventually, repeated participation in the process will help to reconstitute the interests and even the identities of the participants in the process.

As noted by Abram and Antonia Chayes, even where states enunciate arguments against norms, or seek to explain their non-compliance, they are still, not always voluntarily, engaging with the norms, interpreting and interacting with them:[6]

> States are under the practical necessity to give reasons and justifications for suspect conduct. These are reviewed and critiqued not only in formal dispute settlement processes but also in a variety of other venues, public and private, formal and informal, where they are addressed and evaluated. In the process, the circumstances advanced in mitigation or excuse of non-performance are systematically addressed. Those that seem to have substance are dealt with; those that do not are exposed. Often the upshot is agreement on a narrower and more concrete definition of the required performance, adapted to the circumstances of the case. At all stages, the putative offender is given every opportunity to conform. Persuasion and argument are the principal engines of this process, but if a party persistently fails to respond, the possibility of diffuse manifestations of disapproval or pressures from other actors in the regime is present in the background.

A state's perception of reputational costs associated with non-compliance with international norms can also be a factor in a state's internalisation of norms.[7]

According to Harold Koh, internalisation of norms occurs not only in legal but also social and political fora:[8]

> Social internalization occurs when a norm acquires so much public legitimacy that there is widespread general obedience to it. Political internalization occurs when political elites accept an international norm, and adopt it as a matter of government policy. Legal internalization occurs when an international norm is incorporated into the domestic legal system through executive action, judicial interpretation, legislative action, or some combination of the three.

Social movement theory focuses especially on the role played by social movements in stimulating changes in state behaviour, including, for example, by raising norms in litigation against the state.[9] As is evident from the above descriptions, these theories share similar views on the methods that promote

---

6   Abram Chayes and Antonia Handler Chayes *The New Sovereignty: Compliance with International Regulatory Agreements* (Harvard University Press, Cambridge, 1995) at 26.
7   Andrew T Guzman "Reputation and International Law" (2005–2006) 34 Ga J Int'l & Comp L 379 at 387.
8   Koh "Why Do Nations Obey International Law?" above n 4, at 2656–2657.
9   Margaret E Keck and Kathryn Sikkink *Activists Beyond Borders* (Cornell University Press, Ithaca, 1998).

states' internalisation of norms, being social, political and legal actions that compel states to interact with norms. Such actions might include law making processes, such as parliamentary select committees in the New Zealand context; politically influential protest; indigenous-state engagements, including Treaty settlement negotiations; shadow reports to, or statements in, international human rights bodies; and, of most relevance here, claims in domestic courts or tribunals, such as the Waitangi Tribunal.

There are four important points to note here about the processes that lead to potential state internalisation of norms. First, non-state actors, including NGOs, can initiate such processes. Second, these processes can be legal in nature, such as legal argument reliant on the Declaration in courts, but need not be. Protest and argumentation in political contexts can also be functionally important. Third, non-state actors might best initiate a number of political and legal strategies simultaneously to facilitate state engagement with norms. While some activities might be more effective than others to stimulate state responses, multiple approaches can deepen a state's interaction with norms. Fourth, as noted above, a state's rejection of a norm in political and legal fora does not halt a state's internalisation of a norm. Indeed, some scholars claim that norm rejection is a relatively standard "step" in a state's internalisation of norms. Risse and Sikkink write:[10]

> [w]e count the denial phase as part of the socialization process because the fact that the state feels compelled to deny the charges demonstrates that a process of international socialization is already under way. If socialization were not yet underway, the state would feel no need to deny the accusations that are made.

There is some evidence to suggest that New Zealand is already en route to internalising some of the norms in the Declaration, albeit perhaps only those norms that do not seriously, or are not perceived to, threaten New Zealand's sovereignty or private property regime.[11] In 2010, for example, it reversed its earlier rejection of the Declaration, with official records of the time noting that endorsement would enhance New Zealand's reputation and meet recommendations made by the UN Human Rights Council (HRC) during its universal periodic review of New Zealand.[12]

Māori and other non-state actors' activities continue to persistently compel New Zealand to engage with the Declaration in multiple ways, for example, in

---

10   Thomas Risse and Kathryn Sikkink "The Socialization of International Human Rights Norms into Domestic Practices: Introduction" in Thomas Risse, Stephen C Ropp and Kathryn Sikkink (eds) *The Power of Human Rights: International Norms and Domestic Change* (Cambridge University Press, Cambridge, 1999) 1, at 23.
11   Sheryl Lightfoot "Emerging International Indigenous Rights Norms and 'Over-Compliance' in New Zealand and Canada" (2010) 62(1) Political Science 84–104.
12   Pita Sharples "UNPFII Opening Ceremony New Zealand Statement" (Speech delivered at the United Nations Permanent Forum on Indigenous Issues, New York, 19 April 2010).

shadow reports and statements before international human rights bodies,[13] in claims to the courts[14] and Waitangi Tribunal,[15] in select committees,[16] and through the establishment of bodies to monitor New Zealand's compliance with the Declaration.[17]

C. Background to Whaia te Mana Motuhake Report

The Whaia te Mana Motuhake inquiry concerned a claim by the New Zealand Māori Council (the Council) that the Crown had breached the principles of the Treaty of Waitangi by unilaterally initiating and undertaking a review of the legislation that established the Council, the Maori Community Development Act 1962 (the Development Act). The Development Act established "districts" throughout New Zealand and processes for appointing representatives of these districts that together comprised the Council as a national body with a mandate to give advice to government on a range of policy matters affecting Māori.

The Council sought to have the Waitangi Tribunal take into account the Declaration when determining whether the Crown had breached the principles of the Treaty of Waitangi. The Council particularly relied on the Declaration with respect to its claim that the Crown had interfered with Māori self-government and mana motuhake rights by initiating the review of the Development Act. The Council claimed that the principles of the Treaty, the Act itself and the Declaration required that any review of Māori organisations, including statutory bodies such as the Council, should be led by Māori. An important element of the claim was that the Council had been established pursuant to a "historic self-government pact" between Maori and the Crown. The Council argued Māori should decide

---

13 For example, see the shadow reports submitted by Peace Movement Aotearoa and Aotearoa Indigenous Rights Trust to the UN Human Rights Committee in February 2016 for the March 2016 review of New Zealand's compliance with the International Covenant on Civil and Political Rights <http://tbinternet.ohchr.org/_layouts/treatybodyexternal/TBSearch.aspx?Lang=En&CountryID=124>.
14 For example, in *Takamore v Clarke* [2012] NZSC 116; *New Zealand Maori Council v Attorney General* [2013] NZSC 6; and *Paki v Attorney General* [2014] NZSC 118.
15 See, *Whaia te Mana Motuhak: In Pursuit of Mana Motuhake* (Wai 2417, 2015).
16 See for example Dr Carwyn Jones, Associate Professor Claire Charters, Andrew Erueti, Professor Jane Kelsey "Māori Rights, Te Tiriti o Waitangi and the Trans-Pacific Partnership Agreement" (2016) submission to Foreign Affairs, Defence and Trade Select Committee on International treaty examination of the Trans-Pacific Partnership Agreement (TPPA) <https://www.parliament.nz/en/pb/sc/submissions-and-advice/document/51SCFDT_EVI_00DBSCH_ITR_68247_1_A496119/andrew-erueti>.
17 Such as the Iwi Chairs Forum's establishment of an independent mechanism to monitor the government's implementation of the UN Declaration on the Rights of Indigenous Peoples in 2015. See Report of the Monitoring Mechanism regarding the implementation of the UN Declaration on the Rights of Indigenous Peoples in Aotearoa/New Zealand (2016) A/HRC/EMRIP/2016/CRP.4.

what changes they want to their self-government institutions even where those institutions are provided for in legislation.

The Crown conceded during the hearing that any review of the Council and relevant sections of the Development Act should be led by Māori. However, given changes in representation of Māori, especially the establishment of many new iwi representative groups, the Crown argued that a broader range of Māori should be included in decision making on the Council's reform. The Council successfully requested the Waitangi Tribunal to authorise the preparation of expert evidence on the relevance of the Declaration to the claim, which I prepared and then presented during the hearing. I focused on the Māori right to autonomy to lead a review of the Council free from Crown interference or control.

D. Case Study: Using the Declaration in Waitangi Tribunal Hearings

1. The Declaration and Human Rights

My evidence first sought to establish the authority of the Declaration. The objective was to persuade the Waitangi Tribunal that, despite not being "binding" on New Zealand, there are sound legal reasons for the Waitangi Tribunal to rely on it. To do this, I focused on the legitimacy of the Declaration, namely the reasons why it is legally authoritative rather than legally binding. I pointed out that it is the most supported and comprehensive of legal instruments describing the rights of indigenous peoples and that declarations are recognised within the United Nations as "solemn instrument[s] resorted to only in very rare cases relating to matters of major and lasting importance where maximum compliance is expected."[18] This point is reflected in the status of another declaration, the Universal Declaration of Human Rights.[19] I outlined some of the key justifications for the normative weight of the Declaration, including:

> The UN General Assembly's authority to adopt declarations is sourced in Article 13(1)(b) of the Charter of the United Nations (UN Charter), to assist with the realisation of human rights and freedoms. The UN Charter constitutes the United Nations.

Under the UN Charter all states are required to respect and promote human rights. The Declaration informs these duties.

The Declaration reflects a global consensus on the rights of Indigenous peoples with 143 states voting for it in the UN General Assembly. Only four states voted

---

18 Economic and Social Council *Report of the Commission on Human Rights* (18th Sess, March-April 1962) UN Doc E/3616/Rev 1, para 105.
19 *Universal Declaration of Human Rights*, GA Res 217A (III), UNGAOR, 3rd Sess, Supp No 13, UN Doc A/810 (1948) 71.

against the Declaration and all (including New Zealand) changed their position to one of support within three years of the General Assembly's adoption of it.

Many of the rights expressed in the Declaration reflect rights and freedoms included in widely ratified human rights treaties, including those ratified by New Zealand. For example, rights to non-discrimination, culture, property and, importantly for this inquiry, the right to self-determination contained in Article 1 of the International Covenant on Civil and Political Rights (ICCPR) and the International Covenant on Economic, Social and Cultural Rights (ICESCR).

World-renowned international lawyers that comprise the International Law Association concluded that the Declaration "includes several key provisions which correspond to existing State obligations under customary international law".

With respect to New Zealand specifically, the close relationship between the substance of the Declaration and the Treaty of Waitangi was acknowledged by the government in its statement in support of the Declaration and by the Supreme Court.

Human rights institutions the world over have cited the importance of the Declaration including New Zealand institutions such as the Human Rights Commission and previous Waitangi Tribunal reports.[20]

2. Process Legitimacy

Next I highlighted the legitimacy that attaches to the Declaration as a result of the processes that gave rise to it. In terms of procedure, I stressed that the Declaration text was negotiated over two decades and included states, indigenous peoples, international institutions, non-governmental organisations and academics, amongst others. In addition, I made the point that the Declaration has been considered by many UN bodies.[21] Over the two decades from the mid-1980s until 2007, the Declaration was considered or approved in its various forms by a multitude of bodies – all comprised of states or their appointees and, in one case, indigenous peoples' representatives – before its final adoption by the UN General Assembly. These bodies included the UN Working Group on Indigenous Populations (comprised of state-appointed experts on human rights), the UN Sub-Commission on the Protection and Promotion of Human Rights (comprised of state-appointed experts on human rights), the (former) UN Commission on Human Rights (comprised of states), the UN Open-Ended Inter-sessional Commission on Human Rights Working Group on the draft Declaration on the Rights of Indigenous Peoples (comprised of states with indigenous peoples' participation), the UN Human Rights Council (the UN's principal multi-lateral

---

20 See, for example, Waitangi Tribunal *Ko Aotearoa Tenei: A Report into Claims Concerning New Zealand Law and Policy Affecting Māori Culture and Identity* (Wai 262, 2011) at 233.
21 Claire Charters, Brief of Evidence, 20 January 2014 (doc A 10) (Wai 2417, 2015), at [24].

state human rights institution), the UN General Assembly's Third Committee on Social, Humanitarian and Cultural Issues, which focuses on human rights (multilateral state institution) and then, finally, the UN General Assembly itself on 13 September 2007 (the highest-level and most inclusive state body of the UN).

3. Substance Legitimacy: The Normative Weight of the Declaration

I then highlighted that the Declaration responds to historical discrimination against indigenous peoples under colonial regimes and international law and that, as many authors have noted, international law historically and discriminatorily excluded indigenous peoples from recognition as sovereigns and "peoples".[22] In its acknowledgment of an indigenous peoples' right to self-determination, the Declaration goes some way to remedying that historical injustice.

4. The Declaration's Influence Internationally and Domestically

Next I focused on the influence of the Declaration internationally and domestically, highlighting that it has become the standard against which state activities are assessed at the domestic and international levels.

(i) International Law

At the international level, I highlighted how the Declaration has been used as an authoritative guide on the content of the rights of indigenous peoples by institutions such as the UN General Assembly, the UN Human Rights Council, the UN Economic and Social Council, the World Intellectual Property Office, UN human rights treaty bodies, the International Labour Organization, by UN special procedures, the UN Food and Agricultural Organisation, the World Health Organisation, the World Bank, the UN Development Programme, the UN Working Group on the issue of human rights and transnational corporations and other business enterprises, institutions associated with the Convention on Biodiversity, environmental institutions, regional courts such as the Inter-American Court of Human Rights and, of course, indigenous specific bodies such as the UN Expert Mechanism on the Rights of Indigenous Peoples, the Special Rapporteur on the Rights of Indigenous Peoples and the UN Permanent Forum on Indigenous Issues.

Given international human rights treaties ratified by states are binding, I cited specific examples of human rights treaty bodies endorsing and applying the Declaration in their observations, responses to communications from individuals

---

22 See Antony Anghie *Imperialism, Sovereignty and the Making of International Law* (Cambridge University Press, Cambridge, 2004) and Patrick Macklem "Indigenous Recognition in International Law: Theoretical Observations" (2009) 30 Mich J Int'l Law 177. See also Patrick Macklem *The Sovereignty of Human Rights* (Oxford University Press, New York, 2015).

and general recommendations or comments. Equally, I stressed comments made to New Zealand by other states to implement the Declaration in the Human Rights Council's Universal Periodic Review process.[23]

While the jurisprudence of regional human rights bodies such as the Inter-American Court of Human Rights and the African Commission on Human and Peoples' Rights is not binding on New Zealand, it illustrates that indigenous peoples' rights are being applied in concrete ways. Both regional bodies have recognised, for example, states' duties to demarcate and title indigenous peoples' rights to their lands, territories and resources under their own indigenous legal systems. Similarly, I thought it relevant to mention the World Bank's policies on indigenous peoples' rights, which draw on the Declaration, not least because the World Bank has significant power to compel states to comply with its policies when they seek loans.

I also considered that the Waitangi Tribunal might be influenced by case law from other jurisdictions that cite positively and rely on the Declaration, including cases from other common law jurisdictions such as Belize.[24]

I provided detail of criticisms of New Zealand's failures to respect indigenous peoples' rights by international human rights treaty bodies, the UN Human Rights Council and the UN Special Rapporteur on the Rights of Indigenous Peoples to drive home the point that New Zealand cannot avoid international oversight of its approach to Māori rights. It also served to highlight that if the Waitangi Tribunal failed to recognise and apply indigenous peoples' rights under international law, it might well be subject to similar criticism when New Zealand is reviewed by international human rights bodies.

(ii) Domestic Law

To illustrate that international law can be relevant to the interpretation and application of the common law, I first cited extracts from the Court of Appeal to the effect that "so far as its wording allows, legislation should be read in a way which is consistent with New Zealand's international obligations",[25] and that international instruments can be taken into account by courts when developing

---

23 See Natalie Baird's chapter in this book.
24 *Cal v Attorney General* Claims Nos 171/2007, 172/2007, 18 October 2007 (Supreme Court of Belize). Since the finalisation of my expert evidence, the Caribbean Court of Appeal affirmed the lower court's decision to recognise Mayan land rights. See Press Release, University of Arizona Indigenous Peoples Law and Policy Program, 22 April 2015, "Maya Indigenous Peoples of Belize Win".
25 Citing *New Zealand Airline Pilots' Association Inc v Attorney-General* [1997] 3 NZLR 269, 289 (CA), per Keith J. In the immigration context, refer *Puli'uvea v Removal Review Authority* (1996) 2 HRNZ 510 (CA); *Tavita v Minister of Immigration* [1994] 2 NZLR 257 (CA) and *Zaoui v Attorney-General* [2006] 1 NZLR 289 (SC).

the common law.[26] I also noted that the Court of Appeal has observed that "[l]egitimate criticism could extend to the New Zealand courts if they were to accept the argument that, because a domestic statute giving discretionary powers in general terms does not mention international human rights norms, or obligations, the Executive is necessarily free to ignore them."[27] The latter point was also made to, once again, make the point that the Waitangi Tribunal's decisions might be reviewed by international human rights bodies.

To stress the influence of the Declaration domestically, I cited a number of cases that refer to the Declaration, including the Supreme Court decisions of *New Zealand Māori Council v the Attorney General*[28] and *Takamore v Clarke*.[29]

The New Zealand Māori Council v Attorney General concerned the Council's objection to the Crown's establishment of a mixed-ownership model of formerly state owned enterprises engaged in energy generation and, especially, the potential for Māori rights to freshwater to be compromised as a result. The Supreme Court in its single unanimous decision doubted whether the Declaration adds to the principles of the Treaty when it is statutorily recognised in legislation.[30] I argued that this suggested that the Supreme Court is of the view that the principles of the Treaty are co-extensive with the rights and freedoms expressed in the Declaration. Moreover, the Supreme Court also accepted that "the Declaration provides some support for the view that those principles should be construed broadly."[31]

The other notable decision was *Takamore v Clarke*, which concerned a dispute between Mr Takamore's wife, Denise Clarke, and Mr Takamore's Tūhoe whānau as to where Mr Takamore should be buried given Takamore died intestate and left no clear indication as to where he wanted to be buried. The whānau argued that he should be buried in accordance with tikanga Māori. A principal legal issue was the extent to which the common law could accommodate tikanga Māori. The decision was ultimately decided by the Supreme Court in Denise Clarke's favour.

Noting that both the Court of Appeal and the Supreme Court had cited the Declaration positively, I explained, that Elias CJ, in the Supreme Court, cited the Declaration as evidence of "the importance placed on the repatriation of the dead by Indigenous peoples."[32] In relation to the Court of Appeal decision, I noted that the majority also cited the Declaration as recognising the need to safeguard both the individual and the collective rights of indigenous peoples.[33] I argued that this

---

26 *Hosking v Runting* [2005] 1 NZLR 1 (CA) and *Lange v Atkinson* [1998] 3 NZLR 424.
27 *Tavita v Minister of Immigration* [1994] 2 NZLR 257 (CA).
28 *New Zealand Māori Council v Attorney General* [2013] NZSC 6.
29 *Takamore v Clarke* [2012] NZSC 116.
30 At [92].
31 At [63.1].
32 At [63.2].
33 *Takamore v Clarke* [2012] 1 NZLR 573 at [252].

indicated the common law relating to burial needs to give greater consideration to the collective nature of indigenous peoples' rights. Finally, on the status of the Declaration in New Zealand law, the Court of Appeal noted that while it is non-binding, "New Zealand announced its support of the Declaration in 2010" and that New Zealand "is a party to the international human rights covenants on which the Declaration is based" and that an authority on the Declaration, Professor Elsa Stamatopoulou, observes that "the Declaration does not in fact contain any new cultural human rights, but restates, in one systematic text, human rights contained in previously adopted international instruments and confirmed through the case law of international bodies."[34]

I then cited a number of positive references to the Declaration by the Waitangi Tribunal that "to the extent that rights declared in the [Declaration] may be recognised consistent with the jurisdiction and procedures of the Tribunal, then this Tribunal should do so."[35] In a similar vein, I noted obligations on Parliament to take into account international legal obligations when making laws and the numerous times that the Declaration has been referenced in Parliament.[36]

The Waitangi Tribunal's statutory mandate is to assess Crown actions against the principles of the Treaty of Waitangi.[37] It was important to make the case that the principles of the Treaty can and should be read consistently with the Declaration.[38] Many high-level governmental persons had also noted the synergies between the instruments, which I mentioned in the evidence. Of especial note, the Hon Pita Sharples (then Minister of Māori Affairs), during his expression of support for the Declaration at the UN, on behalf of New Zealand, had stated that, "[t]he Declaration contains principles that are consistent with the duties and principles inherent in the Treaty, such as operating in the spirit of partnership and mutual respect."[39] I also highlighted the similarities between Treaty principles and the Declaration, albeit noting that the Declaration with its 46 articles is more explicit, specific and express in outlining Indigenous peoples' rights than the Treaty principles.[40]

---

34 At [253].
35 Judge Caren Fox, Presiding Officer, *Memorandum of Directions (No 7)* in relation to Wai 2200 (3 December 2010).
36 At paras 72 and 79, citing the New Zealand Cabinet Manual (Wellington, 2008), 1 and the Guidelines provided by the Legislation Advisory Committee *Guidelines on Process and Content of Legislation* 2001 with subsequent amendments (Wellington), at 135. For an example of references to the Declaration in Parliament, see the debate on the Marine and Coastal Area (Takutai Moana) Act 2011 <http://www.parliament.nz/ennz/pb/debates/debates/49HansD_20110308_00000716/marine - and-coastal-area-takutai-moana-bill-—-second-reading>.
37 Treaty of Waitangi Act 1975.
38 Claire Charters, Brief of Evidence, 20 January 2014 (doc A 10) (Wai 2417, 2015) at [81]-[85].
39 Rt Hon Pita Sharples, New York (19 April 2010).
40 Claire Charters, Brief of Evidence, 20 January 2014 (doc A 10) (Wai 2417, 2015) at [84].

I devoted considerable attention to the relevance of s 20 of the New Zealand Bill of Rights Act (BORA), which includes the right to culture, to the interpretation of the Treaty and, in turn, the role of the Declaration in New Zealand law. Section 20 of the BORA, which mirrors article 27 of the International Covenant on Civil and Political Rights, states that:[41]

> A person who belongs to an ethnic, religious or linguistic minority in New Zealand shall not be denied the right, in community with other members of that minority, to enjoy the culture, profess and practise the religion, or to use the language, of that community.

While there is little jurisprudence on section 20 in New Zealand case law, albeit with notable exceptions such as in *Takamore*, its potential relevance to cases involving Māori culture is significant.[42] As Paul Rishworth comments: "[o]nce it is accepted that culture may involve matters ranging from commercial exploitation of natural resources by minorities to mechanisms of social control and conflict resolution, the reach of s 20 is broad indeed."[43] This is especially true, given that BORA imposes legally enforceable obligations on the Executive whereas the Treaty of Waitangi ordinarily requires statutory recognition to be enforceable. Elias CJ states in *Takamore* that:[44]

> It would however be paying lipservice to the importance of culture recognised by the New Zealand Bill of Rights Act and in particular the importance of Māori society and culture in New Zealand (derived from the Treaty of Waitangi and recognised in modern New Zealand legislation) to conclude that the wishes of the spouse will always prevail over other interests.

Section 20 of the BORA could function as an important vehicle to incorporate Declaration rights into New Zealand jurisprudence if New Zealand courts and tribunals interpret the right to culture in a way that is consistent with the Declaration, which is exactly what international human rights treaty bodies have done. As stated in my evidence:[45]

> Most articles in the Declaration are closely related to Indigenous individuals' and peoples' rights not to be denied the right to enjoy their culture, from rights to lands, territories and resources, to self-determination and to determination of their own representative institutions. Accordingly, s 20 BORA can easily be

---

41 ICCPR, art 27.
42 Fleur Adcock "Maori and the Bill of Rights Act: A Case of Missed Opportunities" (2013) 11 NZJPIL 183.
43 Rishworth "Minority Rights", at 401.
44 *Takamore v Clarke* [2012] NZSC 116, at [101].
45 Claire Charters, Brief of Evidence, 20 January 2014 (doc A 10) (Wai 2417, 2015) at [91].

interpreted to "cover" or even to "incorporate" many of the rights expressed in the Declaration into New Zealand law.

I then illustrated ways in which the UN Human Rights Committee has interpreted the right to culture consistently with indigenous peoples' rights under the Declaration, such as to protect indigenous peoples' rights to their lands, territories and resources, to consultation and free, prior and informed consent, and to self-determination.[46]

(iii) The Right to Self-determination and the Waitangi Tribunal Hearing

The remainder of my evidence focused on the specific issue before the Waitangi Tribunal, namely showing that the Declaration, especially the right to self-determination and related articles, supported the Council's claim that Māori should determine the constitution of their institutions. I relied on articles that support indigenous autonomy and, especially article 33, which states, "Indigenous peoples have the right to determine the structures and to select the membership of their institutions in accordance with their own procedures." I also referred to the articles on free, prior and informed consent and related international jurisprudence, given the Council's concern that government might proceed and unilaterally impose its reforms under the Development Act.

E. The Waitangi Tribunal Report and Findings on the Declaration

The Waitangi Tribunal found for the Council especially with respect to the need for Māori to determine their own processes with respect to the constitution of their own Māori institutions. In doing so, the Waitangi Tribunal relied on the Declaration in many places in its report to "assist in the interpretation of and application of [. . .] Treaty principles."[47] As this quote suggests, the Declaration was not authoritative in and of itself, which the Waitangi Tribunal addressed explicitly. It clarified:[48]

> our jurisdiction is to assess Crown actions against the principles of the Treaty. It is not our role to make findings on whether the Crown has acted inconsistently with [the Declaration]. However, both the claimants and the Crown accept that [the Declaration] articles are relevant to the interpretation of the principles of the Treaty of Waitangi. Because the New Zealand Government has now affirmed [the

---

46 At [92]-[97]. Relevant material cited includes UN Doc HRI/GEN/1/Rev.1 at 38 (1994); CCPR/C/AUS/CO/5, 2 April 2009, para 13; CCPR/C/MEX/CO/5, 17 May 2010, para 22; CCPR/C/95/D/1457/2006, 24 April 2009; CCPR/C/NZL/CO/5, 7 April 2010, para 19; *Apirana Mahuika et al v New Zealand* Comm No 547/1993 UN Doc CCPR/C/70/D/547/1993 (2000).
47 *Whaia te Mana Motuhake: In Pursuit of Mana Motuhake* (Wai 2417, 2015) at 47.
48 At 55.

Declaration], the obligations described in its articles are a circumstance we can take into account in assessing the Crown's actions. [The Declaration] is therefore relevant to the manner in which the principles of the Treaty of Waitangi should be observed by Crown officials. This is particularly the case where [the Declaration] articles provide specific guidance as to how the Crown should be interacting with Māori or recognising their interests.

In considering various arguments made about the relevance of the Declaration, the Waitangi Tribunal noted the importance of UN declarations generally; that the Declaration "merely restates for the most part, human rights contained in other international instruments";[49] that it is "routinely referred to by international institutions";[50] and that there is extensive New Zealand case law referencing the Declaration. Citing New Zealand's statement of support for the Declaration in 2010, the Waitangi Tribunal notes that it envisages that the government will respect the Treaty, "as further elucidated by any relevant articles of [the Declaration], subject to any lawful limitations."[51] It also cited earlier comments by the Waitangi Tribunal, including that it is "perhaps the most important international instrument ever for Maori people",[52] and references to the Declaration in judgments of New Zealand Court of Appeal and Supreme Court.[53]

The Waitangi Tribunal went on to group many of the Declaration's articles under various Treaty principles, including kāwanatanga, rangatiratanga, partnership, active protection, equity and equality and right to development. Clearly this schema could be of use in subsequent claims to the Waitangi Tribunal.

The Waitangi Tribunal referred multiple times to the Declaration. In a key passage where the Declaration was especially important to the Waitangi Tribunal's approach, it states that:[54]

> in our view, reading the Treaty principles as informed by the Declaration, we think it is correct that Māori should decide what changes they want to their self-government institutions, even where those institutions are provided for in legislation. Having decided what is wanted or needed, Māori must then discuss implementation with the Crown, because the Crown would need to arrange the necessary funding or legislation. Collaboration occurs because the Crown has a duty to satisfy itself that the requested funding or legislation is reasonable and can be met by Parliament and/or the public purse. Also, in Dr Charters' evidence, the Crown would need to satisfy itself that legislative changes are supported by the Māori groups who will be affected by them, before it promotes legislation to give effect to them.

49 At 51.
50 At 51.
51 At 54.
52 At 54.
53 At 54–55.
54 At 364–365.

The Waitangi Tribunal decided that "the Crown's decision in 2013 to proceed with a Crown-led review, leading to unilateral Crown decisions about Maori self-government institutions, was not consistent with the rights affirmed in the Declaration."[55] In its recommendations the Tribunal also recommended that reform should be Council-led and negotiated with the Crown.

F. Conclusion

In conclusion, I have argued that by using the Declaration in a variety of legal and political fora, advocates can contribute to state internalisation of its norms. By explaining how the Declaration can be used in Māori legal claims in the Waitangi Tribunal, based on my evidence in Wai 2417, I hope to encourage other advocates to promote state internalisation by articulating arguments based on it.

---

55 At 510.

8
The UN Special Procedures and Indigenous Peoples' Rights

*Fleur Te Aho**

A. Introduction

The United Nations Human Rights Council's (HRC) special procedures are one mechanism for advancing implementation of the UN Declaration on the Rights of Indigenous Peoples (the Declaration).[1] The special procedures are a collection of independent experts charged by the UN with monitoring and promoting human rights around the world. The experts have an express mandate regarding indigenous peoples' rights. In 1993 the UN Commission on Human Rights (CHR) called on all thematic experts to pay particular attention to the situation of indigenous peoples within the framework of their mandates.[2] Subsequently, in 2001 the mandate of the UN Special Rapporteur on the Rights of Indigenous Peoples (Special Rapporteur) was established to investigate and report on indigenous peoples' rights.[3] Importantly for rights implementation, the special procedures have been praised for their efficacy in the realisation of human rights. Former UN Secretary-General Kofi Annan described the special procedures as the "crown jewel" of the UN human rights machinery and Amnesty International has called them "a critical element in the implementation of international human

---

[*] Lecturer, Faculty of Law, University of Auckland.
[1] *United Nations Declaration on the Rights of Indigenous Peoples* GA Res 61/295, A/RES/61/295 (2007).
[2] *International Year of the World's Indigenous People* CHR Res 1993/30, E/CN.4/RES/1993/30 (1993) at [2].
[3] The title of the original mandate – UN Special Rapporteur on the situation of human rights and fundamental freedoms of indigenous people – was revised in 2010 to refer to "peoples", in line with the Declaration, and was shortened to the "Special Rapporteur on the Rights of Indigenous Peoples". Human Rights Council *Human Rights and Indigenous Peoples: Mandate of the Special Rapporteur on the Rights of Indigenous Peoples* HRC Res 15/14, A/HRC/RES/15/14 (2010).

rights standards."[4] In this chapter, I argue that the special procedures are uniquely placed to foster implementation of the Declaration, although there are challenges associated with leveraging the mechanism in Aotearoa New Zealand as elsewhere. The findings draw on empirical research regarding the mechanism's domestic influence, including 18 semi-structured interviews carried out between 2010 and 2011 with, among others, Māori rights advocates, the two former UN Special Rapporteurs on Rights of Indigenous Peoples, current and former members of the UN Office of the High Commissioner for Human Rights (OHCHR), a member of Aotearoa New Zealand's Parliament, and representatives of the New Zealand Human Rights Commission (NZHRC).[5] In Part B, I examine the special procedures' mandate regarding indigenous peoples. In Part C, I outline the key tools at the experts' disposal for fulfilling their indigenous mandate. Part D suggests some strategies for leveraging the special procedures to help realise the rights affirmed in the Declaration in Aotearoa New Zealand.

B. The Special Procedures' Indigenous Mandate

The special procedures have a broad mandate to help realise international indigenous rights norms. The special procedures have evolved from their haphazard creation to become one of the HRC's primary instruments for monitoring and advancing state conformity to international human rights norms, alongside the HRC's Universal Periodic Review process. The special procedures were first established in the late 1960s on an ad hoc basis by the former Commission on Human Rights (the HRC's predecessor),[6] and now come under the authority of the HRC. The mandates are created either on a country-specific basis, such as in respect of the Central African Republic[7] or Myanmar,[8] or on a thematic basis,

---

4   Kofi Annan, UN Secretary-General *Secretary-General Urges Human Rights Activists to "Fill Leadership Vacuum", Hold World Leaders to Account, in Address to International Day Event* SG/SM/10788 (2006); Amnesty International *Organization of the Work of the Session: Written Statement Submitted by Amnesty International, a Non-Governmental Organization in Special Consultative Status* E/CN.4/2006/NGO/250 (2006) at 2.

5   Fleur Adcock "The UN Special Rapporteur on the Rights of Indigenous Peoples and New Zealand: A Study in Compliance Ritualism" (2012) 10 NZYIL 97; Fleur Adcock "The United Nations Special Procedures and Indigenous Peoples: A Regulatory Analysis" (PhD Dissertation, The Australian National University, 2013). Except regarding the two former Special Rapporteurs on indigenous peoples who consented to be named, in this chapter the names of the interviewees (and in one instance the city of the interview) have been anonymised in order to protect the identity of the interviewees.

6   *UN Economic and Social Council Res 1235 (XLII)* 42 UN ESCOR Supp (No. 1) 17, E/4393 (1967) at [2]-[3].

7   *Technical assistance to the Central African Republic in the field of human rights* HRC Res 24/34, A/HRC/RES/24/34 (2013).

8   Office for the High Commissioner for Human Rights *Situation of human rights in Myanmar* CHR Res 1992/58 (1992).

concerning issues as diverse as the right to food, arbitrary detention, cultural rights and transnational corporations.[9] The experts hold their positions either as Special Rapporteurs, Independent Experts or members of Working Groups.[10] The general role of the current 56 special procedures mandates is to examine, monitor and report on human rights violations. But the specific roles of these experts are established and defined by their individual enabling resolutions. The resolutions often grant the experts significant licence.[11] Awareness-raising is a central feature of the experts' function. Notably, the experts also have a role in helping to bring about tangible human rights improvements.[12]

The mandate-holders enjoy an unusual position within the UN human rights system. They are independent. They are not representatives of their government, the UN Secretary General or particular rights groups.[13] They are not UN staff members – they serve in their personal capacities – and do not receive salaries.[14] However, they are considered UN "experts on mission";[15] the UN pays mandate-holders a per diem allowance and some travel expenses;[16] and mandate-holders receive some (albeit slender) personnel, policy, research and logistical support from the OHCHR.

There were two landmarks in the development of the experts' mandate regarding indigenous peoples. The first was the CHR's Resolution 1993/60, which, as noted, explicitly recognised the relevance of indigenous rights concerns to the mandates of all thematic special procedures (their relevance to country mandates was not mentioned).[17] The recommendation was issued to further the UN's International Year of the World's Indigenous People in 1993.[18] A number

9   For a complete list see UN Office of the High Commissioner for Human Rights *Thematic mandates* <www.ohchr.org/EN/HRBodies/SP/Pages/Themes.aspx>.
10 Ted Piccone *Catalysts for Rights: The Unique Contribution of the UN's Independent Experts on Human Rights* (The Brookings Institution, Washington DC, 2010) at 27.
11 Menno T Kamminga "The Thematic Procedures of the UN Commission on Human Rights" (1987) 34 NIL Rev 299 at 322; See also Joanna Naples-Mitchell "Perspectives of UN Special Rapporteurs on their Role: Inherent Tensions and Unique Contributions to Human Rights" (2011) 15(2) IJHR 232 at 234.
12 Joanna Naples-Mitchell, above n 11 at 240.
13 Human Rights Council *Code of Conduct for Special Procedures Mandate-holders of the Human Rights Council* A/HRC/Res/5/2 (2007), art 3 [Code of Conduct]; Manual of Operations of the Special Procedures of the Human Rights Council (August 2008) at [9] [Manual of Operations].
14 Manual of Operations, above n 13, at [10].
15 Convention on Privileges and Immunities of the United Nations 1 UNTS 15 (opened for signature 13 February 1946, entered into force 17 September 1946); Manual of Operations, above n 13, at [13]-[15]. See generally Ingrid Nifosi *The UN Special Procedures in the Field of Human Rights* (Intersentia, Antwerpen; Oxford, 2005) at 49–55.
16 Ted Piccone "The Contribution of the UN's Special Procedures to National Level Implementation of Human Rights Norms" (2011) 15(2) IJHR 206 at 224.
17 *International Year of the World's Indigenous People* CHR Res 1993/30, E/CN.4/RES/1993/30 (1993) at [2].
18 *International Year for the World's Indigenous People* GA Res 45/164, A/RES/45/164

THE UN SPECIAL PROCEDURES AND INDIGENOUS PEOPLES' RIGHTS   155

of thematic mandate-holders have heeded the CHR's recommendation, although the degree and quality of that attention has depended highly on the individual mandate-holder. To take just one example, while the expert on racism has devoted sizeable attention to the human rights situation of indigenous peoples, the expert on the sale of children has not.[19]

The second landmark was the creation of the thematic mandate of the Special Rapporteur on the Rights of Indigenous Peoples on 24 April 2001. It was established by a consensus resolution of the CHR, despite the strong objections of the governments of Aotearoa New Zealand, the United States of America, Canada, Australia and Russia.[20] An indigenous-focused special procedures mandate was a long-standing demand of indigenous peoples that had been raised at various international conferences, including the World Conference on Human Rights in 1993.[21] The Special Rapporteur's enabling resolution afforded the expert a broad mandate to investigate, and provide suggestions on how to prevent and remedy specific violations of indigenous peoples' human rights.[22] Later revisions to the mandate have emphasised the Special Rapporteur's role in securing the "effective" protection of indigenous peoples' rights. For example, since 2002 the Special Rapporteur has been encouraged to identify ways to overcome "obstacles to the full and effective protection" of indigenous peoples' rights (with some slight revision to this wording in later years), and in

---

(1990). It was a call later repeated by the CHR, and echoed in resolutions of the CHR's Sub-Commission on the Promotion and Protection of Human Rights, see *Working Group on Indigenous Populations of the Sub-Commission on the Promotion and Protection of Human Rights, and the International Decade of the World's Indigenous Peoples* CHR Res 2004/58, E/CN.4/RES/2004/58 (20 April 2004) at [4]; *Working Group on Indigenous Populations*, Sub-Commission on the Promotion and Protection of Human Rights Res 2006/13, A/HRC/Sub.1/RES/2006/13 (2006) at [5].

19 United Nations Commission on Human Rights *Report by Mr Maurice Glélé-Ahanhanzo, Special Rapporteur on Contemporary Forms of Racism, Racial Discrimination, Xenophobia and Related Intolerance: Addendum Mission to Colombia* E/CN.4/1997/71/Add.1 (1997) at [6], [8], [10], [12]-[14], [17]-[19], [21]-[23], [31]-[33], [46]-[57], [59]-[64], [67]-[68]; United Nations Commission on Human Rights *Report by Mr Maurice Glélé-Ahanhanzo, Special Rapporteur on Contemporary Forms of Racism, Racial Discrimination, Xenophobia and Related Intolerance on his Mission to Brazil from 6 to 17 June 1995, Submitted Pursuant to Commission on Human Rights resolutions 1993/20 and 1995/12* E/CN.4/1996/72/Add.1 (1995) at [32], [37], [60], [61], [70].

20 *Human Rights and Indigenous Peoples* CHR Res 2001/57, E/CN.4/RES/2001/57 (2001); Victoria Tauli-Corpuz and Erlyn Ruth Alcantara *Engaging the UN Special Rapporteur on Indigenous People: Opportunities and Challenges* (Tebtebba Foundation, Philippines, 2004) at 5–6.

21 Interview with Rodolfo Stavenhagen, Former United Nations Special Rapporteur on the Rights of Indigenous People (2001–2008) (The author, Skype Interview, 19 April 2011); Jens Dahl, *The Indigenous Space and Marginalized Peoples in the United Nations* (Palgrave Macmillan, London, 2012) at 61–62.

22 *Human Rights and Indigenous Issues* CHR Res 2001/57, UN Doc E/CN.4/RES/2001/57 at para 1.

2005 the expert was requested to prepare a study on best practices regarding implementation of the expert's general and country recommendations.[23] Three experts have held the role of Special Rapporteur on the Rights of Indigenous Peoples since its creation: Rodolfo Stavenhagen, a noted Mexican sociologist (June 2001 to April 2008); James Anaya, a leading American international law expert of Apache and Purepecha descent (May 2008 to June 2014); and, since 2014, Victoria Tauli-Corpuz, a Kankanaey Igorot leader and activist from the Philippines.

The mandate of the Special Rapporteur has a special relationship with the Declaration. The normative framework that informs the mandate of the Special Rapporteur is drawn from an extensive collection of instruments, including treaties and declarations of the UN General Assembly, as well as customary international law. But the Declaration is *the* guiding instrument. Following the adoption of the Declaration in 2007, the HRC requested the Special Rapporteur "[t]o promote the [Declaration] and international instruments relevant to the advancement of the rights of indigenous peoples, where appropriate."[24] Anaya expressly embraced the Declaration as the guiding framework for his work as Special Rapporteur,[25] whether or not the particular state he was examining endorsed it.[26] Anaya's approach did not meet with public resistance from states. Anaya has remarked that he received "no push back at least outwardly, no one went on record saying that I should not do that, no one went on record saying 'that

---

23 *Human Rights and Indigenous Issues,* CHR Res 2002/65, E/CN.4/RES/2002/65 (2002) at [2]; *Human Rights and Indigenous Issues,* CHR Res 2003/56, E/CN.4/RES/2003/56 (2003) at [2]; *Human Rights and Indigenous Issues* CHR Res 2004/62, E/CN/4/RES/2004/62 (2004) at [3]; *Human Rights and Indigenous Issues* CHR Res 2005/51, E/CN/4/RES/2005/51 (20 April 2005) at [2]; *Human Rights and Indigenous Peoples: Mandate of the Special Rapporteur on the Situation of Human Rights and Fundamental Freedoms of Indigenous People* HRC Res 6/12, A/HRC/RES/6/12 (2007), at [1](a); *Human Rights and Indigenous Peoples: Mandate of the Special Rapporteur on the Rights of Indigenous Peoples,* above n 3, at [1](a); *Human Rights and Indigenous Peoples: Mandate of the Special Rapporteur on the Rights of Indigenous Peoples* HRC Res 24/9, A/HRC/24/9 (2013) at [1].

24 *Human Rights and Indigenous Peoples: Mandate of the Special Rapporteur on the Situation of Human Rights and Fundamental Freedoms of Indigenous People* HRC Res 6/12, A/HRC/RES/6/12 (2007) at [1](g); *Human Rights and Indigenous Peoples: Mandate of the Special Rapporteur on the Rights of Indigenous Peoples,* above n 3, at [1](g).

25 James Anaya *Promotion and Protection of All Human Rights, Civil, Political, Economic, Social and Cultural Rights, Including the Right to Development: Report of the Special Rapporteur on the Situation of Human Rights and Fundamental Freedoms of Indigenous People* A/HRC/9/9 (11 August 2008) at [34]-[43] [*Special Rapporteur Report to the Human Rights Council 2008*]. See also James Anaya *Report of the Special Rapporteur on the Rights of Indigenous People* A/68/317 (14 August 2013) at [3], [57] [*Special Rapporteur Report to the General Assembly 2013*].

26 Interview with James Anaya, Former United Nations Special Rapporteur on the Rights of Indigenous People (2008–2014) (The author, Telephone Interview, 24 January 2011, updated by email 5 July 2013).

is not the standard', so from the very beginning I have used the Declaration as the benchmark."[27] This approach is evidenced in all of Anaya's reports, including his studies on operationalising the Declaration in 2008, 2009, 2010 and 2013.[28] Anaya's approach is an example of what Ingrid Nifosi has described as the special procedures "augmenting the legal force of soft law instruments by constantly urging states to comply with them and monitoring such compliance."[29] She argues that such approaches "have established a sort of *mandatory significance* of such instruments which is in between the exhortative power of a UN Declaration and the legal force of a human rights Convention."[30] The boldness of Anaya's explicit embrace of the Declaration as the guiding framework in his dealings with all states is noteworthy. Anaya has commented that having the standards in the Declaration agreed on "is an advantage I have over my predecessor."[31] But even prior to its adoption, Stavenhagen drew on the draft Declaration in performing his role as Special Rapporteur. In his first thematic study in 2002, Stavenhagen described the draft Declaration as "undoubtedly the most important human rights document for indigenous peoples" and went on to reference its provisions on natural resources, institutional structures and customs, and indigenous membership in the report.[32] Tauli-Corpuz has also made the Declaration the key benchmark for her work. In her first thematic study in 2014, Tauli-Corpuz described the Declaration as "[t]he principal normative framework for the mandate" and she devoted attention in that report to challenges to its practical implementation.[33] Her subsequent thematic studies have applied key articles in the Declaration to the issues of socio-economic development, the position of indigenous women and the impact of international investment and free trade on indigenous peoples.[34]

27 Interview with James Anaya, above n 26.
28 *Special Rapporteur Report to the Human Rights Council 2008*, above n 25; James Anaya *Report of the Special Rapporteur on the Situation of Human Rights and Fundamental Freedoms of Indigenous People* A/64/338 (2009); James Anaya *Interim Report of the Special Rapporteur on the Situation of Human Rights and Fundamental Freedoms of Indigenous People* A/65/264 (2010) [*Special Rapporteur Report to the General Assembly 2010*]; James Anaya *Promotion and Protection of All Human Rights, Civil, Political, Economic, Social and Cultural Rights, Including the Right to Development: Report of the Special Rapporteur on the Situation of Human Rights and Fundamental Freedoms of Indigenous People* A/HRC/23/40 (2013).
29 Ingrid Nifosi, above n 15, at 134.
30 At 134 (emphasis in original).
31 Interview with James Anaya, above n 26.
32 Rodolfo Stavenhagen *Report of the Special Rapporteur on the Situation of Human Rights and Fundamental Freedoms of Indigenous People, Mr Rodolfo Stavenhagen, Submitted Pursuant to Commission Resolution 2001/57* E/CN.4/2002/97 (2002) at [15], [55], [78], [99].
33 Victoria Tauli Corpuz *Report of the Special Rapporteur on the Rights of Indigenous Peoples, Victoria Tauli Corpuz* A/HRC/27/52 (2014) [6], [17]-[47] [*Special Rapporteur Report to the General Assembly 2014*].
34 General Assembly *Transmission of the Report of the Special Rapporteur of the Human Rights*

Even with the establishment of the mandate of the Special Rapporteur, all special procedures experts retain a role in advancing the realisation of indigenous peoples' rights, which some experts have embraced. Coordination and collaboration on indigenous rights issues between the Special Rapporteur and other experts occurs on an erratic basis. There is no formal process for collaboration; when it happens, it takes place informally according to the interests and agendas of the individual experts. Stavenhagen recalled exchanging information on the position of indigenous women with the expert on violence against women "very often", for example.[35] According to Anaya, coordination between the experts is "complicated" by their differing working methods, which are considered in the next section.[36]

C. The Key Tools for Fulfilling the Indigenous Mandate

The special procedures draw on an assorted toolset to perform their mandate to advance the realisation of indigenous rights. All the core mechanisms the experts wield are dialogue-based. The special procedures rely on dialogue-based mechanisms because states are not obliged to cooperate with the special procedures' experts in their work and the experts do not have the authority to coerce compliance with their recommendations. The same instrument that is the ultimate authority for the creation of the special procedures – the UN Charter – also affirms the principles of national sovereignty and non-interference in domestic affairs.[37] Acting within these constraints the experts have sought to leverage the dialogue-based mechanisms available to them to help progress the realisation of indigenous rights. While the individual working styles of the special procedures experts differ, there are a number of commonalities.

Shaming is the overriding mechanism engaged by the experts, with dialogue-building and capacity-building the two other significant tools invoked. In this context, shaming relies on the state being made aware in private or in public that it is not complying with international indigenous rights and that this non-compliance is disapproved of – the idea being that this disapproval will shame or embarrass states into compliance. At the very least, knowing that its indigenous rights situation is being monitored may prevent a state from allowing a situation

---

Council on the Rights of Indigenous Peoples A/69/267 (2014); Victoria Tauli Corpuz *Report of the Special Rapporteur on the Rights of Indigenous Peoples, Victoria Tauli Corpuz* A/HRC/30/41 (2015); Victoria Tauli Corpuz *Report of the Special Rapporteur of the Human Rights Council on the Rights of Indigenous Peoples on the impact of international investment and free trade on the human rights of indigenous peoples* A/70/301 (2015) [*Special Rapporteur Report to the General Assembly 2015*].

35 Interview with Rodolfo Stavenhagen, above n 21.
36 Interview with James Anaya, above n 26.
37 Charter of the United Nations, art 2(7).

of concern to escalate, even if it does not resolve the rights issue. Crucially, shaming requires that the state concerned cares about whether it has a positive or negative indigenous rights reputation. A state may be concerned about its reputation for upholding indigenous rights for a host of reasons: to maintain investment and aid flows, ensure stability within the state, or maintain an image as a responsible member of the international community.

Shaming permeates the experts' country missions and reports, communications, "special" missions and reports on specific cases, as well as media releases. Most experts conduct country missions, where they undertake country visits to investigate specific human rights violations and report their findings and recommendations following those missions to the HRC and sometimes the UN General Assembly.[38] The Special Rapporteur on the Rights of Indigenous Peoples has embraced this working method. The state being visited must consent to the mission.[39] States may outright refuse to permit an expert to conduct a visit, neglect to respond to an expert's request to visit or consistently delay an agreed visit. Some states have issued standing invitations, meaning that in principle the state is willing to receive a country visit from any thematic special procedures mandate-holder. The New Zealand government issued a standing invitation to the special procedures in 2004.[40] However, even where a state has issued a standing invitation, state consent to each visit is still required.[41]

Hundreds of missions have been undertaken to countries from across the world. In 2013 alone, experts conducted 79 country missions to 66 countries and territories.[42] Most special procedures experts conduct two country visits per year, with each mission lasting around one to two weeks, visiting the capital and other sites of concern.[43] However, Anaya, for example, generally secured funding to conduct at least three missions per year.[44] Occasionally the experts undertake country missions jointly.[45] The factors that can influence whether a

---

38   See Ted Piccone *Catalysts for Rights*, above n 10, at 9–11.
39   *Code of Conduct*, above n 13, art 11(b).
40   Office for the High Commissioner for Human Rights "Standing Invitations" (20 March 2016) <http://spinternet.ohchr.org/_Layouts/SpecialProceduresInternet/StandingInvitations.aspx>.
41   *Code of Conduct*, above n 13, art 11(b).
42   Office for the High Commissioner for Human Rights "United Nations Special Procedures: Facts and Figures 2013" (February 2014) <http://www.ohchr.org/Documents/HRBodies/SP/Facts_Figures2013.pdf> at 13.
43   *Manual of Operations*, above n 13, at [53]; Ted Piccone "The Contribution of the UN's Special Procedures to National Level Implementation of Human Rights Norms", above n 16, at 212.
44   Interview with James Anaya, above n 26.
45   Christophe Golay, Claire Mahon and Ioana Cismas "The Impact of the UN Special Procedures on the Development and Implementation of Economic, Social and Cultural Rights" (2011) 15(2) IJHR 299 at 309.

country mission is undertaken include:⁴⁶

> considerations of geographical balance, the expected impact of the visit and the willingness of national actors to cooperate with the mandate-holder, the likelihood of follow-up on any recommendations made . . . [and] recent or proposed visits by other special procedures mandate-holders.

The agenda for each country mission is determined by the relevant expert, often with the assistance of the OHCHR.⁴⁷ The experts meet with a wide range of actors during the missions. These include state representatives, such as members of the executive, legislature and judiciary, as well as regional and local authorities; members of the national human rights institution, if one exists; NGOs and victims of human rights violations; the UN and other inter-governmental agencies with a local presence; academics and business actors, where relevant; and the domestic press. If there are indigenous rights concerns, the experts will generally meet with indigenous leaders and communities, as well as indigenous individuals who have experienced rights violations. During the visits the experts also receive written submissions, documents and other information from different sources, often in quantities impossible to digest in the timeframe or 10,000 word limit available for the report on the mission.⁴⁸

Country missions help to break down the linguistic, financial and visa barriers that inhibit indigenous peoples' access to the UN, because they bring the UN to indigenous peoples. The experts' ability to shuttle "between these two worlds – the [UN] headquarters, as centre, and the field, as periphery" distinguishes the special procedures from myriad other UN human rights mechanisms.⁴⁹ For example, UN human rights treaty bodies do not generally conduct on-site country visits.⁵⁰

In addition to the missions, experts receive information on allegations of human rights violations and issue "communications" that request state governments to clarify the facts. Communications are a fundamental aspect of

---

46 For other considerations see the *Manual of Operations,* above n 13, at [57].
47 At [64]. Commentators have suggested that initially governments exercised significant say over the Special Rapporteur on indigenous peoples' itinerary and meetings, although now the Special Rapporteur on indigenous peoples typically has more influence. In 1998, special procedures adopted terms of reference for their country visits, providing for freedom of movement and inquiry amongst other things, which act as a guide to governments in the conduct of visits. See Manual of Operations, above n 13, at annex III.
48 Interview 9 with Former Bureaucrat at the UN Office of the High Commissioner for Human Rights, Geneva (The author, Telephone Interview, 6 September 2010).
49 Oliver Hoehne "Special Procedures and the New Human Rights Council – A Need for Strategic Positioning" (2007) 4(1) EHRR 48 at 56.
50 See Nigel Rodley "The United Nations Human Rights Council, its Special Procedures and its Relationship with Treaty Bodies: Complementarity or Competition?" (2003) 25 HRQ 882 at 61.

most experts' shaming repertoire, although the shaming techniques engaged are more indirect because they are, at least initially, private communications between the experts and the state (and in some cases, companies).[51] Communications take two forms: urgent appeals or letters of allegation. Urgent appeals "communicate information in cases where the alleged violations are time-sensitive in terms of involving loss of life, life-threatening situations or either imminent or ongoing damage of a very grave nature" that require urgent intervention.[52] Letters of allegation "communicate information about violations that are alleged to have already occurred" and are of a less urgent nature.[53] Since the creation of the Special Rapporteur on the Rights of Indigenous Peoples mandate, the Special Rapporteur has issued around 400 communications to states, most frequently directing its communications to Mexico, Colombia, Chile, India and Guatemala.[54] Communications can include reference to individual cases, general trends and patterns, violations affecting a particular group, the content of legislation incompatible with international human rights standards, and rights violations that have occurred or are ongoing or that have a high risk of occurring. They can be sent by one expert alone or, more commonly, jointly with others.[55] While

---

51 *Special Rapporteur Report to the General Assembly 2013*, above n 25, at [34].
52 *Manual of Operations*, above n 13, at [43].
53 At [46]. Communications comprise a large portion of many thematic experts' work and feature in some country experts' working methods too. Communications in the thousands have been sent to all regions of the world; during 2013, a total of 528 communications were sent to the governments of 117 countries. See Office for the High Commissioner for Human Rights, above n 42, at 10. Some are also sent to non-government actors, such as companies. See Office for the High Commissioner for Human Rights "Special Rapporteur on the Rights of Indigenous Peoples" <www.ohchr.org/EN/Issues/IPeoples/SRIndigenousPeoples/Pages/CommunicationsReports.aspx>.
54 Office for the High Commissioner for Human Rights "Special Rapporteur on the Rights of Indigenous Peoples" <www.ohchr.org/EN/Issues/IPeoples/SRIndigenousPeoples/Pages/Commun-icationsReports.aspx>.
55 See *Manual of Operations*, above n 13, at [28]-[48]; Office for the High Commissioner for Human Rights "Special Procedures of the Human Rights Council" <www.ohchr.org/EN/HRBodies/SP/Pages/Introduction.aspx>. Whether an expert intervenes on the basis of information received is at the discretion of the expert. Given the volume of cases experts receive most are not able to respond to every situation. See James Anaya *Report of the Special Rapporteur on the Situation of Human Rights and Fundamental Freedoms of Indigenous People, James Anaya* A/HRC/12/34 (15 July 2009) at [34] [*Special Rapporteur Report to the Human Rights Council 2009*]. Since 2007 the assessment of whether to act has been guided by the admissibility criteria set out in the special procedures' Code of Conduct. See *Code of Conduct*, above n 13, arts 9 and 10. The experts will usually look to "the reliability of the source and the credibility of information received; the details provided; and the scope of the mandate", although the specific requirements will depend on the expert. See Office for the High Commissioner for Human Rights "Special Procedures of the Human Rights Council: Communications" See also *Manual of Operations*, above n 13 at [38]-[42]; Office for the High Commissioner for Human Rights "Special Procedures of the Human Rights Council: Urgent Appeals and Letters of Allegation on Human Rights Violations" <http://www2.

many states have failed to ratify the protocols permitting UN human rights treaty bodies to review individual complaints, the special procedures can send communications to any state.⁵⁶

Anaya also took the innovative step of occasionally conducting country missions to investigate specific indigenous rights violations, known as "special" missions, in those cases that demanded targeted action.⁵⁷ This working method

---

ohchr.org/english/bodies/chr/special/docs/communicationsbrochure_en.pdf>. In contrast to other human rights mechanisms, information regarding an alleged rights violation can be provided to the expert by any person or organisation, and no relationship to the alleged victim or victims is necessary; the experts can send communications regardless of whether the alleged victim has exhausted all domestic remedies; and a detailed legal argument regarding the case is not required. The emphasis is on rapid action to protect victims and potential victims. See *Manual of Operations*, above n 13 at [38], [39], [42]; Office for the High Commissioner for Human Rights "Special Procedures of the Human Rights Council" <www.ohchr.org/EN/HRBodies/SP/Pages/Introduction.aspx>. For discussion, see Christophe Golay, Claire Mahon and Ioana Cismas, above n 45 at 307; Allison L Jernow "Ad Hoc and Extra-Conventional Means for Human Rights Monitoring" (1996) 28 JILP 785 at 802.

56 See Nigel Rodley, above n 50, at 63–65.
57 Most of the special country missions conducted by Anaya were to Central and South America, namely Panama, Peru, Costa Rica and Guatemala. See James Anaya *Report of the Special Rapporteur on the Situation of Human Rights and Fundamental Freedoms of Indigenous People, James Anaya: Observations on the Situation of the Charco la Pava Community and Other Communities Affected by the Chan 75 Hydroelectric Project in Panama* A/HRC/12/34/Add.5 (7 September 2009); James Anaya *Informe del Relator Especial sobre la Situación de los Derechos Humanos y las Libertades Fundamentales de los Indígenas, S James Anaya: Observaciones sobre la Situación de los Pueblos Indígenas de la Amazonía y los Sucesos del 5 de Junio y Días Posteriores en las Provincias de Bagua y Utcubamba, Perú* A/HRC/12/34/Add.8 (18 August 2009) [*Special Rapporteur Observations on Peru 2009*]; James Anaya *Informe del Relator Especial sobre los Derechos de los Pueblos Indígenas, James Anaya: La Situación de los Pueblos Indígenas Afectados por el Proyecto Hidroeléctrico El Diquís en Costa Rica*, A/HRC/18/35/Add.8 (11 July 2011); James Anaya *Report of the Special Rapporteur on the Situation of Human Rights and Fundamental Freedoms of Indigenous People, James Anaya: Observations on the Situation of the Rights of the Indigenous People of Guatemala with Relation to the Extraction Projects, and other Types of Projects, in their Traditional Territories* A/HRC/18/35/Add.3 (7 June 2011) [*Special Rapporteur Observations on Guatemala 2011*]; James Anaya *Report of the Special Rapporteur on the Situation of Human Rights and Fundamental Freedoms of Indigenous People, James Anaya: The situation of indigenous peoples' rights in Peru with regard to the extractive industries* A/HRC/27/52/Add.3 (7 May 2014). Anaya also produced a special report on the Australian Government's Northern Territory Emergency Response (NTER) programme following his standard country mission there. The NTER programme, a collection of legislation and initiatives ostensibly developed to address child sexual abuse, included the compulsory acquisition of five-year leases for exclusive possession to the lands of more than 64 Aboriginal communities and a regime of compulsory income management for those receiving social security benefits. See Northern Territory Emergency Response Act 2007 (Cth), s 31; Social Security and Other Legislation Amendment (Welfare Reform and Reinstatement of Racial Discrimination Act) Act 2010 (Cth). The special report enabled Anaya to dedicate focused attention to the complex programme, aspects of which he found to be "racially discriminatory and incompatible with Australia's international human rights obligations". See James Anaya *Report by the Special Rapporteur on the Situation of*

THE UN SPECIAL PROCEDURES AND INDIGENOUS PEOPLES' RIGHTS   163

allows impressive speed in responding to rights concerns. Anaya's special mission to Peru in 2009 occurred a week after he issued a press release regarding violent clashes between indigenous protestors and police, which in turn had been issued only days after the clashes had begun.[58] Other experts have undertaken similar missions on a smaller scale. For example, in 2007 Stavenhagen undertook a joint mission with the expert on housing to Mexico to examine indigenous rights issues regarding the construction of the Parota hydroelectric project, producing joint findings and recommendations on the issue that are reported in the expert on housing's communications report.[59] Yet, Anaya is alone in including the technique as part of his standard working methods and in publishing a separate special report on his missions.

In addition to drawing attention to their general and special country visits, the special procedures experts engage the media to publicise especially flagrant or urgent rights violations that they become aware of, bypassing the communications and country mission processes at least initially.[60] This step is generally only taken in the most serious of cases; the special procedures' Manual of Operations encourages it to be used as a means of last resort.[61] The Special Rapporteur on the Rights of Indigenous Peoples has issued public statements on concerns, including the Chilean Government's response to protests by indigenous peoples in Rapa Nui,[62] a hunger strike by Chief Theresa Spence of the Attawapiskat First Nation in Canada,[63] and a proposal to repeal core laws and policies concerning the Sami in Norway.[64]

Human Rights and Fundamental Freedoms of Indigenous People, James Anaya: Situation of Indigenous Peoples in Australia A/HRC/15/37/Add.4 (1 June 2010) at appendix B [37].

58 *Special Rapporteur Observations on Peru 2009*, above n 57, at [2], [42]-[47].
59 Miloon Kothari *Report of the Special Rapporteur on Adequate Housing as a Component of the Right to an Adequate Standard of Living, and on the Right to Non-Discrimination in this Context, Miloon Kothari: Summary of Communications Sent and Replies Received from Governments and Other Actors* A/HRC/7/16/Add.1 (4 March 2008) at [72]-[100].
60 See *Special Rapporteur Report to the Human Rights Council 2009*, above n 55, at [35]; James Anaya *Report of the Special Rapporteur on the Rights of Indigenous Peoples, James Anaya: Extractive Industries Operating Within or Near Indigenous Territories* A/HRC/18/35 (11 July 2011) at [19] [*Extractive Industries Report by the Special Rapporteur 2011*]; James Anaya *Report of the Special Rapporteur on the Rights of Indigenous Peoples, James Anaya* A/HRC/21/47 (6 July 2012) at [18] [*Special Rapporteur Report to the Human Rights Council 2012*]; *Special Rapporteur Report to the General Assembly 2013*, above n 25, at [31]. See generally Christophe Golay, Claire Mahon and Ioana Cismas, above n 45 at 308.
61 *Manual of Operations*, above n 13 at [49]-[51].
62 *Extractive Industries Report by the Special Rapporteur 2011*, above n 60, at [19].
63 James Anaya *Report of the Special Rapporteur on the Rights of Indigenous Peoples, James Anaya: Extractive Industries and Indigenous Peoples* A/HRC/24/41 (1 July 2013) at [20] [*Extractive Industries Report by the Special Rapporteur 2013*]; Office for the High Commissioner for Human Rights "Canada: UN Expert Calls for Meaningful Dialogue with Aboriginal Leaders After Weeks of Protests" (Media Release, 8 January 2013).
64 James Anaya "Norway Could Lose Lead in the Recognition and Protection of Indigenous

Dialogue-building can be engaged through each of these tools as well. The experts' statements and reports can act as a witness to rights violations and some experts offer praise for positive developments to encourage states. But dialogue-building is most evident in the experts' efforts to improve knowledge regarding the substance of international indigenous rights. The experts do this above all through their thematic studies on issues or themes relevant to their mandates. The experts' thematic studies are included in their annual and special reports to the HRC and UN General Assembly. They are focused on awareness-raising,[65] with several experts developing analytical frameworks or guidelines regarding particular rights issues in their reports.[66] The studies are produced by thematic special procedures experts, and occasionally by country experts. A wide variety of actors are generally invited to contribute to the studies, including indigenous peoples, governments and NGOs.[67] Indigenous peoples sometimes request topics for study by the experts. For example, in 2011 the Pacific Indigenous Caucus requested that the Special Rapporteur on the Rights of Indigenous Peoples "study climate change and [indigenous peoples'] rights in the Pacific region."[68] Many of the experts conduct questionnaires or surveys to collect the views of relevant actors, including Anaya's questionnaire on the impact of extractive industries operating within or near indigenous territories, and Stavenhagen's questionnaire on domestic legislation, policies and programmes regarding indigenous peoples' rights.[69] Expert seminars, conferences and meetings also feed into many of the thematic studies.[70] Unlike the country reports, and occasionally the

Peoples' Rights – UN Expert" (Public Statement, 28 October 2011) <http://unsr.jamesanaya.org/notes/norway-could-lose-its-lead-in-the-recognition-and-protection-of-indigenous-peoples-rights>.

65 *Manual of Operations,* above n 13 at [106]. See generally Gerd Oberleitner, *Global Human Rights Institutions: Between Remedy and Ritual* (Polity, Cambridge; Oxford; Boston, 2007) at 59–60.

66 See CHR *Preliminary Report of the Special Rapporteur on the Right to Education, Ms Katarina Tomasevski, Submitted in Accordance with Commission on Human Rights Resolution 1998/33*, UN Doc E/CN.4/1999/49 (13 January 1999) at [51]-[74]. See generally Christophe Golay, Claire Mahon and Ioana Cismas, above n 45, at 300-301.

67 See *Extractive Industries Report by the Special Rapporteur 2013*, above n 63, at annex [21]; *Special Rapporteur Report to the Human Rights Council 2012*, above n 60, at [35].

68 Indigenous Peoples' Center for Documentation, Research and Information, *Update No 94-95 – January/April* (April 18 2011) <http://cendoc.docip.org/collect/upd_en/index/assoc/HASH01c4.dir/Upd94-95_eng.pdf> at 14.

69 *Extractive Industries Report by the Special Rapporteur 2011*, above n 60, at [27]; Rodolfo Stavenhagen *Report of the Special Rapporteur on the Situation of Human Rights and Fundamental Freedoms of Indigenous People, Rodolfo Stavenhagen, Submitted in accordance with Commission Resolution 2001/65* E/CN.4/2004/80 (26 January 2004) at [7].

70 See *Special Rapporteur Report to the General Assembly 2013*, above n 25, at [42]; Rodolfo Stavenhagen *Report of the Special Rapporteur on the Situation of Human Rights and Fundamental Freedoms of Indigenous People, Mr Rodolfo Stavenhagen: Conclusions and Recommendations of the Expert Seminar on Indigenous Peoples and the Administration of*

communications, the thematic studies do not contain recommendations directed at specific states. Typically, they contain conclusions and recommendations directed at states and the international system more generally.

The Special Rapporteur on the Rights of Indigenous Peoples is a key source of thematic studies on indigenous peoples' rights, conducting studies on issues across the world.[71] Since the creation of the Expert Mechanism on the Rights of Indigenous Peoples (EMRIP), which has the singular role of providing thematic expert advice to the HRC on indigenous rights concerns, the Special Rapporteur has made the production of thematic studies a secondary aspect of the mandate's work.[72] Nevertheless, the Special Rapporteur has produced a host of thematic studies. Generally, a different theme has been studied each year, although particular attention has been given to the content of the international instruments relevant to indigenous peoples' rights,[73] development projects and agendas,[74] and the rights of indigenous peoples in Asia.[75] The Declaration is a key feature of these studies. One of the main issues focused on in these studies has been the impact of extractive industries on indigenous peoples. This is regarded by Anaya as "one of the foremost concerns of indigenous peoples worldwide, and possibly also the most pervasive source of the challenges to the full exercise of their rights."[76] Anaya expressed an intention to elaborate a set of guidelines or principles to guide protection of indigenous rights in this context, building on John Ruggie's – the former expert on transnational corporations – "Guiding

---

Justice E/CN.4/2004/80/Add.4 (27 January 2004) at 2.

71 See generally Jennifer Preston and others *The UN Special Rapporteur: Indigenous Peoples Rights: Experiences and Challenges* (International Work Group for Indigenous Affairs, Copenhagen, 2007) at 18–20.

72 *Special Rapporteur Report to the Human Rights Council 2009,* above n 55, at [13].

73 See Rodolfo Stavenhagen, above n 32; James Anaya, above n 28; *Special Rapporteur Report to the General Assembly 2014,* above n 33.

74 Rodolfo Stavenhagen *Report of the Special Rapporteur on the Situation of Human Rights and Fundamental Freedoms of Indigenous People, Rodolfo Stavenhagen, Submitted in accordance with Commission Resolution 2001/65* E/CN.4/2003/90 (21 January 2003); *Special Rapporteur Report to the Human Rights Council 2009,* above n 55; James Anaya *Report of the Special Rapporteur on the Situation of Human Rights and Fundamental Freedoms of Indigenous People, James Anaya* A/HRC/15/37 (19 July 2010) [*Special Rapporteur Report to the Human Rights Council 2010*]; *Report to the General Assembly 2010,* above n 28; James Anaya *Report of the Special Rapporteur on the Rights of Indigenous Peoples to the General Assembly* A/66/288 (10 August 2011); *Special Rapporteur Report to the Human Rights Council 2012,* above n 60; *Extractive Industries Report by the Special Rapporteur 2013,* above n 63; *Transmission of the Report of the Special Rapporteur of the Human Rights Council on the Rights of Indigenous Peoples,* above n 34; *Special Rapporteur Report to the General Assembly 2015,* above n 34.

75 Rodolfo Stavenhagen *Report of the Special Rapporteur on the Situation of Human Rights and Fundamental Freedoms of Indigenous People, Rodolfo Stavenhagen: General Considerations on the Situation of Human Rights and Fundamental Freedoms of Indigenous Peoples in Asia* A/HRC/6/15/Add.3 (1 November 2007).

76 *Extractive Industries Report by the Special Rapporteur 2011,* above n 60, at [57].

Principles on Business and Human Rights."[77] Accordingly, his final thematic study in 2013 included a set of "[c]onditions for getting to and sustaining indigenous peoples' agreement to extractive activities promoted by the State or third party business enterprises."[78]

In addition to shaming and dialogue-building, capacity-building is employed through the special procedures' technical advisory assistance, which forms part of the experts' mandate to promote best practice. Capacity-building differs from the technique of shaming in that it is proactive rather than simply reactive, developing capacity to avoid further rights violations rather than only responding to existing violations. In fact, positive encouragement is an important component of capacity-building. It differs from dialogue-building, in particular the technique of improving knowledge, because although it builds knowledge and dialogue, actual assistance is provided to a state or other actor to realise particular rights. Not all special procedures experts provide technical advisory assistance. However, the Special Rapporteur on the Rights of Indigenous Peoples' mandate expressly encourages the expert to provide technical advisory assistance to states.[79] The Special Rapporteur fulfils this aspect of the mandate through "encouraging domestic legal, administrative, and programmatic reforms that comply with the standards of the [Declaration] and other relevant human rights instruments."[80] Anaya seized on this working method. Suggestions regarding processes and laws for appropriately consulting with indigenous peoples dominated his technical advisory work, including in respect of Chile in 2009 and 2012,[81] Colombia in 2010,[82] Guatemala in 2011,[83] Peru in 2011 and 2012,[84] and Brazil in 2012.[85] The provision of technical advice often, although

---

77 At [62], [74]-[76], [89]; *Special Rapporteur Report to the Human Rights Council 2012*, above n 60, at [74]-[75], [86]-[89].
78 *Extractive Industries Report by the Special Rapporteur 2013*, above n 63, at [41]-[78].
79 *Human rights and indigenous peoples: mandate of the Special Rapporteur on the Rights of Indigenous Peoples*, above n 3, at [1](f).
80 The University of Arizona Indigenous Peoples Law and Policy Program "The Role of the UN Special Rapporteur on the Rights of Indigenous Peoples within the United Nations Human Rights System: A Handbook for Indigenous Leaders in the United States" (2012) <http://unsr.jamesanaya.org/docs/data/UNSR-Handbook-USA.pdf> at 19.
81 James Anaya *Relator Especial de Naciones Unidas sobre la Situación de los Derechos Humanos y las Libertades Fundamentales de los Indígenas: Principios Internacionales Aplicables a la Consulta en Relación con la Reforma Constitucional en Materia de Derechos de los Pueblos Indígenas en Chile* A/HRC/12/34/Add.6 (24 April 2009) [*Special Rapporteur Report on Chile 2009*]; *Extractive Industries Report by the Special Rapporteur 2013*, above n 63, at annex [9].
82 *Special Rapporteur Report to the Human Rights Council 2010*, above n 74, at [16].
83 *Special Rapporteur Observations on Guatemala 2011*, above n 57, at [8]-[10].
84 *Special Rapporteur Report to the Human Rights Council 2012*, above n 60, at [10]; *Special Rapporteur Report to the General Assembly 2013*, above n 25, at [11].
85 *Special Rapporteur Report to the Human Rights Council 2012*, above n 60, at [10]; *Special Rapporteur Report to the General Assembly 2013*, above n 25, at [11].

not always, involves a short visit to the state concerned. It can be ongoing. For example, Anaya provided advice to the Ecuadorian Government on several occasions between 2008 and 2011, suggesting content for new constitutional provisions affirming indigenous peoples' collective rights, as well as providing comments on new legislation aimed at bettering indigenous peoples' access to justice and coordinating indigenous justice systems with the national justice system.[86] Given the cooperative nature of this work, it is dependent on states first requesting assistance, which (as the examples above show) several have.[87] The Special Rapporteur also builds the capacity of other actors to realise indigenous peoples' rights, notably indigenous peoples themselves and international bodies, including the OHCHR, the UN Educational, Scientific and Cultural Organization, the UN Development Programme, the Food and Agriculture Organization of the UN, the International Finance Corporation of the World Bank Group and the World Intellectual Property Organization.[88]

D. Strategies for Using the Special Procedures to Implement the Declaration in Aotearoa New Zealand

A range of strategies are open to actors seeking to use these tools of the special procedures to advance implementation of the Declaration in Aotearoa New Zealand. Three strategies are highlighted in this Part, drawing on my empirical research regarding the special procedures' domestic influence in Aotearoa New Zealand. Aotearoa New Zealand has already had two country missions from the Special Rapporteur in 2005 and 2010, as well as a mission from the Working Group on Arbitrary Detention in 2014.[89] All three reports on these missions

---

86 James Anaya *Report of the Special Rapporteur on the Situation of Human Rights and Fundamental Freedoms of Indigenous People, S James Anaya: Summary of Cases Transmitted to Governments and Replies Received* A/HRC/9/9/Add.1 (15 August 2008) at annex 1 [*Special Rapporteur Communications Report 2008*]; James Anaya *Report by the Special Rapporteur on the Situation of Human Rights and Fundamental Freedoms of Indigenous People, James Anaya: Observations on the Progress Made and Challenges Faced in the Implementation of the Constitutional Guarantees of the Rights of Indigenous Peoples in Ecuador* A/HRC/15/37/Add.7 (13 September 2010) at [11]-[12]; *Extractive Industries Report by the Special Rapporteur 2011*, above n 60, at [13].

87 See *Special Rapporteur Report on Chile 2009*, above n 81; *Extractive Industries Report by the Special Rapporteur 2013*, above n 63, at annex [9]; *Special Rapporteur Report to the Human Rights Council 2010*, above n 74, at [16].

88 See *Extractive Industries Report by the Special Rapporteur 2013*, above n 63, at annex [11]; *Special Rapporteur Report to the Human Rights Council 2012*, above n 60, at [11], [14]; *Extractive Industries Report by the Special Rapporteur 2011*, above n 60, at [6], [14]; *Special Rapporteur Report to the Human Rights Council 2009*, above n 55, at [15].

89 Rodolfo Stavenhagen *Report of the Special Rapporteur on the Situation of Human Rights and Fundamental Freedoms of Indigenous People, Rodolfo Stavenhagen: Mission to New Zealand* E/CN.4/2006/78/Add.3 (13 March 2006) [*Stavenhagen Report on New Zealand*]; James Anaya *Report of the Special Rapporteur on the Situation of Human Rights and Fundamental*

were critical of the human rights situation of Māori. Stavenhagen and Anaya raised concerns regarding, amongst other things, the domestic insecurity of Māori rights; barriers to Māori political participation; insufficient consultation with Māori on decisions affecting them; infringements on land rights, in particular in relation to the foreshore and seabed; the lack of accord given to Waitangi Tribunal recommendations; flaws in the Treaty settlement process; and the overrepresentation of Māori in negative socio-economic indicators.[90] Criminal justice was the focus of the Working Group on Arbitrary Detention's mission, which drew attention to the overrepresentation of Māori in the criminal justice system and "found indications of bias at all levels of the criminal justice process."[91] Its recommendations included that the government "intensify its efforts to tackle the root causes" of this bias.[92]

The government's response to these reports swung from harsh criticism to little comment. Its public response to Stavenhagen's report was vitriolic, denouncing the report as "selective", "disappointing", "narrow" and full of errors.[93] The government made no public comment following the release of Anaya's advance report and made only a dry formal statement on the final report before the HRC, expressing appreciation for the report, acknowledging some of the report's concerns and stating that it was "already acting on many of his recommendations and will continue to draw on the report over time".[94] Regarding the Working Group on Arbitrary Detention's criticisms on the position of Māori, while the government saw no evidence of institutional racism,[95] when the final report was presented to the HRC it stated that the overrepresentation of Māori in the criminal justice system was an issue of concern that it was working to address.[96]

Freedoms of Indigenous People, James Anaya: The Situation of Maori People in New Zealand A/HRC/18/35/Add.4 (31 May 2011) [*Anaya Follow-up Report on New Zealand*]; Working Group on Arbitrary Detention *Report of the Working Group on Arbitrary Detention, Addendum, Mission to New Zealand* A/HRC/30/36/Add.2 (6 July 2015).

90 *Stavenhagen Report on New Zealand,* above n 89, at [76]-[82]; *Anaya Follow-up Report on New Zealand,* above n 89, at [66]-[85].

91 *Report of the Working Group on Arbitrary Detention, Addendum, Mission to New Zealand,* above n 89, at [93].

92 At [105](e). See also [105](j), (n), and (o).

93 Michael Cullen, Deputy Prime Minister "Response to UN Special Rapporteur Report" (press release, 4 April 2006).

94 Dell Higgie, New Zealand Government Representative "Webcast 18th Session of the Human Rights Council. Statement of Special Rapporteur and Interactive Dialogue" (Webcast of the 18th Session of the HRC, 21 September 2011) < http://unsr.jamesanaya.org/videos/webcast-18th-session-of-the-human-rights-council-statement-of-special-rapporteur-and-interactive-dialogue>.

95 "Maori offenders not targetted [sic] – minister" *Radio New Zealand* (online ed, New Zealand, 8 April 2014).

96 Office for the High Commissioner for Human Rights "Human Rights Council holds interactive

The New Zealand government has also been the subject of several communications from special procedures experts, two of which were issued by the Special Rapporteur on the Rights of Indigenous Peoples. In 2007, Stavenhagen, jointly with the experts on terrorism and human rights defenders, issued a communication to the Government concerning the arrest of Māori activists suspected of terrorism-related offences, as part of the police operation carried out in various parts of the country called Operation 8.[97] In 2012, Anaya acting alone sent an allegation letter to the New Zealand government concerning the alleged exclusion of a family collective, the Mangakāhia Whānau, from the Treaty settlement process as a product of the Government's policy of negotiating Treaty settlements with large Māori groupings.[98] The New Zealand Government responded promptly and substantively to each of the communications, although it largely dismissed the concerns.[99]

Elsewhere, I have found that the special procedures' recommendations have influenced the New Zealand government's behaviour towards Māori imperfectly but perceptibly. However, the impact has been largely superficial. Even where the government has taken outward steps in agreement or alignment with the special procedures' recommendations, it has developed techniques to avoid giving effect to the rights behind them.[100] Analysis of the experts' influence inspired the strategies identified below. I focus here on techniques that may be adopted by indigenous rights advocates and the special procedures experts, while conscious that many of the impediments to the special procedures' impact are a product of states' lack of political will and institutional constraints.[101]

First, if the special procedures are to foster implementation of the rights in the Declaration, the special procedures experts need to be bold in advocating the core rights affirmed in that instrument. In many respects this already occurs. For example, both the Special Rapporteurs' reports on Aotearoa New Zealand expertly raised concerns and offered recommendations regarding important Māori land and resource rights, participation in decision-making, rights to

dialogue on arbitrary detention and contemporary forms of slavery" (14 September 2015)
97   *Special Rapporteur Communications Report 2008*, above n 86, at [339]-[357].
98   James Anaya *Report of the Special Rapporteur on the Rights of Indigenous Peoples, James Anaya: Communications Sent, Replies Received and Observations 2013* A/HRC/24/41/Add.4 (2 September 2013) at [121]-[124]; *Communications Report of Special Procedures* A/HRC/22/67 (20 February 2013) at 78.
99   *Special Rapporteur Communications Report 2008*, above n 86, at [349]-[356]; Letter from Brian Wilson to James Anaya (18 October 2012) and Letter from Brian Wilson to James Anaya (6 November 2012) accessible through *Communications Report of Special Procedures*, above n 98, at 78.
100 "The UN Special Rapporteur on the Rights of Indigenous Peoples and New Zealand: A Study in Compliance Ritualism", above n 5.
101 "The United Nations Special Procedures and Indigenous Peoples: A Regulatory Analysis", above n 5.

culture and social welfare and development.[102] All these categories of rights are affirmed in the Declaration. However, one right for which there remains greater scope for bold advocacy is the right to self-determination. The right to self-determination is the cornerstone of indigenous peoples' claims and of the Declaration.[103] Self-determination claims (and its te reo Māori equivalents of tino rangatiratanga and mana motuhake) were raised with Stavenhagen and Anaya in Aotearoa New Zealand.[104] Yet, the two Special Rapporteurs adopted different approaches to this right. Stavenhagen's 2006 report on Aotearoa New Zealand pushed the right to self-determination in its comments on iwi and hapū governance structures, self-governing social programmes, constitutional reform and implementation of the Declaration.[105] Anaya was more restrained in his references to the right in Aotearoa New Zealand. In his press statement and preliminary note he commented that "[t]he principles of the Treaty provide a foundation for Māori self-determination based on a real partnership between Māori and the New Zealand State".[106] He also referred to the right in articulating the purpose of the Declaration.[107] However, the language of self-determination disappeared in his final report on the mission, beyond a scene-setting remark regarding the meaning of tino rangatiratanga.[108] Avoiding use of the language of self-determination in the country report may be a deliberate tactic to avoid provoking the ire of the government and keep it at the meeting table. Recognition of the right to self-determination may be viewed as too ambitious or unrealistic;[109] after all the New Zealand Government did publicly voice concerns regarding the

---

102 *Stavenhagen Report on New Zealand*, above n 89, at [83]-[103]; *Anaya Follow-up Report on New Zealand*, above n 89, at [68]-[85].

103 Declaration art 3. See Michael Dodson quoted in Craig Scott "Indigenous Self-Determination and Decolonization of the International Imagination: A Plea" (1996) 18 Hum Rts Q 814 at 814; James Anaya *Indigenous Peoples in International Law* (2nd ed, Oxford University Press, New York, 2004) 7 at 97.

104 See Letter from Peace Movement Aotearoa to Rodolfo Stavenhagen (Special Rapporteur on the Rights of Indigenous Peoples) regarding the Rights and Fundamental Freedoms of Māori (23 November 2005) <www.converge.org.nz/pma/sr-pma05.pdf> at 2, 10-11; Ruth Berry "Maori Denied Rights, UN Man Told" *The New Zealand Herald* (online ed, Auckland, 21 November 2005); "Tuhoe Assured UN Visitor on Apartheid – Kruger" *The New Zealand Herald* (online ed, Auckland, 30 July 2010).

105 *Stavenhagen Report on New Zealand*, above n 89, at [18], [42], [80], [84], [94], [102].

106 James Anaya "New Zealand: More to be done to Improve Indigenous People's Rights, Says UN Expert" (Press Statement, 23 July 2010); James Anaya *Report of the Special Rapporteur on the Situation of Human Rights and Fundamental Freedoms of Indigenous People, James Anaya, Addendum, Preliminary Note on the Mission to New Zealand (18 to 24 July 2010)* A/HRC/15/37/Add.9 (26 August 2010) at [3] [*Preliminary Note on New Zealand 2010*].

107 "New Zealand: More to be Done to Improve Indigenous People's Rights, Says UN Expert", above n 106; *Preliminary Note on New Zealand 2010*, above n 106, at [4].

108 *Anaya Follow-up Report on New Zealand*, above n 89, at [8].

109 The special procedures' Manual of Operations calls for the experts' recommendations to be "attainable" and "realistic", see *Manual of Operations*, above n 13 at [98].

inclusion of a right to self-determination in the Declaration.¹¹⁰ Or it could be that strong autonomy claims are seen as capable of expression using alternative concepts, such as the right to culture.¹¹¹ But the reports could have more impact if the right to self-determination is positioned at the forefront of discussions and is reflected in its stronger, more autonomous, dimensions. In part this is because more Māori may use the reports.

Secondly, if the special procedures experts' reports and thematic studies are to play a role in fostering implementation of the Declaration it is vital that Māori and indigenous rights advocates use the reports supporting the rights articulated in the Declaration in their negotiations and lobbying. Māori and indigenous rights advocates in Aotearoa New Zealand have engaged with the special procedures mechanism: providing information to special procedures experts requesting them to take action, such as through the communications procedure or calling on them to undertake country missions,¹¹² meeting with special procedures experts during their country missions,¹¹³ and praising their reports.¹¹⁴ What is needed is leverage of the experts' findings and recommendations by a larger base of actors.

In Aotearoa New Zealand there has been minimal use of the Special Rapporteurs' reports by Māori and even less use of them by other actors. Some prominent Māori who are highly conversant with the UN human rights system and aware of the experts' reports elected not to read them or, having read them, did not choose to use them.¹¹⁵ The Special Rapporteurs' reports have been used most on the international stage, such as by an indigenous organisation and

---

110 See Karen Engle "On Fragile Architecture: The UN Declaration on the Rights of Indigenous Peoples in the Context of Human Rights" (2011) 22(1) EJIL 141 at 146 n 14.
111 Karen Engle *The Elusive Promise of Indigenous Development: Rights, Culture, Strategy* (Duke University Press, Durham (NC), 2010) at 3.
112 Interview 1 with Member of the NZHRC (The author, Wellington, 5 May 2011); Interview 3 with Member of the NZHRC (The author, Wellington, 3 May 2011); Interview 4 with Māori Academic (The author, Wellington, 4 May 2011); Interview 6 with Māori Rights Advocate (The author, city confidential, 3 June 2011).
113 See *Stavenhagen Report on New Zealand,* above n 89, at [3]-[5].
114 See Moana Jackson "The United Nations on the Foreshore: A Summary of the Report of the Special Rapporteur" (5 April 2006) Converge <www.converge.org.nz/pma/mj050406.htm>; Interview 5 with Māori Rights Advocate (The author, Christchurch, 6 May 2011); Interview 6 with Māori Rights Advocate, above n 112; Adam Gifford "UN Report Shouldn't be Lost in Upheaval" (24 February 2011) Waatea News Update <http://waatea.blogspot.com.au/2011/02/te-puni-kokiri-seeks-quake-role.html>; Tracey Whare, trustee of Aotearoa Indigenous Rights Trust (under the banner of Incomindios) "Webcast 18th Session of the Human Rights Council. Statement of Special Rapporteur and Interactive Dialogue" (Webcast of the 18th Session of the HRC, 21 September 2011) <http://unsr.jamesanaya.org/videos/webcast-18th-session-of-the-human-rights-council-statement-of-special-rapporteur-and-interactive-dialogue>.
115 Interview 2 with Member of New Zealand Parliament (The author, Wellington, 5 May 2011); Interview 4 with Māori Academic, above n 112; Interview 5 with Māori Rights Advocate, above n 114.

other domestic human rights NGOs to inform their shadow reports to human rights treaty bodies and in interventions before the EMRIP.[116] However, as one Māori human rights lawyer identified, it is domestic leverage of the reports that is central, and more local actors, particularly Māori lawyers, need to use the reports.[117] While in opposition government, the Māori Party referenced Stavenhagen's report in Parliament and in media releases on several occasions.[118] But this practice subsided when the Party entered into a formal coalition government with the National Party in late 2008.[119] The NZHRC has referenced the Special Rapporteur's recommendations in its domestic race relations reports,[120] as well as using them "to drive the issue" of Māori representation in local government domestically.[121] But a public appraisal of the Government's implementation of Anaya's recommendations has not materialised from the NZHRC or elsewhere. And a member of the NZHRC reflected that it had found the experts' reports "difficult to mobilise ... through New Zealand."[122] Neither Anaya nor Stavenhagen's report on Aotearoa New Zealand is cited in domestic case law. Only a handful of academics refer to the mandate.[123] The absence of high-

---

116 See Jennifer Preston and others, above n 71 at 36, 40; Peace Movement Aotearoa "NGO Information for the 48th session of the Committee on Economic, Social and Cultural Rights" (April 2012) Converge <www.converge.org.nz/pma/CESCR48-PMA.pdf> at [43], [49]; Aotearoa Indigenous Rights Trust and others "Joint submission to the Universal Periodic Review of New Zealand: Indigenous People's Rights and the Treaty of Waitangi" (10 November 2008) Converge <www.converge.org.nz/pma/towupr09.pdf> at [12], [13], 3 n 6, [35], 8 n 17, [47]-[49]; Peace Movement Aotearoa "NGO Report to the Committee on the Elimination of Racial Discrimination" (21 May 2007) <http://www.converge.org.nz/pma/CERD71-PMA.pdf> at [18]-[20], [38]; Interview 6 with Māori Rights Advocate, above n 114.
117 Interview 6 with Māori Rights Advocate, above n 114.
118 See (5 April 2006) 630 NZPD 2519; Māori Party "Too Slow Too Furious" (Press Release, 1 June 2006); Māori Party "Maori Party Welcomes New UN Special Rapporteur" (Press Release, 1 April 2008).
119 Interview 2 with Member of New Zealand Parliament, above n 115.
120 See NZHRC *Tūi Tūi Tuituiā: Race Relations in 2012* (May 2013) at 100; NZHRC *Tūi Tūi Tuituiā: Race Relations in 2011* (March 2012) at 34–37; NZHRC *Tūi Tūi Tuituiā: Race Relations in 2006* (March 2007) at 15.
121 Interview 1 with Member of the NZHRC, above n 112.
122 Interview 3 with Member of the NZHRC, above n 112.
123 See Jacinta Ruru "Finding Support for a Changed Property Discourse for Aotearoa New Zealand in the United Nations Declaration on the Rights of Indigenous Peoples" (2011) 15 LCLR 951 at 973–974; Roderic Pitty "The Unfinished Business of Indigenous Citizenship in Australia and New Zealand" in Klaus Neumann and Gwenda Tavan (eds) *Does History Matter? Making and Debating Citizenship, Immigration and Refugee Policy in Australia and New Zealand* (ANU E Press, Canberra, 2009) 25 at 38–39; Fleur Adcock "Indigenous Peoples Rights Under International Law: The Year in Review" (2011) 9 NZYIL 296 at 296–299; Fleur Adcock and Claire Charters "Indigenous Peoples' Rights Under International Law: The Year in Review" (2010) 8 NZYIL 203 at 206–207. Non-academic texts have also referred to the experts' reports, see also Robert Kirkness "A Proud Democratic Tradition?" NZLawyer (17 August 2007) <www.nzlawyermagazine.co.nz/Archives/Issue71/F4/tabid/422/Default.aspx>; Fleur Adcock "Aotearoa (New Zealand)" in Cæcilie Mikkelsen (ed) *The Indigenous*

profile Māori rights advocates pushing for action on the reports, bar some public statements by leading Māori lawyer Moana Jackson regarding Stavenhagen's report, is striking.[124]

Thirdly, the special procedures experts, Māori and indigenous rights advocates could use the New Zealand Government's self-perception as a world leader in human rights and indigenous rights to gain traction for the Declaration rights promoted in the experts' reports.[125] Part of the reason why the government so vividly rejects international interference in its domestic affairs regarding Māori is because it promotes the idea that it is a human rights and indigenous rights leader. As a result it struggles with information – such as that set out in the experts' reports – that conflicts with or may tarnish that self-image. This was evident in the government's response to both Special Rapporteurs' visits. For example, when discussing Anaya's visit, the Prime Minister stated, "New Zealand actually has a very well defined and established set of rules when it comes to dealing with indigenous rights and I think we're a leader in that field."[126] In the government's formal response to Stavenhagen's report, it projected the state as an archetype of harmonious ethnic relationships, asserting that "Māori, like all New Zealanders, live in a contemporary democracy that is, by any standards, participatory and inclusive . . . discrimination is an anathema to New Zealanders."[127] The view that Aotearoa New Zealand is a world leader in human rights and indigenous rights is widely embraced, domestically and internationally.[128] Compared to other states, Aotearoa New Zealand's positive human rights record may be generally well-deserved. But it contains many blind spots in its recognition of indigenous peoples' (and others') claims. The government's interest in maintaining that self-image could be harnessed as a tool for persuading it to become "an innovator to lead

---

    World 2012 (IWGIA, Copenhagen, 2012) 224 at 229–230.
124 See Moana Jackson, above n 114. Māori academic Rawiri Taonui urged that attention be given to Anaya's report. Rawiri Taonui is cited in "UN Report Shouldn't be Lost in Upheaval", above n 114.
125 "The UN Special Rapporteur on the Rights of Indigenous Peoples and New Zealand: A Study in Compliance Ritualism", above n 5.
126 Adam Bennett "UN Visitor Checks NZ Race Relations" *The New Zealand Herald* (online ed, Auckland, 20 July 2010).
127 Don Mackay, New Zealand Permanent Representative "Human Rights Council: Presentation of Report by Special Rapporteur on the Situation of the Human Rights and Fundamental Freedoms of Indigenous Peoples" (Statement to the Human Rights Council, Geneva, 19 September 2006).
128 See Waitangi Tribunal *Ko Aotearoa Tēnei: A Report into Claims Concerning New Zealand Law and Policy Affecting Māori Culture and Identity – Te Taumata Tuarua Volume 1* (Wai 262, 2011) at 98; Carlos Vázquez, the Country Rapporteur for New Zealand, closing remarks in UN Committee on Elimination of Racial Discrimination "Committee on Elimination of Racial Discrimination Considers Report of New Zealand" (Media Release, 22 February 2013) at Concluding Remarks.

the pack" in the continuous improvement of its indigenous rights recognition.[129] This could harbour benefits, both for the New Zealand government's indigenous rights conformity and potentially that of other states, who are compelled to "catch up with the leader".[130]

E. Conclusion

The special procedures are uniquely positioned to advance the rights affirmed in the Declaration. They enjoy a broad mandate to promote the realisation of international indigenous rights. This is buttressed by the CHR's 1993 resolution recognising the relevance of indigenous rights concerns to the mandates of all thematic special procedures and the creation of the mandate of the Special Rapporteur on the Rights of Indigenous Peoples in 2001, which has the Declaration as its guiding normative instrument. The special procedures draw on an assorted set of dialogue-based tools to carry out their mandate, primarily shaming, but dialogue-building and capacity-building are also used. Actors can engage various strategies to mobilise the special procedures to advance implementation of the Declaration in Aotearoa New Zealand. The special procedures experts can advocate the core rights in the Declaration, such as the right to self-determination. Māori and indigenous rights advocates can use the reports' support for the rights in the Declaration in their negotiations and lobbying. The special procedures experts, Māori and Māori-rights advocates can also endeavour to use the strength of the New Zealand government's self-perception as a world leader in human rights and indigenous rights against itself. The suggestion is not that the special procedures are *the* answer to calls for significant, substantive, improvement in Māori enjoyment of their rights under the Declaration. Far from it. The special procedures experts are hampered institutionally, financially and – as a body that derives from and operates within an international legal framework that continues to both reflect and constitute colonial power interests – ideologically.[131] Rather, I have argued that the special procedures are one of a collection of tools at the disposal of Māori and Māori-rights advocates to help realise the rights so hopefully affirmed in the Declaration. The responsibility is now with us to do so.

---

129 John Braithwaite and Peter Drahos *Global Business Regulation* (Cambridge University Press, Cambridge, 2000) at 615.
130 At 615.
131 "The United Nations Special Procedures and Indigenous Peoples: A Regulatory Analysis", above n 5, at 228–277.

9
The World Conference on Indigenous Peoples 2014

*Tracey Whare**

A. Introduction

The adoption of the UN Declaration on the Rights of Indigenous Peoples (the Declaration) in 2007 provided a new normative framework for indigenous peoples' rights.[1] The Declaration was heralded as a major step towards the promotion and protection of indigenous peoples' rights as well as an opportunity to reframe the often fraught relationship between states and indigenous peoples. However, following its adoption many governments carried on with business as usual with little or no change to their national policy and legislative frameworks. In response, indigenous advocates – including Māori – continued to attend UN fora to lambaste their respective governments for the lack of concerted effort to affect change at the national level.[2] Not only was criticism raised by indigenous advocates themselves, but concern was also raised by the then UN Special Rapporteur on the Rights of Indigenous Peoples, James Anaya.[3] A lack of political will at the national level to implement the Declaration and states' references to the non-binding nature of the Declaration led to little substantive change.

---

* LLM candidate, Raukawa and Te Whānau a Apanui. From March 2012 to December 2014, I served as the Secretariat of the Indigenous Global Coordinating Group, the body established to coordinate indigenous participation in the World Conference on Indigenous Peoples.
1 *United Nations Declaration on the Rights of Indigenous Peoples* GA Res 61/95, A/Res/61/95 (2007).
2 See, for example, collective statement of First Nations of Canada and non-governmental organisations delivered by Cheryl Maloney during the 7th session of the Permanent Forum on Indigenous Issues 2008; statement of the Pacific caucus delivered by Catherine Davis during the 8th session of the Permanent Forum on Indigenous Issues 2009; and the statement of the Navajo Nation Human Rights Commission delivered by Duane Yazzie during the 3rd session of the Expert Mechanism on the Rights of Indigenous Peoples 2010. All statements available online at <http://www.docip.org/Online-Documentation.32.0.html>.
3 See Anaya's annual statements delivered to the UN Permanent Forum on Indigenous Issues <http://unsr.jamesanaya.org/statements>.

However, an opportunity arose that signaled a potential change to this approach. On 21 December 2010, the UN General Assembly adopted a resolution to organise a General Assembly high-level "special session" to be known as the World Conference on Indigenous Peoples (World Conference) to be held in New York, on 22–23 September 2014.[4] The objective of the conference was expressed in broad terms: "to share perspectives and best practices on the realization of the rights of indigenous peoples" and the resolution also included a specific reference to "pursue the objectives of the Declaration."[5] Could this conference provide an opportunity for states to commit to concrete actions in relation to the Declaration? What further commitments and reforms could the UN system make to realise the rights in the Declaration? What were the risks, especially given that any resulting text would have to be negotiated with and agreed to by indigenous peoples *and* states?

The reference to a "World Conference" in the resolution caused consternation among some indigenous peoples. Previous World Conferences organised by the UN were stand-alone events with regional preparatory meetings and pre-conference meetings. Significant financial resources were allocated to them and each had their own technical secretariat. In comparison, as noted, the indigenous special session was "to be known" as a World Conference.[6] Clearly states envisaged this conference as involving considerably fewer resources with a much more limited focus. Indigenous peoples were understandably sceptical about states' motives. Indeed, while the idea of a World Conference had been mooted by indigenous peoples for a number of years, the resolution came as a complete surprise given that indigenous peoples did not participate in its drafting.

B. Indigenous Response to the World Conference Resolution: Three Priorities

Indigenous peoples needed to meet and consider the implications of the World Conference resolution. In January 2012, an open-ended "brainstorming meeting" was held in Copenhagen.[7] The term "open-ended" was used to reflect that the meeting was held to kick-start preparations and that further discussion among indigenous peoples was anticipated. The meeting was attended by UN experts and indigenous advocates from the seven geo-political regions of Africa, the Arctic, Asia, Latin America and the Caribbean, North America, the Pacific and Russia. The meeting provided a much needed opportunity to table questions and concerns, as well as receive briefings from UN staff about what previous General

---

4   *Indigenous issues* GA Res 65/198, A/Res/65/198 (2010).
5   At paragraph 8.
6   At paragraph 8.
7   Rapporteur Report on the Copenhagen meeting Jan 2012, copy held on file with author.

Assembly conferences had achieved. The briefings referenced the make-up and content of previous conferences as well as their outcomes.

Three main priorities for indigenous peoples came out of the brainstorming meeting. First, indigenous peoples wanted to ensure that the World Conference would not undermine the standards established in the Declaration.[8] Secondly, indigenous peoples demanded their full and active participation in the World Conference organisation and outcome.[9] Thirdly, it was expected that the World Conference would advance state implementation of the Declaration.[10] Critical to all objectives was the appointment of an "indigenous co-facilitator" during the preparatory stages to work alongside a state-appointed facilitator. Prior conferences had effectively been run by states with non-state actors operating at the margins, but indigenous peoples did not see this as appropriate, given their desire to be active participants in a process that was addressing their rights. Indigenous peoples did not consider it necessary to provide any reasoning as to why their participation in the process should be greater than that afforded to non-state actors in previous special sessions. It was simply a given in light of the Declaration's strong standards calling for indigenous peoples' effective participation in decisions affecting them.

The meeting also decided to establish the Indigenous Global Coordinating Group (the GCG), to facilitate indigenous participation. The GCG was comprised of representatives of the seven geo-political regions, as well as the indigenous women's caucus and the indigenous youth caucus. I initially served as one of the interim Pacific representatives on the GCG, but vacated that position when asked to be its Secretariat. The GCG was a crucial tool employed by indigenous peoples over the three years leading up to the World Conference. It engaged in lobbying, carried out fundraising to ensure indigenous participation and activities were resourced, established a communication platform to share information globally and agreed upon activities and strategies as required. Without the GCG, it would not have been possible for indigenous peoples to address the political challenges that arose during the process or proactively participate in all parts of the process.

C. *Ensuring Indigenous Peoples' Equal Participation in the World Conference*

An early victory for indigenous peoples was achieved with the appointment by the President of the General Assembly (PGA)[11] of two co-facilitators to lead

---

8   Resolution of the Open-ended Indigenous Peoples' Brainstorming Meeting on the World Conference on Indigenous Peoples 2014 Copenhagen, Denmark, 13–14 January 2012, copy held on file with author.
9   At preambular paragraph 3 and paragraph 1.
10 Above n 8, at 5.
11 Nassir Abdelaziz Al-Nasser of Qatar. This arrangement proved to be more challenging in

the process leading up to the conference, Luis Alfonso de Alba, Permanent Representative of Mexico, and John Henriksen, an indigenous Sami and representative of Norway's Sami Parliament. The appointment of co-facilitators is not a new development within the UN system, but normally co-facilitators are state representatives. In this instance, an indigenous representative was appointed to reflect the unique and important role that indigenous peoples would play in the conference. The appointment of a non-state co-facilitator was made possible because of the openness of the PGA to such an appointment as well as the effective lobbying of key state representatives such as Ambassador de Alba himself. Indigenous peoples supported the appointments because they ensured that: in the initial stages, a precedent was established that indigenous peoples and states were to be afforded active and equal roles; there would be an open and current flow of information; and the preparations and the conference itself would have their proactive collective input.

The first challenge was to ensure that the three key priorities of indigenous peoples were protected in the General Assembly "modalities resolution" which would outline the conference's aims and plans.[12] Indigenous peoples wanted to ensure the conference itself was more than a "talkfest" and that it delivered concrete outcomes. It was expected, as with prior conferences, that the World Conference would result in an "outcome document", setting out goals and concrete actions. The GCG was in New York to lobby states during the drafting of the resolution. As with any UN resolution, there were a number of challenges raised by states.[13] China's national policy on Taiwan meant that it does not consider the indigenous peoples of Taiwan to be distinct from the general population of both Taiwan or indeed China; the United States noted its preference to engage only with "federally-recognised tribes", while the Russian Federation – which declined to meet with the GCG – was opposed to an indigenous co-facilitator and argued that only states should participate. This gave the GCG a sense of the political climate and tensions within which the rest of the preparatory work for the conference would take place.

On 17 September 2012, the UN General Assembly adopted the World Conference modalities resolution.[14] Key components were:

2013 and 2014 when a new Ambassador was serving as PGA.
12   A further resolution was necessary because the resolution establishing the conference was only general in nature.
13   These specific national challenges were not directly communicated to indigenous advocates, but rather they were gleaned from secondary sources, such as informal bilateral discussions with other states. In addition, indigenous advocates also took note of what was said and what was not said by such states when they delivered statements during meetings that focused on indigenous peoples' rights, such as the Permanent Forum on Indigenous Issues.
14   *Organization of the high-level plenary meeting of the sixty-ninth session of the General Assembly, to be known as the World Conference on Indigenous Peoples* GA Res 66/296, A/

- The meeting would be held in New York on Monday 22 September 2014 and the afternoon of Tuesday 23 September 2014;
- There would be two plenary sessions, the opening and closing sessions;
- There would be three interactive roundtables and one informal panel discussion;
- Summaries of the roundtables and the panel discussion would be presented by the co-chairs at the closing session. Participants in the roundtables and the informal panel discussion would include states, UN agencies, indigenous peoples, civil society and national human rights institutions;
- The PGA would organise an informal interactive hearing no later than June 2014 in order to provide input into the preparatory process. Indigenous peoples, UN agencies, academia, national human rights institutions, parliamentarians, civil society and states were encouraged to participate; and
- The World Conference meeting would result in an action orientated outcome document. The PGA would prepare the draft text on the basis of consultations with states and indigenous peoples and would take into account the views emerging from the preparatory processes and the interactive hearing. A consultation process would be convened to provide input for sufficient consideration by states and agreement by the General Assembly prior to the meeting itself.

While the formal components of the conference meeting were important, the main focus for indigenous peoples was the preparation and completion of the outcome document. With its focus on "action orientated" outcomes, it was hoped that the document would be focused on states' concrete, practical commitments to implement the Declaration.

The World Conference modalities resolution provided that indigenous peoples have input via the June 2014 "informal interactive hearing" and other "preparatory processes" including indigenous-led preparatory meetings. It was also understood by indigenous peoples that the drafting of the outcome document would take place in the months leading up to the World Conference and that in order to influence its content, indigenous peoples would need to agree upon key priority areas they wanted to see reflected in the document as well as commit to active lobbying of states in New York during the months leading up the World Conference.

Within the GCG, the North American Indigenous Peoples' caucus (Canada and the US) voiced their concern that the process set out in the modalities resolution was unworkable given the meeting's status was less than that of a fully-fledged

---

Res/66/296 (2012).

World Conference and that it could potentially undermine indigenous peoples' rights. They wanted to take a more precautionary approach to the process. The other members of the GCG took the view that the World Conference modalities resolution was workable and that indigenous peoples could continue to lobby for stronger outcomes during the implementation of the resolution.

D. *The Alta Outcome Document*

Between November 2012 to April 2013 the seven regional caucuses met as well as the two thematic "women" and "youth" caucuses.[15] Each meeting produced an "outcome document" or "declaration". The priorities that came out of each meeting were varied but they canvassed several core themes including the right to self-determination, violence against women, conflict and militarisation, lands, waters, resources and traditional livelihoods, culture and spirituality, extractive industries, the disaggregation of data, and an optional protocol to the Declaration, as well as greater reporting by states at the international level on the implementation of the Declaration and international oversight.

While the nine documents produced during the respective preparatory meetings had their own standing, they were also part of a larger initiative to create a global indigenous position. This was seen as important because the nine regional and thematic documents canvassed a wide array of issues which needed to be distilled into a shorter, more focused document. The reason for this was strategic; in order for indigenous peoples to effectively engage with states, a common and clear platform of priorities needed to be created to ensure that those issues of most importance to indigenous peoples were captured in the final UN document.

The Sami Parliament of Norway generously offered to host a global conference of indigenous peoples in June 2013. The object was to produce an indigenous document that would influence the content of the World Conference outcome document. The conference was attended by over 600 delegates and observers. The meeting took place over three days during the Arctic summer, meaning there were 24 hours of sunlight each day. This had the unsettling effect of creating equal amounts of jet lag and endless energy among the participants. The drafting process had begun in May when nominated drafters from each of the regions and thematic caucuses met in Madrid for two days. As a result of that meeting and ongoing drafting, a "draft outcome document" was tabled at the Alta conference. It was this document that was revised by the drafters and the meeting as a whole during the Alta conference. On the final day of the

---

15 The GCG raised funds so that all the regional caucuses as well as the two thematic caucuses could hold their own preparatory meetings. Funding was sourced from a mixture of private US foundations, UN agencies and governments.

conference, the "Alta outcome document" was adopted by consensus followed by much celebration.[16] The Alta outcome document set out the principles by which indigenous peoples would engage in the World Conference. Reference was made to the provisions of the Declaration that affirm indigenous peoples' equal participation in decisions affecting them.

The Alta outcome document was comprised of four themes. These were: 1) indigenous peoples' lands, territories, resources, oceans and waters; 2) implementation of the rights of indigenous peoples; 3) United Nations support for the implementation of indigenous peoples' rights; and 4) indigenous peoples' priorities for development with free, prior and informed consent (FPIC). Each theme contained detailed recommendations. For example, the theme of UN action for the implementation of indigenous rights called for an international mechanism to provide oversight and redress in relation to treaties, agreements and other constructive arrangements.

While the adoption of the Alta outcome document was a historic moment for indigenous peoples, in order for it to be taken up by states in the remaining preparatory work, it needed to be championed at the UN. A number of indigenous focused UN meetings were held before the World Conference. Members of the GCG who attended those meetings committed to lobbying states and meeting participants to ensure the Alta outcome document was reflected in the reports and resolutions of those meetings. They also wanted to ensure that the Alta outcome document was in the forefront of states' minds during the remaining preparatory work of the World Conference and that it was given a UN reference number. The significance of a UN reference number meant that the document would be submitted to the UN by states who supported it, thus giving it greater "state legitimacy" and ensuring its consideration in the drafting of the final UN outcome document.

E. UN Lobby Efforts – Led by the GCG

The first UN meeting after the Alta conference was the Expert Mechanism on the Rights of Indigenous Peoples (EMRIP). The Alta outcome document was submitted to the EMRIP Secretariat and tabled as a "conference room paper". Indigenous advocates called for the EMRIP to endorse the Alta outcome document, that it serve as the basis for the drafting of the conference's outcome document, and that its themes be the themes for the conference.[17] During the EMRIP session,

---

16   The Alta Outcome Document was tabled at the 67th session of the General Assembly, where it received an official UN reference. *Letter dated 10 September 2013 from the Permanent Representatives of the Plurinational State of Bolivia, Denmark, Finland, Guatemala, Mexico, New Zealand, Nicaragua, Norway and Peru to the United Nations addressed to the Secretary-General* GA 67/994, A/67/994 Annex (2013).
17   See, for example, the statement of the GCG delivered by Ghazali Ohorella during the 6th

EMRIP expert Chief Wilton Littlechild prepared a paper describing how many of the recommendations set out in the Alta outcome document reflected EMRIP's previous studies and advice.[18] The EMRIP's report to its parent body, the Human Rights Council (HRC), recommended that the General Assembly "consider" the Alta outcome document themes as *the* themes for the conference and that the outcome document "be considered" in the drafting of the final outcome document.[19] There was concern that the EMRIP had not adopted stronger language, given the Alta outcome document was the only global indigenous position on the conference coupled with the fact that the process that indigenous advocates had undertaken to bring it to fruition had been open, long-term and inclusive. The next opportunity to lobby states was the 24th session of the HRC in September 2013. A panel discussion on the conference was held to raise its profile amongst states and emphasise indigenous peoples' core concerns. As a result of lobbying efforts, the HRC adopted a resolution, although again the wording of the resolution was not as strong as was hoped for. The HRC resolution took note of the Alta outcome document and recommended that its themes be "taken into account" when considering the themes for the World Conference.[20]

The next significant UN meeting was the Third Committee of the UN General Assembly which has an annual resolution on the rights of indigenous peoples. Lobbying efforts resulted in a resolution, recommending that the four themes of the Alta outcome document be taken into account when considering the specific themes for the round-table and interactive panel discussions for the World Conference, and that the Alta outcome document "be taken into account" when preparing the World Conference outcome document.[21]

The year 2013 was very productive for indigenous peoples. In particular, the Alta outcome document was filled with concrete recommendations that could be incorporated in the World Conference outcome document. The new PGA, John Ashe of Antigua and Barbuda, had taken office in mid-September and it was expected that he would begin to implement the remaining work by appointing two co-facilitators by the end of 2013. There was an expectation from both states

session of the Expert Mechanism on the Rights of Indigenous Peoples 2013, statement of the Indigenous Peoples Organisations Network of Australia delivered by Brian Wyatt during the 6th session of the Expert Mechanism on the Rights of Indigenous Peoples 2013 and the statement of the International Indian Treaty Council delivered by Andrea Carmen during the 6th session of the Expert Mechanism on the Rights of Indigenous Peoples.
18 *Compilation of Recommendations, Conclusions and Advice from Studies Completed by the Expert Mechanism on the Rights of Indigenous Peoples* A/HRC/EMRIP/2013/CRP.1 (2013).
19 Indigenous advocates had lobbied the EMRIP experts for stronger language – that is, that the Alta outcome document not merely be considered, but be *the* basis for the conference outcome document. See, *Report of the Expert Mechanism on the Rights of Indigenous Peoples on its sixth session (Geneva, 8–12 July 2013)* A/HRC/24/49 (2013).
20 *Human rights and indigenous peoples* HRC Res 24/10, A/HRC/Res/24/10 (2013).
21 *Rights of indigenous peoples report of the Third Committee* A/68/453 (2013).

and indigenous peoples that precedent would be followed and that the PGA would appoint one state facilitator and one indigenous facilitator. However, as the year ended with no clear direction from the PGA, questions were raised as to why the process had stalled.

F. Problems with the Implementation of the World Conference Modalities Resolution

On 29 January 2014, the PGA circulated to states an "aide memoire" outlining three options regarding the appointment of co-facilitators. Option 1 proposed two state co-facilitators and one indigenous advisor; option 2 proposed two state co-facilitators and one indigenous co-facilitator; and option 3 proposed no co-facilitators with all consultations being undertaken by the PGA personally. The majority of the GCG responded by proposing that one state co-facilitator and one indigenous co-facilitator be appointed as was initially agreed or that the proposed PGA options be amended to ensure that equal numbers of indigenous representatives were appointed alongside state representatives to the same roles and that all would participate on an equal footing. The North American Indigenous Peoples' Caucus and the North American Youth Caucus did not agree with the majority of the GCG, and did not sign on to the letter sent by the GCG to the PGA. This was unfortunate, given that up until that point all regions and caucuses had worked collectively through the GCG. However, each region and caucus was free at any point in the process to take their own position. The PGA then circulated a second "aide memoire" on 26 February 2014.[22] This stated that there would be no co-facilitators. Instead, there would be two parallel consultation processes, one for states and one for indigenous "groups", and that indigenous groups could also make their views known to states via "informal briefings". The aide memoire also stated that consultations would begin the following week on 3 March.

This proposal was quickly rejected by indigenous peoples for being inconsistent with: the right to participate in decision-making; the principles of openness and transparency; and the World Conference modalities resolution. The seven regional caucuses responded directly to the PGA, noting that his proposed consultation process was inconsistent with the right of indigenous peoples to participate in matters affecting them. The North American Indigenous Peoples' Caucus called for the cancellation of the World Conference and withdrew from the process. Several states, supportive of indigenous peoples' equal participation in the process, such as Mexico, Guatemala and New Zealand, held bilateral meetings with the PGA calling on him to amend the consultation process. The PGA however was not dissuaded. He circulated a letter on 5 March 2014 confirming that Andrej

---

22 Copy on file with author.

Logar, Permanent Representative of Slovenia, and Eduardo Ulibarri, Permanent Representative of Costa Rica, would assist him with consultations.

After lobbying by states supportive of indigenous peoples' participation, as well as a strong push by indigenous peoples during the 13th session of the UN Permanent Forum on Indigenous Issues, the PGA changed his decision. He would now appoint four advisers – two state advisers and two indigenous advisers – to assist him with consultations. On the basis of the consultations, the PGA would then prepare a draft outcome document for the consideration of states and indigenous peoples which would form the basis of the negotiations on the final outcome document. Indigenous peoples responded by welcoming the confirmation that there would only be one consultation process which included both states and indigenous peoples on an equal footing. Les Malezer and Myrna Cunningham – both leading figures in the international indigenous movement – were nominated to fill the roles of indigenous advisers.[23] The first round of consultations was scheduled in June 2014. With only four days before the first round of consultations, indigenous advocates quickly arranged for representatives to be present in New York. Due to the extremely tight time frame, the African region was unable to participate, but joined in a collective statement on behalf of all the regions that was tabled. As the North American Indigenous Peoples' Caucus had withdrawn from the process they did not participate. However, a number of North American tribes and NGOs participated under their own mandates in the first and successive rounds of consultations.

G. Drafting of the World Conference Outcome Document

The first draft of the outcome document, prepared by the four advisers to the PGA, formed the basis for the first round of informal consultations. There were further informal consultations in July and August and each time a new version of the draft outcome document was tabled taking into account the views expressed by states and indigenous peoples. As each round of consultations progressed, statements by indigenous peoples become more focused and technical, addressing specific word changes and calling on states to support the same.

The meetings were also structured so that each indigenous region was able to speak to each paragraph. This worked well, as it provided each region with an opportunity to comment on the draft in a methodical fashion and encouraged specific technical input. It also allowed regions to collaborate with other regions and present their positions collectively, and it ensured that there was plenty of time for states to take the floor. State participation varied; those supportive of the preparatory process, such as the Nordic states, Canada, Australia, New Zealand

---

23 John Henriksen had by that time confirmed that he no longer wished to be considered for the role of indigenous co-facilitator.

and the United States (CANZUS states) and Latin American states engaged, while others did not. Asian and African states were either absent during the meetings or did not take the floor. However, the lack of engagement by some states did not deter indigenous peoples who had arranged a lobby presence in New York from June to September 2014.

The lobby team was comprised of indigenous advocates from all of the seven geo-political regions and the women's caucus. Each advocate was chosen by their respective caucus, although some caucuses chose to share the position amongst a number of individuals. The team met daily to collectively review versions of the outcome document, to lobby states and to strategise. They also met regularly with a group of states known as "friends of the World Conference", coordinated by Mexico. Given these states were well-versed in the political climate and the technical language of drafting UN documents, they were able to provide useful feedback to the lobby team and the lobby team in turn was able to convey their views and priorities. The two indigenous advisers carried out a dual role; they worked closely with the two state advisers in the drafting of the outcome document and they assisted the PGA's office with logistical arrangements relating to the World Conference, such as accreditation processes and the number of potential participants. The lobby team was also called upon by the PGA's office to provide input into logistical arrangements. While this had not been foreseen as a role they would carry out, they did so in order to ensure that indigenous peoples' expectations about the process and the meeting itself were met.

The lobby team were acutely aware of the short timeframe that remained and the work required to find consensus amongst states on the content of the outcome document. The lobby team prioritised rights and issues from the Alta outcome document in order to ensure that they were included in the final outcome document. Prioritised areas were:

- Cluster 1 – international oversight mechanism, permanent status for indigenous peoples within the UN and other international measures;
- Cluster 2 – lands, territories and resources and demilitarisation;
- Cluster 3 – national policy direction;
- Cluster 4 – indigenous women, youth and children; and
- Cluster 5 – traditional knowledge and livelihoods.

Different regions took on responsibility for specific clusters which involved drafting language and producing non-papers. Non-papers were used to explain the relevance and importance of the rights that each cluster addressed and explained specific mechanisms to implement such rights. The non-papers were informally circulated to states and received positive feedback, as they were viewed as useful detailed explanations of indigenous peoples' priorities.

From June to August 2014, the lobby team, working closely with the friends of the World Conference and the indigenous advisers, advocated for the priority clusters and reviewed draft language. After the last round of consultations in August, a final draft outcome document was prepared by the PGA's office. The outcome document then entered its final stage. This was an intergovernmental process whereby states and the four advisers participated. Indigenous peoples were concerned that there could be significant changes made to the text during this process. It was a difficult period, as the ability to directly influence the content of the outcome document was now in the hands of states. Many states who had not presented their positions during the informal consultations sought to make changes. However, the indigenous advisers and the friends of the World Conference were clear about the priorities of indigenous peoples, and worked to uphold those priorities and were able, in most instances, to reject significant changes.

With only days remaining before the conference was due to take place, the final outcome document was translated and disseminated by the UN. Indigenous advocates turned their focus to logistical matters to ensure that all seven geopolitical regions were represented in New York. The Russian Federation stopped a number of indigenous advocates from leaving Russia and were reported to have harassed and assaulted others.[24] This was taken up during the meeting by both indigenous peoples and states, as there were concerns that such actions would lead to the advocates prosecution and potential incarceration. However, once the conference was over, the harassment and potential prosecutions disappeared.

The main objective of the conference was the formal adoption of the outcome document. This was scheduled for the first day. Only a few indigenous advocates were able to sit alongside states in the General Assembly hall, and the majority were seated in the viewing area or in overflow rooms. Nevertheless, when the gavel sounded confirming the adoption of the outcome document, indigenous advocates celebrated. What had been achieved was historic, both in relation to the content of the outcome document and the way the process had been implemented to reflect the status of indigenous peoples and their right of active and effective participation in decisions affecting them. The outcome document itself reflected many of the priorities that had been set out in the Alta outcome document and the highest body of the UN had committed to concrete actions at both the national and international level.

The outcome document, both in its content and the process by which it was

---

24 See Greenpeace Russia "The Absent Russians at the World Conference on Indigenous Peoples" (23 September 2014) Greenpeace <http://www.greenpeace.org/russia/en/news/23-09-2014_Russia_WCIP/> and Rick Kearns "Russia Prevented Indigenous Leaders From Going to World Conference" (31 October 2014) Indian Country Today <http://indiancountrytodaymedianetwork.com/2014/10/31/russia-prevented-indigenous-leaders-going-world-conference-157616>.

created, addressed the three core priorities that indigenous peoples had identified at the beginning of the process – the rights enshrined in the Declaration were upheld, indigenous peoples participated fully and actively in the process, and states committed to concrete actions to implement the Declaration. Each priority area was tested, but indigenous peoples and those states supportive of indigenous peoples' rights maintained a clear and principled approach and were constantly present, which addressed those states that resisted indigenous peoples' participation in the conference.

The outcome document embraces two overarching principles. First, operative paragraph (OP) 2 states that the indigenous regional and caucus outcome documents as well as the Alta outcome document can be referenced to support the implementation of the Conference's outcome document. Secondly, OP 4 reaffirms the rights of indigenous peoples and the principles of the Declaration. These two principles acknowledge the importance of the preparatory documents, as well as the fact that the conference outcome document cannot be implemented so as to diminish or redefine the rights and principles of the Declaration.

The recommendations of the outcome document can be divided into four groups: 1, legislative and policy; 2, lands, territories and resources; 3, the environment and livelihoods; and 4, social measures. The legislative and policy recommendations are set out in OPs 3, 7, 6, 8, 10 and 30. Three are of particular importance. OP 3 provides for the FPIC of indigenous peoples before the adoption and implementation of legislative or administrative measures that may affect them. It is a reiteration of the right as set out in the Declaration, though its inclusion in the outcome document is important given the ongoing challenges faced by indigenous peoples in their desire to shape their own destiny in the absence of discriminatory laws and policies. Applying this recommendation in the context of Aotearoa New Zealand, would herald a major change in the way that law and policy is determined. It sets a much higher standard than consultation and gives Māori a significant say in how governance would be implemented. OP 7 complements OP 3 by focusing on achieving the ends of the Declaration by promoting awareness of the Declaration amongst the general population. There is scant information available from the New Zealand government on the Declaration and its implications for indigenous peoples' rights. This operative paragraph places an active onus on the government to engage in proactive communication about the Declaration, particularly amongst politicians, the judiciary and the civil service. OP 8 is a useful recommendation in that it focuses on a national action plan. As the outcome document touches upon a myriad of issues, such a plan would be a useful way of prioritising recommendations from the outcome document that are particularly pertinent to Māori. Not only does this recommendation commit to developing a national action plan or other similar strategies, it also commits to its implementation. This provides an excellent opportunity for Māori to take the initiative in drafting this document to clearly reflect areas of priority and to hold the government to account for its implementation. Such a plan has the capacity to be monitored both at the national and international level.

The second group of recommendations, OPs 20, 21, 23 and 24, relate to land, territories and resources. OP 20 states that the indigenous peoples' FPIC must be obtained prior to the approval of projects affecting their lands, territories or other resources. This recommendation, coupled with OP 24 which relates to business entities operating with transparency and in a socially and environmentally responsible manner, places a clear onus on the government to develop and implement law and policy that not only recognises these rights, but also ensures indigenous peoples including Māori are positioned as active decision makers in relation to their lands, territories and resources. While frameworks of co-management in Aotearoa New Zealand could be considered as models that realise these rights, it is clear that the right of FPIC is a game changer and requires a much greater level of input and weight to be given to Māori as key decision makers.

The third group of recommendations, OPs 22, 25–27 and 34–36, relate to the environment and livelihoods. While some of these recommendations are not as strongly worded as those already discussed, OPs 25 and 36 are relevant to the New Zealand context. OP 25 commits the government to developing policies, programmes and resources to support indigenous peoples' occupations, traditional subsistence activities, economies, livelihoods, food security and nutrition. This outcome reflects article 20 of the Declaration, which focuses on the maintenance and development of indigenous political, economic and social systems or institutions as well as indigenous means of subsistence and development. This OP could bolster support for Māori means and ways of living. OP 36 states that indigenous peoples' knowledge and strategies to sustain their environment be taken into account when developing national and international approaches to climate change mitigation and adaptation. Current negotiations on climate change are reluctant to include or work within a human rights framework. However, this recommendation could be used to ensure that indigenous peoples' rights become *the* normative framework within which such policy directives and decisions are made with respect to indigenous peoples.

The last group of recommendations relate to social measures. These are OPs 9 and 15–18. OP 9 specifically mentions indigenous persons with disabilities and notes that policies and programmes aimed at their welfare must be developed in conjunction with them. Particular reference is made to legal, policy and institutional structures. Given New Zealand has ratified the UN Convention on Persons with Disabilities, this recommendation can be used by Māori to garner greater support for indigenous persons with disabilities.

Another pertinent recommendation is OP 18, which relates to violence and discrimination and the strengthening of legal, policy and institutional frameworks. This recommendation can also be used by those advocating for greater change to some of the most vulnerable groups within Māori society.

It could be argued that parts of the outcome document simply reiterate the Declaration. At face value, this is correct. However, given the need to ensure the outcome document did not limit or redefine the rights set out in the Declaration, incorporating portions of it verbatim into the outcome document and referencing those as "agreed to language" was a specific strategy employed by indigenous peoples. The outcome document delivers on many of the pressing issues that indigenous peoples set out in the Alta outcome document. While not all issues were addressed, for example self-determination and demilitarisation, the adoption of numerous concrete proposals that support the Declaration and provide frameworks for the realisation of rights cannot be overlooked. As governments are prone to make statements yet fail to carry out them out, it is incumbent upon Māori to take a proactive role in bringing these commitments to life. Failure to do so will allow the government to carry on business as usual in the mistaken belief that New Zealand's current constitutional and legal structure already meets these needs.

H. Conclusion

As an indigenous advocate and active participant in the conference preparations, I had time to reflect on the accomplishments that were achieved. Many lessons are evidently clear, such as the importance of sufficient resources, long-term forward planning, consensus building among indigenous advocates through a structured and representative body, and focused lobbying. Other lessons that have been learnt along the way include the need for enduring and sustained mental focus to stay on task, the ability to respond quickly and decisively to new developments in strategic ways, and the necessity of building respectful and long-term relationships with states and other key players, such as the President of the General Assembly. This process has shown what can be accomplished when there is a strong collective will and an openness to marry principle and pragmatism. It has required a new way of working and it has achieved some positive results. For example, during the negotiations on the Declaration, indigenous advocates relied upon caucus meetings prior to and during the UN meetings to plan and strategise. In comparison, preparations for the World Conference involved substantial fundraising, various meetings at the regional and international level, and an international indigenous coordinating body, as well as concerted and focused lobbying in New York in the lead up to the World Conference. The process was clearly not perfect and did not meet all indigenous peoples' expectations. However, it did provide a strong foundation and plenty of leverage to effect change. The next challenge lies in the follow up and implementation of the outcome document, meaning that Māori, particularly those who engaged in the process, have an ongoing role to play and a responsibility to share this achievement with their whānau, hapū and iwi.

10

The Declaration in the Universal Periodic Review: Current Status and Future Prospects

Natalie Baird[*]

A. Introduction

This chapter considers the way in which the United Nations Declaration on the Rights of Indigenous Peoples (the Declaration) has been used in the context of the UN Human Rights Council's (HRC) Universal Periodic Review (UPR) mechanism. The primary focus is on the New Zealand experience, but some reference is also made to the experience of Australia, Canada and the United States (together with New Zealand, "the CANZUS states") in their UPR reviews.

The chapter notes the positive use of the Declaration in the UPR process, in particular in supporting the ultimately successful calls for CANZUS states to endorse the Declaration. The use of the Declaration in the UPR is also contributing to the mainstreaming of the Declaration and giving it a certain amount of visibility in the HRC beyond processes which are specific to indigenous peoples. The references to the Declaration in the UPR are, for the most part, reaffirming the international consensus on the Declaration. This is significant, given that the Declaration represents the most robust elaboration of indigenous rights at the international level and was negotiated by states and indigenous peoples.

With indications of endorsement of the Declaration from all four CANZUS states now achieved, the way in which the Declaration is being used in the UPR is changing. Before the reversal of CANZUS states' positions, most references to the Declaration by NGOs and other states called on the relevant CANZUS state to indicate its support for the Declaration. Now that this milestone has been achieved, the recommendations to New Zealand and other CANZUS states mostly call for "implementation" of the Declaration. Beyond this general call, however, to date there has been a distinct lack of specificity in

---

[*] Senior Lecturer, School of Law, University of Canterbury, New Zealand. I am grateful for the research assistance provided by Rachael Harris, and also for the feedback of the participants at the Symposium that preceded this volume.

recommendations which invoke the Declaration.

This chapter therefore explores the potential of the UPR to support implementation of the Declaration on the ground in New Zealand. It notes the general recommendations to CANZUS states to implement the Declaration and considers whether more specificity would be useful and, if so, how this might be achieved. In doing so, it recalls that the ultimate aim of the UPR is to improve the human rights situation on the ground, and queries whether the UPR is a useful tool to achieve implementation of the Declaration on the ground in New Zealand. Part B of this chapter provides an overview of the UPR mechanism and its key features. Part C considers use of the Declaration in the UPR process to date, drawing in particular on the experience of the CANZUS states. Part D explores the New Zealand experience in a little more depth. Part E considers the future prospects of using the UPR mechanism as a tool to support implementation of the Declaration and makes suggestions as to how the UPR can be more effectively used.

In sum, the chapter concludes that although the UPR mechanism is a useful advocacy tool to support implementation of the Declaration, it is limited by some of its key features, including its wide focus on all human rights, the fact that it is a mechanism established and run by diplomats, and its practical constraints in terms of page limits and the time available for dialogue with states. However, there is some scope for better use of the UPR to support implementation of the Declaration and this should certainly be explored by both NGOs and states. In particular, states and NGOs should be encouraged to use the Declaration as the framework through which to view all indigenous rights issues. Ultimately, though, the UPR is unlikely to be very effective in fostering the level of detail or the degree of specificity now needed at the international level to support implementation of the Declaration in Aotearoa New Zealand.

B. *The Universal Periodic Review Mechanism*

The UPR, first initiated in 2008, involves a review by the HRC of the human rights records of all 193 UN member states once every four-and-a-half years. Forty-two states are reviewed each year, with 14 states being reviewed in three two-week sessions. The review is intended to be cooperative and conducted in an objective, transparent, non-selective, constructive, non-confrontational and non-politicised manner.[1] It is an inter-governmental process, involving the country under review and driven by UN member states.[2] Here, the UPR process can be contrasted with both the UN human rights treaty bodies and the UN special procedures, such as the UN Special Rapporteur on the Rights of

---

1   A/HRC/RES/5/1 (2007), Annex, at [3(b)] and [3(g)].
2   A/HRC/RES/5/1 (2007), Annex, at [3(d)] and [3(e)].

Indigenous Peoples, both of which generally comprise independent human rights experts rather than the (mostly) non-expert diplomats who are the key actors in the UPR.

Another contrast with the treaty bodies is that the UPR is not to be "overly burdensome" to the state under review or "overly long."[3] Three documents form the basis of the review. The length of each is carefully prescribed. The first report is the 20-page national report prepared by the state under review. This report can be contrasted with the periodic state reports to treaty bodies which are considerably longer and significantly more detailed. The second document for the UPR is a 10-page compilation by the UN Office of the High Commissioner for Human Rights (OHCHR) of the information contained in various other UN reports. The third report is a 10-page summary report prepared by OHCHR summarising "credible and reliable information provided by other stakeholders" including NGOs and national human rights institutions (the stakeholder summary).[4] The information provided by these stakeholders is itself limited, with a single NGO able to submit a report no longer than 2,815 words (around five pages), and a coalition of two or more NGOs able to submit a report no longer than 5,630 words (around ten pages).[5]

The basis or yardstick for assessing a state's compliance with its human rights obligations and commitments is the UN Charter,[6] the Universal Declaration of Human Rights,[7] human rights instruments to which the particular state is party, and voluntary pledges and commitments made by States.[8]

The review itself is conducted in Geneva in the HRC's Working Group on the UPR, comprised of all 47 member states of the HRC. The review is facilitated by three HRC members, each from a different regional group and drawn by lot (known as the "troika"). UN member states who are not members of the HRC may also participate. Other stakeholders – primarily NGOs – may attend the review, although they cannot participate in the crucial interactive dialogue. This dialogue is a three-and-a-half hour verbal exchange between the state being reviewed and the Working Group. It begins with an oral presentation by the state of its report. Other states then make statements which may include recommendations for the state being reviewed. The state under review may indicate its response to recommendations at the time of the dialogue, or, more commonly, may take time to decide its position and provide its response when the HRC adopts the "outcome report" some three to four months later.

3   A/HRC/RES/5/1 (2007), Annex, at [3(h)] and [3(i)].
4   A/HRC/RES/5/1 (2007), Annex, at [3(m)].
5   OHCHR "A Practical Guide for Civil Society: Universal Periodic Review" (undated), 14.
6   Charter of the United Nations.
7   *Universal Declaration of Human Rights*, GA Res 217A (III), UNGAOR, 3rd Sess, Supp No 13, UN Doc A/810 (1948) 71.
8   A/HRC/RES/5/1 (2007), Annex, at [1].

From an advocacy perspective, the significant output of the interactive dialogue is the set of recommendations made to the state under review plus the formal State response. The recommendations accepted by the state are essentially a commitment by the state to take the action recommended. At the next review, four-and-a-half years later, these accepted recommendations are a key basis for the review.

All of the above largely describes the Geneva side of the UPR process. However, a very real question with any international human rights mechanism is to consider how it can make a difference on the ground. A legitimate question to ask is whether a process which happens in Geneva can really work to improve human rights on the ground domestically. Here it is relevant to note that a key focus during the second cycle of the UPR has been on whether the recommendations from the first cycle have been implemented. Particularly relevant here is the actions of individual states in implementing the recommendations in between their individual UPR reviews. It is this implementation at home which will really improve human rights on the ground, not a three-and-a-half hour dialogue in Geneva.

Assessments of the UPR mechanism to date have largely been positive.[9] The UPR mechanism has had some notable successes. One of the most common recommendations accepted and acted upon by states has been recommendations to ratify outstanding human rights treaties. The UPR has also been successfully leveraged by NGOs campaigning on discrete issues. For example, during the first cycle of the UPR, and largely as a result of a concerted campaign by the LGBT community, a significant number of recommendations were made to and accepted by states on the decriminalisation of same-sex consensual conduct.[10] A further

---

9   See, for example, Alex Conte "Reflections and Challenges: Entering into the Second Cycle of the Universal Periodic Review" (2011) 9 NZYBIL 187; Elvira Dominguez Redondo "Universal Periodic Review: Is There Life Beyond Naming and Shaming in Human Rights Implementation?" (2012) New Zealand Law Review 673; Rosa Freedman "New Mechanisms of the UN Human Rights Council" (2011) 29 Netherlands Quarterly of Human Rights 289; Edward McMahon and Marta Ascherio "A Step Ahead in Promoting Human Rights? The Universal Periodic Review of the UN Human Rights Council" (2012) 18 Global Governance 231; Connie de la Vega and Tamara Lewis "Peer Review in the Mix: How the UPR Transforms Human Rights Discourse" in M Bassiouni and William A Schabas (eds) *New Challenges for the UN Human Rights Machinery* (Intersentia, Cambridge, 2011), 353–386; Hilary Charlesworth and Emma Larking (eds) *Human Rights and the Universal Periodic Review: Rituals and Ritualism* (Cambridge University Press, Cambridge, 2014). For a contrasting view, see Christian Tomuschat "Universal Periodic Review: A New System of International Law with Specific Ground Rules?" in Ulrich Fastenrath, Rudolf Geiger, Daniel-Erasmus Khan, Andreas Paulus, Sabine von Schorlemer and Christoph Vedder (eds) *From Bilateralism to Community Interest: Essays in Honour of Judge Bruno Simma* (Oxford University Press, New York, 2011) 609–628.

10 For more on this issue, see Frederick Cowell and Angelina Milon "Decriminalisation of Sexual Orientation through the Universal Periodic Review" (2012) 12 Human Rights Law Review 341.

success has arguably been the way in which the UPR can be used to put pressure on states in relation to specific events. In particular, there are opportunities for NGOs to lobby other states on these issues and suggest recommendations which could usefully be made to the state being reviewed. During New Zealand's first review in 2009, Mexico made a recommendation, which was accepted by New Zealand, that New Zealand should "continue the new dialogue between the State and the Maori regarding the Foreshore and Seabed Act of 2004, in order to find a way of mitigating its discriminatory effects through a mechanism involving prior informed consent of those affected."[11] Although at that point New Zealand had already established an independent Ministerial panel to consider the 2004 Act,[12] international attention on an issue assists in keeping pressure on a government. Finally, a major success of the UPR has been the fact that there has been comprehensive state engagement by all UN member states with the process itself.

C. *The Declaration in the UPR*

In light of this brief overview of the UPR mechanism, I now turn to consider the way in which the Declaration has been used in the UPR process. Writing in 2009, James Anaya noted that in the context of the UPR, the Declaration "increasingly functions as a benchmark for examining states' conduct in relation to indigenous peoples within the UPR process."[13] While there does appear to be a gradual trend towards more frequent reference to the Declaration, there are some limitations in the way in which the Declaration is being used and in fact can be used. This section considers use of the Declaration by reference to the experience of the CANZUS states to date, while the next section examines the New Zealand experience in more detail.

Table One summarises the use of the Declaration in the eight UPR reviews of the four CANZUS states to date. Some explanation and caution are required when using the information in Table One. The first point is that sometimes the "outcome report" of the HRC Working Group is produced in a different format, which can be misleading in terms of the number of recommendations. Sometimes several recommendations are grouped into one recommendation on a particular issue (even where it is made by more than one state) and sometimes they are separated out into individual recommendations. For example, in Canada's first review, it is noted as receiving two recommendations on the Declaration, although one of these was made by five different states. In contrast, the United

---

11   A/HRC/12/18 (2009), at [36].
12   See *Pakia ki uta pakia ki tai: Summary Report of the Ministerial Review Panel* (Ministry of Justice, Wellington, 2009) <https://www.beehive.govt.nz/sites/all/files/24845%20A5%20Summary%20online.pdf>.
13   S James Anaya *International Human Rights and Indigenous Peoples* (Aspen Publishers, New York, 2009), 106.

States received eight recommendations, from eight different states, although seven of these all concerned the same topic – the United States' endorsement of the Declaration.

It is also necessary to explain the parameters of the stakeholder submissions.[14] These are summarised by the Office of the High Commissioner for Human Rights in the ten-page stakeholder summary, one of the three key documents for each review. However, this summary is not always a comprehensive summary of NGO submissions. Indeed, given the page limits, it is almost impossible for it to be so, especially where there are a large number of stakeholder submissions.[15] So for example, for New Zealand's 2014 review, the stakeholder summary suggests that just two stakeholders raised the Declaration. However, upon looking at the original stakeholder submissions, it is clear that twelve stakeholders mentioned the Declaration. So, rather than relying on the stakeholder summary to indicate use of Declaration, the original stakeholder submissions have therefore been reviewed.

Another point to note in relation to the stakeholder submissions is that, as noted above, submissions can be by a single organisation or number of organisations. Care therefore needs to be taken in drawing conclusions from either the number of submissions which mentioned the Declaration or the total number of submissions, as these numbers may hide a joint submission by a number of NGOs. For example, one of the twelve submissions referring to the Declaration for New Zealand's second review was a joint submission from the Aotearoa Indigenous Rights Trust and Peace Movement Aotearoa. This submission was supported by another 22 organisations. A final point is that in some cases a stakeholder submission or a recommendation may have used the language of the Declaration although not referred to the Declaration itself. In these situations, it has been included in the Table as an Declaration reference if there is an obvious link to the Declaration, such as use of the language of free, prior and informed consent (FPIC). Inevitably this has involved some judgement calls. It is important to keep in mind though that not every reference to an indigenous issue has been treated as a Declaration reference. There are a number of additional recommendations made to states about the human rights of indigenous peoples, but they are not framed in the context of the Declaration. This is a point to which I return below.

---

14   The original stakeholder submissions are available as background documents by way of a footnote on the official OHCHR UPR documentation webpage for each country.
15   For an illuminating discussion of the work of the OHCHR drafters in support of the UPR process, see Julie Billaud "Keepers of the Truth: Producing 'Transparent' Documents for the Universal Periodic Review" in Hilary Charlesworth and Emma Larking above n 9 at 63–83.

UPR of State (in order of review)	Stakeholder submissions referencing UNDRIP	Number of state recommendations on UNDRIP	States making recommendations on UNDRIP	State response to recommendations
Canada (February 2009)	17 (out of 49)	2 (out of 145)	Austria Bolivia Cuba Denmark Norway Pakistan	Rejected.
New Zealand (May 2009)	8 (out of 17)	3 (out of 64)	Austria Iran Mexico Pakistan	Accepted, with qualification.
United States (August 2010)	9 (out of 96)	8 (out of 228)	Bolivia Finland Ghana Iran Libya New Zealand Nicaragua Venezuela	5/8 Accepted. 2/8 Accepted in part. 1/8 Rejected.[†]
Australia (January/February 2010)	7 (out of 13)	3 (out of 145)	Bolivia Denmark Ghana Guatemala Hungary Norway	1/3 Accepted. 2/3 Accepted in part.
Canada II (February 2013)	10 (out of 47)	4 (out of 162)	Cape Verde Cuba Mexico Togo	Rejected.
New Zealand II (January 2014)	12 (out of 54)	1 (out of 155)	Norway	Accepted, with qualification.
United States II (May 2015)	10 (out of 91)	2 (out of 343)	Bolivia Egypt	Accepted, with qualification.
Australia II (October 2015)	9 (out of 22)	3 (out of 290)	Estonia Hungary Senegal	Rejected.

Table One: CANZUS States and the Declaration (UNDRIP) in the UPR

† This recommendation was presumably rejected because it did not make sense. It recommended "that the [Declaration] be

used as a guide to interpret the State obligations under the Convention relating to indigenous peoples." See A/HRC/16/11 (2011), at [92.204].

So, with these caveats on board, what does the CANZUS experience show us about use of the Declaration in the UPR? The first point to note is that, because of the original CANZUS opposition to the Declaration, initial references to it focused on its endorsement. The first three reviews occurred before each state had reversed its position on the Declaration, and so there were a number of recommendations encouraging the state to endorse the Declaration. Canada received one such recommendation, New Zealand received three and the United States received seven. This type of recommendation is similar to the numerous recommendations most states receive urging them to ratify any outstanding non-ratified treaties. Such recommendations may not necessarily result in improvement to the human rights of individuals and groups, as they are simply about commitment to human rights standards which, given the huge gap between ratification and implementation, may not ultimately lead to any improvement to the human rights situation on the ground. On the other hand, in the specific context of the Declaration, these recommendations were probably a useful additional pressure on CANZUS states to reverse their position.

With the Declaration now endorsed by all four CANZUS states, the dialogue around the Declaration has shifted to implementation. Recommendations to states now tend to refer generally to "implementation" or to the need for a national action plan or a reform process. So, for example, during Australia's first review, Guatemala recommended that Australia launch a constitutional reform process to better recognise and protect the rights of Aboriginals and Torres Strait Islanders which would include a framework covering the principles and objectives of the Declaration.[16] In its second review, Canada received two recommendations (from Cape Verde and Mexico) to adopt a national plan of action to implement the Declaration and two recommendations (from Cuba and Togo) to implement the Declaration.[17]

In terms of the way in which CANZUS states themselves have used the Declaration in their national reports, in seven of the eight reviews, the national report of the state itself has referred to the Declaration. The one exception was Canada's first review. In the other reviews, the state has typically commented generally on the country's position on the Declaration, either foreshadowing a change of position, or noting that the state had moved to endorse the Declaration.

16 A/HRC/17/10 (2011), at [86.107]. This recommendation was accepted by Australia, which noted that it was "committed to pursuing recognition of Indigenous peoples in the Australian Constitution and has appointed an Expert Panel to develop options and lead a wide-ranging national public consultation and engagement program." See A/HRC/17/10/Add.1 (2011), at [4].
17 A/HRC/24/11 (2013), at [128.60], [128.61], [128.66] and [128.67].

In Australia's national report for its second review, it simply noted that "Australia continues to support the [Declaration] as a set of important guiding principles for the Government's engagement with Indigenous Australians."[18] While the national reports all discussed the particular human rights issues facing indigenous peoples, not one of them referred to the relevant Declaration articles while doing so.

It is with the stakeholder submissions that the Declaration is currently being used most innovatively in the UPR process. While many stakeholder submissions in the first three reviews simply called for the state to reverse its position on the Declaration, a handful in those first reviews, and still more since then, refer to individual articles of the Declaration. For example, for Canada's first review, Athabasca Chipewyan First Nation referred to articles 3-5 of the Declaration in relation to land contamination, article 7 in relation to carcinogens and article 32 in relation to failure to consult.[19] Similarly, in Australia's first review, Amnesty International referred to article 27 in connection with leases that do not allow community residents the right of residence.[20] In Canada's second review, the joint submission of the First Nations Child and Family Caring Society of Canada and the Native Youth Sexual Health Network referred to article 7 in support of the assertion that indigenous children and youth have the right to life and to be free from any act of genocide.[21] These references to individual articles are the type of specificity to be encouraged in the future, as they deepen engagement with the content of the Declaration.

This specificity could also be developed by states that regularly make recommendations on the Declaration. As indicated in Table One, states who have made recommendations referring to the Declaration at least twice are Austria, Bolivia, Cuba, Denmark, Ghana, Hungary, Iran, Mexico and Norway. It is these states who are most likely to be receptive to suggestions from NGOs for more regular and more specific reference to the Declaration.

Finally, some comment on how CANZUS states have responded to Declaration recommendations is necessary. As indicated in Table One, New Zealand and the United States have tended towards accepting the Declaration recommendations, although this is sometimes qualified. For example, in its second review, the United States "supported" the two recommendations from Egypt and Bolivia to implement the Declaration,[22] but noted that this support was "consistent with our 2010 Announcement of Support for the Declaration."[23] Australia took a similar

---

18   A/HRC/WG.6/23/AUS/1 (2015), at [39].
19   Submission of Athabasca Chipewyan First Nation (2008), at [16], [19] and [24].
20   Submission of Amnesty International (2010), at 2.
21   Submission of the First Nations Child and Family Caring Society of Canada and the Native Youth Sexual Health Network (JS18) (2012), at 4.
22   A/HRC/30/12 (2015), at [176.322]-[176.323].
23   A/HRC/30/12/Add.1 (2015), at [11].

approach to New Zealand and the United States in its first review, but its approach appears to have hardened somewhat in its second review, where it rejected the Declaration recommendations, along the lines of the Canadian approach. In both its first and second reviews, Canada rejected all recommendations relating to the Declaration. This is partly explicable for its first review which took place in February 2009 before it had reversed its position on the Declaration. However, for its second review, it rejected all four recommendations on the Declaration asserting that the Declaration is "an aspirational, non-binding instrument" but "Canada will continue to work in partnership with Aboriginal peoples on many of the issues addressed in the Declaration, including in the areas of education, economic development, housing, child and family services, access to safe drinking water, and the extension of human rights protection and matrimonial real property protection to First Nations on reserve."[24] It might be suggested that while Canada's approach appears more antagonistic, it is perhaps also more transparent, as it states Canada's position clearly. Indeed, the underlying position of all four states appears to be similar, but Canada is perhaps more honest about its position.

D. New Zealand's UPR Experience in 2014

During New Zealand's first review in 2009, the focus was on urging New Zealand to endorse the Declaration. Now that endorsement has been achieved, it is useful to look at New Zealand's second review in 2014 in some detail and consider how the UPR might be better utilised to support implementation of the Declaration.

1. Use of the Declaration by NGOs

As noted above, it is NGOs who are using the Declaration the most innovatively and creatively in the UPR. Of the 54 NGO submissions for New Zealand's second review, twelve of these made some reference to the Declaration.[25] A number of submissions referred to New Zealand's 2010 endorsement of the Declaration. Two submissions (Human Rights Commission, CEDAW Coalition) simply noted New Zealand's 2010 endorsement of the Declaration. Three other submissions (Te Rūnanga o Te Rarawa, the joint submission of Aotearoa Indigenous Rights Trust and Peace Movement Aotearoa (AIRT/PMA), and the joint submission of Edmund Rice International and Edmund Rice Justice Aotearoa Justice Foundation) also referred to New Zealand's endorsement, but went on to criticise the conditionality of that endorsement. Edmund Rice noted that "the New

---

24 A/HRC/24/11/Add.1 (2013), at [19].
25 Note, however, that the OHCHR stakeholder summary only notes two NGOs as referring to the Declaration. See A/HRC/WG.6/18/NZL/3 (2013), at [26] and [82].

Zealand government does not take their responsibilities under the Declaration sufficiently seriously,"[26] while Te Rūnanga o Te Rarawa noted that New Zealand's position on the Declaration was "a deliberate limitation on evolving New Zealand's legal and constitutional frameworks to align with internationally agreed human rights standards."[27]

Two of the NGOs who critiqued the Government's luke-warm endorsement of the Declaration went on to make reasonably comprehensive use of the Declaration throughout their submissions. The AIRT/PMA submission referred to the right of self-determination and the right to FPIC.[28] Two examples were provided of New Zealand's failure to respect the right to FPIC – the awarding of an exploration permit to Petrobras in 2010[29] and the partial privatisation of state-owned energy companies in 2012-2013. Te Rūnanga o Te Rarawa also referred to the need for FPIC. It called specifically for "a [Declaration] implementation strategy" and for UPR reports to include "mandatory consideration of Indigenous rights as outlined in the [Declaration]."[30] It also called for a national plan of action to achieve the full realisation of the right to Māori health and health quality which is consistent with a rights-based approach to health as outlined in the Declaration, and the need for the rights to education and cultural heritage to be explicitly enshrined in domestic law regulation and policy consistent with the Declaration.[31] Some submissions referred to the Declaration in the context of discrete human rights issues. Two submissions (Edmund Rice and the joint submission of Just Speak and the Wellington Community Justice Project) referred to the Declaration in the context of the over-representation of Māori in the criminal justice system.[32] Two other submissions (Ngāti Huarere ki Whangapoua Trust and Ruawaipu Iwi Te Tiriti Claims Settlement Authority) alleged violation of numerous articles of the Declaration arising from the Treaty claims settlement process, particularly in relation to the Crown policy of selecting those groups with whom it negotiates.[33]

Finally, it is worth noting particularly innovative uses of the Declaration. Three NGOs used the Declaration, rather than other human rights standards, as

---

26 Submission of Edmund Rice International and Edmund Rice Justice Aotearoa Justice Foundation (2013), Appendix One, at [9].
27 Submission of Te Rūnanga o Te Rarawa (2013), at [2.4].
28 Submission of Aotearoa Indigenous Rights Trust and Peace Movement Aotearoa (2013), at 4-7.
29 For comment on the Declaration and its implications for mining in New Zealand, see the chapter by Eruetī and Down in this book.
30 Submission of Te Rūnanga o Te Rarawa (2013), at [3.11]-[3.12].
31 Submission of Te Rūnanga o Te Rarawa (2013), at [3.20] and [3.23].
32 Submission of Edmund Rice International and Edmund Rice Justice Aotearoa Justice Foundation (2013), at [9]-[13]; Submission of Just Speak and Wellington Community Justice Project (2013), at [13]-[17].
33 Submission of Ngāti Huarere ki Whangapoua Trust (2013); Submission of Ruawaipu Iwi Te Tiriti Claims Settlement Authority (2013).

a yardstick for considering the human rights implications of trade, inequality and health for Māori. The submission of "It's Our Future" addressed the likely adverse human rights impacts of the Trans-Pacific Partnership Agreement (TPPA) and noted that, based on experience with investor-state dispute settlement in other free trade agreements, the TPPA is likely to result in breaches of the Declaration, particularly in relation to the environment.[34] In its submission, the Council of Christian Social Services noted that growing income inequality in New Zealand was having a disproportionate impact on Māori and would affect the ability of New Zealand to fulfil its obligations under article 21 of the Declaration.[35] The New Zealand Nurses Organisation focused its submission on the failure of the Government to collect Māori health workforce data and the consequential impact of this on addressing Māori health workforce deficits which in turn impact on the rights of Māori to good health. The submission referred to article 24(2) of the Declaration and argued that the failure to collect Māori health workforce data meant that no confidence could be placed in any Māori health workforce strategy or in achieving health equity for Māori.[36]

2. Use of the Declaration by New Zealand

In its second review, the Government referred to the Declaration only once in its national report. It noted that New Zealand had moved to support the Declaration in April 2010 and that the statement of support "affirmed New Zealand's commitment to the common objectives of the Declaration and the Treaty of Waitangi, which continues to form the basis of the relationship between Māori and the Government."[37] The national report makes it clear that it is the Treaty of Waitangi that is the key framework for the Crown–Māori relationship. Implicitly, it suggests that the Treaty of Waitangi is a preferable alternative to the Declaration in dealing with the rights of Māori.[38] The introduction to the national report notes that the signing of the Treaty was a "seminal event" which established a partnership between British representatives and Māori and which continues to exert "a powerful influence on New Zealand's human rights story."[39] New Zealand identified six key human rights priorities in its national report, the first of which was "[s]trengthening the partnership between Government and Māori by continuing to support Māori to realise their potential

---

34　Submission of "It's Our Future NZ" (2013), at [4.2].
35　Submission of New Zealand Council of Christian Social Services (2013), at [15].
36　Submission of New Zealand Nurses Organisation (2013), at [19]-[22].
37　A/HRC/WG.6/18/NZL/1 (2013), at [20].
38　For similar commentary on Canada's position on UNDRIP, see Benjamin Authers "Representation and Suspicion in Canada's Appearance under the Universal Periodic Review" in Hilary Charlesworth and Emma Larking above n 9 at 169–186, at 183–184.
39　A/HRC/WG.6/18/NZL/1 (2013), at [3].

and continuing the momentum on achieving fair, just and durable settlements of historical claims under the Treaty of Waitangi."[40] Elsewhere in the report, there are references to various human rights issues which specifically affect Māori, including social inequalities,[41] repeal of the Foreshore and Seabed Act 2004,[42] settlement of historical Māori land claims[43] and Māori experience in the criminal justice system.[44]

During the interactive dialogue in the Working Group of the HRC, the Treaty of Waitangi again received considerable emphasis, both by other states in their comments, and by New Zealand in its responses. New Zealand clarified that the Treaty of Waitangi was part of its constitutional arrangements, and that "[t]he arrangements continued to evolve through engagement with Māori and through negotiation and acceptance of new international commitments."[45] There were just two explicit references to the Declaration in the interactive dialogue, with both Norway and Uruguay welcoming New Zealand's statement of support for the Declaration.[46]

New Zealand received one recommendation from Norway to "take concrete measures to ensure the implementation and promotion of the Declaration."[47] New Zealand accepted this recommendation but with a qualification – "[the Declaration] is consistent with the Treaty of Waitangi, which continues to be the central focus for the Government's efforts to resolve issues affecting New Zealand's indigenous people."[48] As noted above, although New Zealand accepted the recommendation, its explanation indicates that its underlying position is in fact quite similar to that of Canada, and as noted by some of the NGO submissions, New Zealand's support for the Declaration is somewhat less than whole-hearted. The Treaty of Waitangi remains the paramount framework for approaching indigenous issues in New Zealand.

It is important to note that, while only one recommendation was received which specifically mentioned the Declaration, a number of other recommendations concern the human rights of Māori. Indeed, the database of UPR-Info which categorises all UPR recommendations identifies 32 other recommendations from the total of 155 recommendations made to New Zealand as addressing "indigenous peoples".[49] While it is good that issues which affect the human rights of Māori

40 A/HRC/WG.6/18/NZL/1 (2013), at [4].
41 A/HRC/WG.6/18/NZL/1 (2013), at [31]-[36].
42 A/HRC/WG.6/18/NZL/1 (2013), at [38]-[39].
43 A/HRC/WG.6/18/NZL/1 (2013), at [40].
44 A/HRC/WG.6/18/NZL/1 (2013), at [41]-[45].
45 A/HRC/26/3 (2014), at [47].
46 A/HRC/26/3 (2014), at [55] and [85].
47 A/HRC/26/3 (2014), at [128.89].
48 A/HRC/26/3/Add.1 (2014), at [24].
49 See <www.upr-info.org>. UPR-Info is a Geneva-based NGO dedicated to promoting the UPR.

are being raised in the UPR process, it would be even better to see them being linked to the specific human rights standards in the Declaration. Considering these issues within the framework of the Declaration, the strongest expression of the rights of indigenous peoples at the international level, would ensure that the UPR process could be used to support meaningful implementation of the Declaration on the ground in New Zealand.

3. The New Zealand Human Rights National Plan of Action 2015–2019

In June 2015, the New Zealand Human Rights Commission launched the New Zealand Human Rights National Plan of Action 2015–2019 (NPA).[50] This is an online interactive tool which aims to monitor the Government's progress implementing recommendations from the 2014 UPR. It sets out the actions the Government is taking in response to each of the recommendations accepted by New Zealand in the 2014 review. It will hopefully evolve into a useful tool to enable NGOs and ordinary New Zealanders to monitor Government progress in implementing the recommendations.

In relation to indigenous rights, the NPA currently lists 34 recommendations as relating to the "population group" of Māori, 29 of which were accepted by the Government and five of which were rejected.[51] The NPA identifies 32 Government "actions" that are identified as responding to these recommendations. Curiously, twelve recommendations (all accepted) are listed as relating to "indigenous rights," with seven Government "actions" identified as responding to these recommendations. All twelve of these "indigenous rights" recommendations are also categorised as relating to the "population group" of Māori, but it could perhaps be argued that all of the 34 recommendations which relate to the population group of Māori should also be categorised as relating to indigenous rights. This different categorisation is itself illustrative

---

It provides capacity-building tools to different actors in the UPR process including states, NGOs and National Human Rights Institutions.

50 See 'New Zealand Human Rights National Plan of Action' <http://npa.hrc.co.nz/#/>.

51 Two of the rejected recommendations were that New Zealand ratify ILO Convention 169 concerning Indigenous and Tribal Peoples in Independent Countries. The third rejected recommendation was that New Zealand "continue to address all forms of political, economic and social discrimination against the Maori and Pacific population by meeting their various demands for constitutional and legal reforms and recognition." The fourth was that New Zealand "enshrine, in the framework of the current constitutional review, the principle of equality between men and women, and redouble efforts to improve the situation of the Māori and the Pacifika in the areas of health and employment on one hand, and strengthen the specific measures taken in their favour to raise the level of education of their children on the other hand." The fifth rejected recommendation was that New Zealand "develop, in partnership with civil society, a national action plan for women with defined targets, to address issues such as violence against women, pay inequality, the situation of Māori and Pacific women, and women with disabilities."

of a failure to consider human rights issues which affect Māori as automatically also being an indigenous rights issue.

One notable feature of the NPA is that it is framed around the UPR recommendations rather than recommendations of the treaty bodies. Although the online tool has a feature which also groups the issues according to treaty body, it does not use the treaty body recommendations as the yardstick. This is perhaps a shortcoming, as the recommendations of the treaty bodies, which are comprised of independent human rights experts, tend to be more specific and measureable than those which emerge from the more political UPR process.

However, it is early days yet with the NPA and, if it comes to be used as a key reference point by Government and NGOs, then this will add some strength to the UPR as a monitoring mechanism for implementation of all human rights in New Zealand. This would then be an additional reason to encourage NGOs and Governments to move towards more specific references to the Declaration in the UPR, so that these can be picked up and monitored in subsequent versions of the NPA.

E. Future Prospects

In his capacity as the UN Special Rapporteur on the Rights of Indigenous Peoples, James Anaya has noted that the UPR is an "important tool" in promoting the rights affirmed in the Declaration.[52] Regular reference to the Declaration certainly confirms the support evident at the time the Declaration was adopted and "indicates an international consensus on the normative expression of the rights of indigenous peoples in a way that is consistent with existing human rights standards."[53] However it is important to consider whether, and if so how, the UPR process might better support implementation of the Declaration on the ground in New Zealand.

The UPR is in many respects a fairly modest tool for promoting implementation of the Declaration. In particular, it is a general human rights mechanism which monitors the entire human rights situation in a given country, across the full spectrum of civil, political, economic, social and cultural rights, as well as the rights of all vulnerable groups including indigenous peoples. As it is also a very constrained process in terms of page limits and time available for the interactive dialogue, there is limited scope for in-depth consideration of indigenous rights issues. Here, the UPR can be contrasted with the UN Special Rapporteur on the Rights of Indigenous Peoples who has been specifically tasked by the HRC with

---

52 A/HRC/9/9 (2008), at [63].
53 Asia Pacific Forum and Office of the High Commissioner for Human Rights *The United Nations Declaration on the Rights of Indigenous Peoples: A Manual for National Human Rights Institutions* (APF and OHCHR, Sydney, 2013), at 47.

promotion of the Declaration.⁵⁴ Similarly, a number of the treaty bodies including the Committee on the Elimination of Racial Discrimination (under CERD), the Human Rights Committee (under ICCPR), the Committee on Economic, Social and Cultural Rights (under ICESCR) and the Committee on the Rights of the Child (under CRC) have been able to ensure much more specific and tailored focus on the situation of indigenous peoples and, increasingly, on the Declaration.⁵⁵ The treaty bodies and the special procedures are also run by independent human rights experts in contrast to the diplomats who are the primary participants in the UPR process and not necessarily experts on indigenous rights or the Declaration itself.

Nevertheless, despite its shortcomings, a notable feature of the UPR process to date is that it appears to have captured the attention of states and many NGOs in a way that the treaty bodies have not. There is an undeniable momentum around the UPR process. The fact that the New Zealand Human Rights Commission has used the recommendations from New Zealand's second UPR as the framework for the NPA, rather than the recommendations of treaty bodies, is an apt illustration of exactly this. While we might rightly be cynical about the reasons for this apparent preference for the "softer" UPR mechanism, the fact remains that it has a certain amount of impetus and it should therefore be leveraged if possible.

Another reason to leverage the UPR, and indeed the other international mechanisms, as much as possible is that the UN's two dedicated bodies on indigenous peoples (the Permanent Forum on Indigenous Issues and the Expert Mechanism on the Rights of Indigenous Peoples) are both precluded by their mandates from considering human rights abuses or commenting adversely on a particular country situation.⁵⁶ The UPR at least enables focus on a country situation and the opportunity to raise particular human rights abuses against indigenous peoples.⁵⁷

A key way in which the UPR could better support implementation of the Declaration is for it to be more regularly referenced in the UPR. While many human rights issues of indigenous peoples are raised in the UPR, most are not framed using the Declaration. For example, the stakeholder summary for Australia's second review notes that 14 of the 22 stakeholder submissions referred to "indigenous related issues",⁵⁸ but, as noted in Table One, only nine of these submissions actually referred to the Declaration. In the New Zealand context, the

---

54 A/HRC/RES/6/12 (2007), at [1(g)]; A/HRC/RES/15/14 (2010), at [1(g)].
55 See chapter by Claire Breen on the Convention on the Rights of the Child in this book.
56 Note that in practice, however, NGOs have been successful in bringing particular situations to the attention of both mechanisms.
57 In terms of documentation, both OHCHR's stakeholder summary and its compilation of other UN information on each state include an "Indigenous peoples" or "Minorities and indigenous peoples" heading, enabling indigenous issues to be separately highlighted.
58 A/HRC/WG.6/23/AUS/3 (2015), at [66].

submission of Action for Children and Youth Aotearoa on New Zealand's second review raised a number of human rights issues concerning Māori children, but referred only to the Convention on the Rights of the Child (CRC).[59] In future UPR submissions, referencing both the Declaration and CRC would be useful.[60] NGOs and indigenous peoples' organisations can play a key role in leading the way here. Non-indigenous NGOs in particular should be encouraged to refer to the standards in the Declaration alongside any related standards in the relevant treaties. Such an approach would eventually result in the Declaration becoming more embedded in the UPR process and being the key interpretation tool for defining the obligations of states and guiding the recommendations with regard to indigenous peoples. It would also "reflect the indivisibility and interconnectedness of human rights – leading to better outcomes for Indigenous people."[61] In addition, the more regularly the Declaration is accepted as the appropriate standard by states, then the stronger the case becomes that it is part of customary international law.[62]

A second way in which the Declaration can be better leveraged in the UPR process is by encouraging more concrete and specific recommendations. One of the reasons why the UPR mechanism appeals to states is that although it enables adverse comment on a particular state, it is relatively non-threatening. The political nature of the process means that any adverse comment is delivered diplomatically rather than confrontationally. The UPR was not intended to be and does not operate as a "naming and shaming" mechanism.[63] The recommendations made to an individual state are essentially bilateral recommendations made in a multilateral forum; they are not in fact the recommendations of the Human Rights Council itself. This arguably gives the recommendations a "softer" and less confrontational nature than the concluding observations made by treaty bodies or the often very direct comments of the Special Rapporteur on Indigenous Peoples. The softer nature of UPR recommendations is perhaps one of the reasons for the high level of state engagement with the process; there is less fear of being explicitly named and shamed.

There has, however, been some critique of the language used by states in their UPR recommendations.[64] Drawing on the work of academic Edward

---

59 Submission of Action for Children and Youth Aotearoa (2013).
60 For a related argument, see the chapter by Claire Breen in this book.
61 Jackie Hartley, Paul Joffe and Jennifer Preston "Hopes and Challenges on the Road Ahead" in Jackie Hartley, Paul Joffe and Jennifer Preston (eds) *Realizing the UN Declaration on the Rights of Indigenous Peoples: Triumph, Hope and Action* (Purich Publishing Ltd, Saskatoon, 2010), 189–194, at 191.
62 On this point, see Claire Charters "The Year in Review: Indigenous Peoples' Rights Under International Law" (2008) 5 NZYBIL 199 at 205–206.
63 See generally Elvira Dominguez Redondo above n 9.
64 See Edward R McMahon "Herding Cats and Sheep: Assessing State and Regional Behavior

McMahon,[65] UPR-Info categorises the recommendations made by states into one of five "action categories" based on the verb used in the recommendation and the nature of the action recommended.[66] Category one (minimal action) includes recommendations where states are asked to "share" or "seek", whereas category five (specific action) includes recommendations such as "ratify", "amend" or "abolish." New Zealand's recommendation to the United States that it "continue its forward movement"[67] on the Declaration was categorised as a category two "continuing action" by UPR-Info. It is a perfect example of a weak and almost meaningless recommendation. Such recommendations do not lead to any change in state action, or improvement of the human rights situation on the ground, which is after all one of the underlying aims of the UPR process. Examples of more concrete recommendations made by states include a recommendation made by Bolivia and accepted by Colombia, that Colombia "take into account the [Declaration] in the implementation of its public policies."[68] And, even more strongly, Mexico recommended and the Russian Federation accepted that it "comply with the principles contained in the [Declaration]."[69]

There is considerable scope for NGO advocacy here. As noted above, some states are more inclined to raise indigenous issues in the interactive dialogue.[70] NGOs should lobby these states with suggestions for very concrete and specific recommendations that might be made to New Zealand using the Declaration as the yardstick.

Finally, the UPR, along with other international human rights mechanisms, is at risk of becoming something which simply occurs periodically in Geneva. Although one of the objectives of the UPR is the improvement of the human rights situation on the ground, there remains quite a gap between what happens in Geneva and translating that into actual human rights improvements on the ground in New Zealand. In follow-up work, NGOs should ensure that they use the recommendations made to and accepted by New Zealand in their lobbying and advocacy at home. NGOs have a significant role to play in ensuring that the

---

in the Universal Periodic Review Mechanism of the United Nations Human Rights Council" (Working Paper, University of Vermont, 2010); Edward R McMahon "The Universal Periodic Review: A Work in Progress – An Evaluation of the First Cycle of the New UPR Mechanism of the United Nations Human Rights Council" (Friedrich Ebert Stiftung, Geneva, September 2012).

65 <https://www.upr-info.org/database/files/Database_Action_Category.pdf>.
66 See <http://www.upr-info.org/database/files/Database_Action_Category.pdf>.
67 A/HRC/16/11 (2011), at [92.205].
68 A/HRC/10/82 (2009), at [87.61]. UPR-Info categorises this as a category four "general action" recommendation.
69 A/HRC/11/19 (2009), at [85.56]; A/HRC/11/19/Add.1/Rev.1 (2009), at 8. UPR-Info classifies this as a category four "general action" recommendation.
70 In this regard, UPR-Info has an excellent database for searching recommending states. See <www.upr-info.org>.

recommendations are used as a platform for action and advocacy in New Zealand, and not just referred to every four-and-a-half years in Geneva. In this regard, the Human Rights Commission's National Plan of Action will hopefully prove to be a useful tool for monitoring implementation of the UPR recommendations accepted by New Zealand and, in so doing, supporting practical implementation of the Declaration.

F. Conclusion

The ultimate aim of the UPR is to improve the human rights situation on the ground. Although the UPR mechanism is a useful advocacy tool to support implementation of the Declaration, it is limited by some of its key features, including its focus on all human rights, the fact that it is a mechanism established and run by diplomats, and its practical constraints in terms of page limits and the time available for dialogue with states. Nevertheless, there is some scope for better use of the UPR. In particular, states and NGOs should be encouraged to refer to the Declaration as the relevant yardstick for considering the human rights of indigenous peoples, including by more regular and more specific reference to its individual articles. There should also be more specificity in the recommendations made to states on indigenous rights issues. In addition, it is important that the UPR process is not simply another international human rights mechanism which operates in Geneva but has no impact beyond. In 2019, when New Zealand is next reviewed under the UPR, it would be heartening to see the Declaration being used by the New Zealand government, other states and NGOs as the primary reference point for all Māori issues. This would mean that the UPR process itself could then more meaningfully assist in supporting implementation of the Declaration in Aotearoa New Zealand.

Appendix:
The United Nations Declaration on the Rights of Indigenous Peoples

Resolution adopted by the General Assembly

61/295. United Nations Declaration on the Rights of Indigenous Peoples

The General Assembly,

Taking note of the recommendation of the Human Rights Council contained in its resolution[1] of 29 June 2006, by which the Council adopted the text of the United Nations Declaration on the Rights of Indigenous Peoples,

Recalling its resolution 61/178 of 20 December 2006, by which it decided to defer consideration of and action on the Declaration to allow time for further consultations thereon, and also decided to conclude its consideration before the end of the sixty-first session of the General Assembly,

Adopts the United Nations Declaration on the Rights of Indigenous Peoples as contained in the annex to the present resolution.

107th plenary meeting
13 September 2007

United Nations Declaration on the Rights of Indigenous Peoples

The General Assembly,

Guided by the purposes and principles of the Charter of the United Nations, and good faith in the fulfilment of the obligations assumed by States in accordance with the Charter,

Affirming that indigenous peoples are equal to all other peoples, while recognizing the right of all peoples to be different, to consider themselves different, and to be respected as such,

Affirming alsothat all peoples contribute to the diversity and richness of civilizations and cultures, which constitute the common heritage of humankind,

---

[1] See Official Records of the General Assembly, Sixty-first Session, Supplement No. 53 (A/61/53), part one, chap. II, sect. A.

Affirming further that all doctrines, policies and practices based on or advocating superiority of peoples or individuals on the basis of national origin or racial, religious, ethnic or cultural differences are racist, scientifically false, legally invalid, morally condemnable and socially unjust,

Reaffirming that indigenous peoples, in the exercise of their rights, should be free from discrimination of any kind,

Concerned that indigenous peoples have suffered from historic injustices as a result of, inter alia, their colonization and dispossession of their lands, territories and resources, thus preventing them from exercising, in particular, their right to development in accordance with their own needs and interests,

Recognizing the urgent need to respect and promote the inherent rights of indigenous peoples which derive from their political, economic and social structures and from their cultures, spiritual traditions, histories and philosophies, especially their rights to their lands, territories and resources,

Recognizing also the urgent need to respect and promote the rights of indigenous peoples affirmed in treaties, agreements and other constructive arrangements with States,

Welcoming the fact that indigenous peoples are organizing themselves for political, economic, social and cultural enhancement and in order to bring to an end all forms of discrimination and oppression wherever they occur,

Convinced that control by indigenous peoples over developments affecting them and their lands, territories and resources will enable them to maintain and strengthen their institutions, cultures and traditions, and to promote their development in accordance with their aspirations and needs,

Recognizing that respect for indigenous knowledge, cultures and traditional practices contributes to sustainable and equitable development and proper management of the environment,

Emphasizing the contribution of the demilitarization of the lands and territories of indigenous peoples to peace, economic and social 3progress and development, understanding and friendly relations among nations and peoples of the world,

Recognizing in particular the right of indigenous families and communities to retain shared responsibility for the upbringing, training, education and wellbeing of their children, consistent with the rights of the child,

Considering that the rights affirmed in treaties, agreements and other constructive arrangements between States and indigenous peoples are, in some situations, matters of international concern, interest, responsibility and character,

Considering alsothat treaties, agreements and other constructive arrangements, and the relationship they represent, are the basis for a strengthened partnership between indigenous peoples and States,

Acknowledging that the Charter of the United Nations, the International Covenant on Economic, Social and Cultural Rights[2] and the International Covenant on Civil and Political Rights,[2] as well as the Vienna Declaration and Programme of Action,[3] affirm the fundamental importance of the right to self-determination of all peoples, by virtue of which they freely determine their political status and freely pursue their economic, social and cultural development,

Bearing in mind that nothing in this Declaration may be used to deny any peoples their right to self-determination, exercised in conformity with international law,

Convinced that the recognition of the rights of indigenous peoples in this Declaration will enhance harmonious and cooperative relations between the State and indigenous peoples, based on principles of justice, democracy, respect for human rights, non-discrimination and good faith,

Encouraging States to comply with and effectively implement all their obligations as they apply to indigenous peoples under international instruments, in particular those related to human rights, in consultation and cooperation with the peoples concerned,Emphasizingthat the United Nations has an important and continuing role to play in promoting and protecting the rights of indigenous peoples,

Believing that this Declaration is a further important step forward for the recognition, promotion and protection of the rights and freedoms of indigenous peoples and in the development of relevant activities of the United Nations

---

2   See resolution 2200 A (XXI), annex.
3   A/CONF.157/24 (Part I), chap. III.

system in this field,

Recognizing and reaffirming that indigenous individuals are entitled without discrimination to all human rights recognized in international law, and that indigenous peoples possess collective rights which are indispensable for their existence, wellbeing and integral development as peoples,

Recognizing that the situation of indigenous peoples varies from region to region and from country to country and that the significance of national and regional particularities and various historical and cultural backgrounds should be taken into consideration,

Solemnly proclaims the following United Nations Declaration on the Rights of Indigenous Peoples as a standard of achievement to be pursued in a spirit of partnership and mutual respect:

Article 1
Indigenous peoples have the right to the full enjoyment, as a collective or as individuals, of all human rights and fundamental freedoms as recognized in the Charter of the United Nations, the Universal Declaration of Human Rights[4] and international human rights law.

Article 2
Indigenous peoples and individuals are free and equal to all other peoples and individuals and have the right to be free from any kind of discrimination, in the exercise of their rights, in particular that based on their indigenous origin or identity.

Article 3
Indigenous peoples have the right to self-determination. By virtue of that right they freely determine their political status and freely pursue their economic, social and cultural development.

Article 4
Indigenous peoples, in exercising their right to self-determination, have the right to autonomy or self-government in matters relating to their internal and local affairs, as well as ways and means for financing their autonomous functions.

---

[4] Resolution 217 A (III)

Article 5
Indigenous peoples have the right to maintain and strengthen their distinct political, legal, economic, social and cultural institutions, while retaining their right to participate fully, if they so choose, in the political, economic, social and cultural life of the State.

Article 6
Every indigenous individual has the right to a nationality.

Article 7
(1) Indigenous individuals have the rights to life, physical and mental integrity, liberty and security of person.
(2) Indigenous peoples have the collective right to live in freedom, peace and security as distinct peoples and shall not be subjected to any act of genocide or any other act of violence, including forcibly removing children of the group to another group.

Article 8
(1) Indigenous peoples and individuals have the right not to be subjected to forced assimilation or destruction of their culture.
(2) States shall provide effective mechanisms for prevention of, and redress for:
    (a) Any action which has the aim or effect of depriving them of their integrity as distinct peoples, or of their cultural values or ethnic identities;
    (b) Any action which has the aim or effect of dispossessing them of their lands, territories or resources;
    (c) Any form of forced population transfer which has the aim or effect of violating or undermining any of their rights;
    (d) Any form of forced assimilation or integration;
    (e) Any form of propaganda designed to promote or incite racial or ethnic discrimination directed against them.

Article 9
Indigenous peoples and individuals have the right to belong to an indigenous community or nation, in accordance with the traditions and customs of the community or nation concerned. No discrimination of any kind may arise from the exercise of such a right.

Article 10
Indigenous peoples shall not be forcibly removed from their lands or territories.

No relocation shall take place without the free, prior and informed consent of the indigenous peoples concerned and after agreement on just and fair compensation and, where possible, with the option of return.

Article 11
(1) Indigenous peoples have the right to practise and revitalize their cultural traditions and customs. This includes the right to maintain, protect and develop the past, present and future manifestations of their cultures, such as archaeological and historical sites, artefacts, designs, ceremonies, technologies and visual and performing arts and literature.
(2) States shall provide redress through effective mechanisms, which may include restitution, developed in conjunction with indigenous peoples, with respect to their cultural, intellectual, religious and spiritual property taken without their free, prior and informed consent or in violation of their laws, traditions and customs.

Article 12
(1) Indigenous peoples have the right to manifest, practise, develop and teach their spiritual and religious traditions, customs and ceremonies; the right to maintain, protect, and have access in privacy to their religious and cultural sites; the right to the use and control of their ceremonial objects; and the right to the repatriation of their human remains.
(2) States shall seek to enable the access and/or repatriation of ceremonial objects and human remains in their possession through fair, transparent and effective mechanisms developed in conjunction with indigenous peoples concerned.

Article 13
(1) Indigenous peoples have the right to revitalize, use, develop and transmit to future generations their histories, languages, oral traditions, philosophies, writing systems and literatures, and to designate and retain their own names for communities, places and persons.
(2) States shall take effective measures to ensure that this right is protected and also to ensure that indigenous peoples can understand and be understood in political, legal and administrative proceedings, where necessary through the provision of interpretation or by other appropriate means.

Article 14
(1) Indigenous peoples have the right to establish and control their educational systems and institutions providing education in their own languages, in a manner appropriate to their cultural methods of teaching and learning.
(2) Indigenous individuals, particularly children, have the right to all levels and forms of education of the State without discrimination.
(3) States shall, in conjunction with indigenous peoples, take effective measures, in order for indigenous individuals, particularly children, including those living outside their communities, to have access, when possible, to an education in their own culture and provided in their own language.

Article 15
(1) Indigenous peoples have the right to the dignity and diversity of their cultures, traditions, histories and aspirations which shall be appropriately reflected in education and public information.
(2) States shall take effective measures, in consultation and cooperation with the indigenous peoples concerned, to combat prejudice and eliminate discrimination and to promote tolerance, understanding and good relations among indigenous peoples and all other segments of society.

Article 16
(1) Indigenous peoples have the right to establish their own media in their own languages and to have access to all forms of non-indigenous media without discrimination.
(2) States shall take effective measures to ensure that State-owned media duly reflect indigenous cultural diversity. States, without prejudice to ensuring full freedom of expression, should encourage privately owned media to adequately reflect indigenous cultural diversity.

Article 17
(1) Indigenous individuals and peoples have the right to enjoy fully all rights established under applicable international and domestic labour law.
(2) States shall in consultation and cooperation with indigenous peoples take specific measures to protect indigenous children from economic exploitation and from performing any work that is likely to be hazardous or to interfere with the child's education, or to be harmful to the child's health or physical, mental, spiritual, moral or social

development, taking into account their special vulnerability and the importance of education for their empowerment.

(3) Indigenous individuals have the right not to be subjected to any discriminatory conditions of labour and, inter alia, employment or salary.

Article 18
Indigenous peoples have the right to participate in decision-making in matters which would affect their rights, through representatives chosen by themselves in accordance with their own procedures, as well as to maintain and develop their own indigenous decision-making institutions.

Article 19
States shall consult and cooperate in good faith with the indigenous peoples concerned through their own representative institutions in order to obtain their free, prior and informed consent before adopting and implementing legislative or administrative measures that may affect them.

Article 20
(1) Indigenous peoples have the right to maintain and develop their political, economic and social systems or institutions, to be secure in the enjoyment of their own means of subsistence and development, and to engage freely in all their traditional and other economic activities.

(2) Indigenous peoples deprived of their means of subsistence and development are entitled to just and fair redress.

Article 21
(1) Indigenous peoples have the right, without discrimination, to the improvement of their economic and social conditions, including, inter alia, in the areas of education, employment, vocational training and retraining, housing, sanitation, health and social security.

(2) States shall take effective measures and, where appropriate, special measures to ensure continuing improvement of their economic and social conditions. Particular attention shall be paid to the rights and special needs of indigenous elders, women, youth, children and persons with disabilities.

Article 22
(1) Particular attention shall be paid to the rights and special needs of indigenous elders, women, youth, children and persons with

disabilities in the implementation of this Declaration.
(2) States shall take measures, in conjunction with indigenous peoples, to ensure that indigenous women and children enjoy the full protection and guarantees against all forms of violence and discrimination.

Article 23
Indigenous peoples have the right to determine and develop priorities and strategies for exercising their right to development. In particular, indigenous peoples have the right to be actively involved in developing and determining health, housing and other economic and social programmes affecting them and, as far as possible, to administer such programmes through their own institutions.

Article 24
(1) 1. Indigenous peoples have the right to their traditional medicines and to maintain their health practices, including the conservation of their vital medicinal plants, animals and minerals. Indigenous individuals also have the right to access, without any discrimination, to all social and health services.
(2) Indigenous individuals have an equal right to the enjoyment of the highest attainable standard of physical and mental health. States shall take the necessary steps with a view to achieving progressively the full realization of this right.

Article 25
Indigenous peoples have the right to maintain and strengthen their distinctive spiritual relationship with their traditionally owned or otherwise occupied and used lands, territories, waters and coastal seas and other resources and to uphold their responsibilities to future generations in this regard.

Article 26
(1) Indigenous peoples have the right to the lands, territories and resources which they have traditionally owned, occupied or otherwise used or acquired.
(2) Indigenous peoples have the right to own, use, develop and control the lands, territories and resources that they possess by reason of traditional ownership or other traditional occupation or use, as well as those which they have otherwise acquired.
(3) States shall give legal recognition and protection to these lands, territories and resources. Such recognition shall be conducted with due respect to the customs, traditions and land tenure systems of the indigenous peoples concerned.

Article 27
States shall establish and implement, in conjunction with indigenous peoples concerned, a fair, independent, impartial, open and transparent process, giving due recognition to indigenous peoples' laws, traditions, customs and land tenure systems, to recognize and adjudicate the rights of indigenous peoples pertaining to their lands, territories and resources, including those which were traditionally owned or otherwise occupied or used. Indigenous peoples shall have the right to participate in this process.

Article 28
(1) Indigenous peoples have the right to redress, by means that can include restitution or, when this is not possible, just, fair and equitable compensation, for the lands, territories and resources which they have traditionally owned or otherwise occupied or used, and which have been confiscated, taken, occupied, used or damaged without their free, prior and informed consent.
(2) Unless otherwise freely agreed upon by the peoples concerned, compensation shall take the form of lands, territories and resources 11equal in quality, size and legal status or of monetary compensation or other appropriate redress.

Article 29
(1) Indigenous peoples have the right to the conservation and protection of the environment and the productive capacity of their lands or territories and resources. States shall establish and implement assistance programmes for indigenous peoples for such conservation and protection, without discrimination.
(2) States shall take effective measures to ensure that no storage or disposal of hazardous materials shall take place in the lands or territories of indigenous peoples without their free, prior and informed consent.
(3) States shall also take effective measures to ensure, as needed, that programmes for monitoring, maintaining and restoring the health of indigenous peoples, as developed and implemented by the peoples affected by such materials, are duly implemented.

Article 30
(1) Military activities shall not take place in the lands or territories of indigenous peoples, unless justified by a relevant public interest or otherwise freely agreed with or requested by the indigenous peoples concerned.
(2) States shall undertake effective consultations with the indigenous

peoples concerned, through appropriate procedures and in particular through their representative institutions, prior to using their lands or territories for military activities.

Article 31
(1) Indigenous peoples have the right to maintain, control, protect and develop their cultural heritage, traditional knowledge and traditional cultural expressions, as well as the manifestations of their sciences, technologies and cultures, including human and genetic resources, seeds, medicines, knowledge of the properties of fauna and flora, oral traditions, literatures, designs, sports and traditional games and visual and performing arts. They also have the right to maintain, control, protect and develop their intellectual property over such cultural heritage, traditional knowledge, and traditional cultural expressions.
(2) In conjunction with indigenous peoples, States shall take effective measures to recognize and protect the exercise of these rights.

Article 32
(1) Indigenous peoples have the right to determine and develop priorities and strategies for the development or use of their lands or territories and other resources.
(2) States shall consult and cooperate in good faith with the indigenous peoples concerned through their own representative institutions in order to obtain their free and informed consent prior to the approval of any project affecting their lands or territories and other resources, particularly in connection with the development, utilization or exploitation of mineral, water or other resources.
(3) States shall provide effective mechanisms for just and fair redress for any such activities, and appropriate measures shall be taken to mitigate adverse environmental, economic, social, cultural or spiritual impact.

Article 33
(1) Indigenous peoples have the right to determine their own identity or membership in accordance with their customs and traditions. This does not impair the right of indigenous individuals to obtain citizenship of the States in which they live.
(2) Indigenous peoples have the right to determine the structures and to select the membership of their institutions in accordance with their own procedures.

Article 34
Indigenous peoples have the right to promote, develop and maintain their institutional structures and their distinctive customs, spirituality, traditions, procedures, practices and, in the cases where they exist, juridical systems or customs, in accordance with international human rights standards.

Article 35
Indigenous peoples have the right to determine the responsibilities of individuals to their communities.

Article 36
(1) Indigenous peoples, in particular those divided by international borders, have the right to maintain and develop contacts, relations and cooperation, including activities for spiritual, cultural, political, economic and social purposes, with their own members as well as other peoples across borders.
(2) States, in consultation and cooperation with indigenous peoples, shall take effective measures to facilitate the exercise and ensure the implementation of this right.

Article 37
(1) Indigenous peoples have the right to the recognition, observance and enforcement of treaties, agreements and other constructive arrangements concluded with States or their successors and to have States honour and respect such treaties, agreements and other constructive arrangements.
(2) Nothing in this Declaration may be interpreted as diminishing or eliminating the rights of indigenous peoples contained in treaties, agreements and other constructive arrangements.

Article 38
States, in consultation and cooperation with indigenous peoples, shall take the appropriate measures, including legislative measures, to achieve the ends of this Declaration.

Article 39
Indigenous peoples have the right to have access to financial and technical assistance from States and through international cooperation, for the enjoyment of the rights contained in this Declaration.

Article 40

Indigenous peoples have the right to access to and prompt decision through just and fair procedures for the resolution of conflicts and disputes with States or other parties, as well as to effective remedies for all infringements of their individual and collective rights. Such a decision shall give due consideration to the customs, traditions, rules and legal systems of the indigenous peoples concerned and international human rights.

Article 41

The organs and specialized agencies of the United Nations system and other intergovernmental organizations shall contribute to the full realization of the provisions of this Declaration through the mobilization, inter alia, of financial cooperation and technical assistance. Ways and means of ensuring participation of indigenous peoples on issues affecting them shall be established.

Article 42

The United Nations, its bodies, including the Permanent Forum on Indigenous Issues, and specialized agencies, including at the country level, and States shall promote respect for and full application of the provisions of this Declaration and follow up the effectiveness of this Declaration.

Article 43

The rights recognized herein constitute the minimum standards for the survival, dignity and wellbeing of the indigenous peoples of the world.

Article 44

All the rights and freedoms recognized herein are equally guaranteed to male and female indigenous individuals.

Article 45

Nothing in this Declaration may be construed as diminishing or extinguishing the rights indigenous peoples have now or may acquire in the future.

Article 46

(1) Nothing in this Declaration may be interpreted as implying for any State, people, group or person any right to engage in any activity or to perform any act contrary to the Charter of the United Nations or construed as authorizing or encouraging any action which would dismember or impair, totally or in part, the territorial integrity or political unity of sovereign and independent States.

(2) In the exercise of the rights enunciated in the present Declaration, human rights and fundamental freedoms of all shall be respected. The exercise of the rights set forth in this Declaration shall be subject only to such limitations as are determined by law and in accordance with international human rights obligations. Any such limitations shall be non-discriminatory and strictly necessary solely for the purpose of securing due recognition and respect for the rights and freedoms of others and for meeting the just and most compelling requirements of a democratic society.

(3) The provisions set forth in this Declaration shall be interpreted in accordance with the principles of justice, democracy, respect for human rights, equality, non-discrimination, good governance and good faith.

Index

Action for Children and Youth Aotearoa
 206–7
Adoption Act 1955 71–72, 74
Africa 18, 27, 28, 36, 37, 39, 185
African Commission of Human and Peoples'
 Rights 120, 145
African Group of States 38, 52
Alta outcome document 180–82, 184–89
Amaltal Fishing Co Ltd v Nelson Polytechnic
 (legal case) 54–55, 57
Amnesty International 152–53, 199
Anaya, James
 human rights model 34–35
 mineral resources 120, 164
 self-determination 170
 Treaty of Waitangi settlement process 169
 Universal Periodic Review (UPR) 195, 205
 UN special procedures 156–57, 158, 159,
  162–63, 164, 165, 166–67, 168, 170, 172,
  173
 World Conference on Indigenous Peoples
  2014 175
Annan, Kofi 152
Aotearoa Indigenous Rights Trust 196, 200
articles of the UN Declaration, discussion of
 Article 3 13, 33, 92
 Article 4 92
 Article 11 39
 Article 12 39, 97
 Article 13 97
 Article 14 96
 Article 15 96–97
 Article 23 39, 92
 Article 24 92
 Article 25 115–16
 Article 26 116

Article 32 116, 117
Article 37 62–63
Article 46 50–52, 62–63, 71
Ashe, John 182–83
Asia
 decolonisation model 24, 36
 human rights model 18, 36
 ILO conventions 27
 mixed-model interpretative approach
  38–39
 UN Declaration negotiations 37
 UN membership 28
 UN special procedures 165
 World Conference on Indigenous Peoples
  2014 176, 185
 see also specific countries
Attorney-General v Ngati Apa (legal case)
 66
Australia
 indigenous peoples' advocacy 24
 racial discrimination 54, 56, 60
 Racial Discrimination Act 57
 Universal Periodic Review (UPR) 197,
  198–99, 200, 206
 UN special procedures 155
 World Conference on Indigenous Peoples
  2014 184–85
 see also CANZUS states
Austria 197, 199

Baird, Natalie 17, 20
*Barton-Prescott v Director-General of Social
 Welfare* (legal case) 64, 73, 84
Bolivia 79, 197, 199, 208
Breen, Claire 19
Bridled Power (Palmer & Palmer) 65

Canada 54
  Canadian Charter of Rights and Freedoms 57
  Canadian Constitution Act 53
  decolonisation model 24, 25
  Supreme Court of Canada 47, 53, 59, 127
  Universal Periodic Review (UPR) 195, 197, 198, 199, 200, 203
  UN special procedures 155, 163
  World Conference on Indigenous Peoples 2014 184–85
  see also CANZUS states; North American Indigenous Peoples' Caucus
CANZUS states 14, 57
  decolonisation model 24–25
  indigenous rights advocacy 18
  mixed-model interpretative approach 35, 39
  Universal Periodic Review (UPR) 191–92, 195, 197, 198, 199
  World Conference on Indigenous Peoples 2014 184–85
  see also specific countries
capacity-building, as a tool for indigenous people's rights 158, 166, 174
Charter of the United Nations 26, 27–28, 142, 158, 193
Charters, Claire 17, 20, 62, 67, 83, 150–51
Chayes, Abram 139
Chayes, Antonia 139
children, indigenous
  Action for Children and Youth Aotearoa 206–7
  Committee on the Rights of the Child 89, 90, 91, 92, 93, 95, 206
  educational rights 90–91, 94–98
  health, rights to 90–94
  international legal framework 87–90
  UN Convention on the Rights of the Child (CRC) 19, 86, 87–91, 94–97, 98, 206–7
Chile 163
Chilwell, Justice 64
China 178
Clarke, Denise 146
collective indigenous rights 14, 19, 44
  children, of 87, 90, 98
  discrimination, and 42, 68
  historical 47, 51–63
  legal cases 84, 146
  UN special procedures 167
colonialism 29, 30, 31, 41
colonisation 18, 30–31, 33
  see also decolonisation model
Columbia 161, 166, 208
Committee on Economic, Social and Cultural Rights 95–96, 206
Committee on the Rights of the Child 89, 90, 91, 92, 93, 95, 206
constructivism 138, 181
Cooke, Robin 50, 64, 101
Court of Appeal, New Zealand 100–1, 145–47
  Attorney-General v Ngati Apa 66
  foreshore and seabed case 66
  Takamore v Clarke (legal case) 68–70, 73, 84
criminal justice system 167, 168, 201, 203
Cropp v A Judicial Committee (legal case) 81
Crown Minerals Act 1991 (CMA) 123–25, 128, 129, 133
Cuba 197, 199
customary international law 80–81, 83, 143, 156, 207

de Alba, Luis Alfonso 178
Declaration on the Granting of Independence to Colonial Countries and Peoples 29
decolonisation model 23, 24–33, 35, 36–38, 40, 41
  see also colonialism; colonisation
Denmark 59, 197, 199
dialogue-building, as a tool for indigenous people's rights 158, 164, 166, 174
  discrimination against non-Māori 45, 56, 71
Down, Sarah 19
Durie, Edward Taihākurei 115, 116

Ecuador 167
education, children's rights to 90–91, 94–98
Elias, Sian 64, 69, 146, 148
Engle, Karen 34, 35, 36, 37, 38, 51
Erueti, Andrew 18
Expert Mechanism on the Rights of Indigenous Peoples (EMRIP) 96, 144, 165, 181–82, 206

Finlayson, Christopher 103
  Foreshore and Seabed Act 66, 129, 195, 203
free, prior and informed consent (FPIC) 14, 19, 23
  decolonisation model, and 39
  indigenous children's rights 89, 90, 92
  self-determination, and 129, 132
  UN Declaration, and 32, 117–19

INDEX

Universal Periodic Review, and 196, 201
World Conference on Indigenous Peoples 2014 181, 187–88
Friendly Relations Declaration 29–30

Geiringer, Claudia 67, 69
Ghana 197, 199
Glazebrook, Susan 84
Gover, Kirsty 15–16, 18–19
Guatemala 161, 183

health, children's rights to 90–94
Hemmes v Young (legal case) 73–74
Henriksen, John 178
High Court of Australia 47, 60
High Court of New Zealand 54–55, 73–74, 82–83, 84
Huakina Development Trust v Waikato Valley Authority (legal case) 64
human rights abuses 30
　business related 20, 122
　natural resources, and 128
　Universal Periodic Review (UPR) 206
　UN special procedures 154, 155, 159, 160
Human Rights Act 1993 57, 72
human rights model 18, 32, 33–40
Hungary 197, 199

Indigenous and Tribal Peoples in Independent Countries (ILO Convention 169) 13, 27, 34, 87
Indigenous Global Coordinating Group (GCG) 177, 178, 179–80, 181, 183
indigenous women, rights of 157–58, 185
　see also women's rights
Inter-American Court of Human Rights 120, 144, 145
International Convention on the Elimination of all forms of Racial Discrimination (ICERD) 57, 59
International Covenant on Civil and Political Rights (ICCPR) 13, 17, 26, 46, 68, 87, 88, 143, 148
International Covenant on Economic, Social and Cultural Rights (ICESCR) 13, 17, 26, 87, 143
International Indian Treaty Council 25, 31–32, 37
International Labour Organization (ILO)
　Convention 105 26–27, 87
　Convention 169 13, 27, 34, 87
Iran 197, 199
Isaac, Wilson 74

Joseph, Philip 64

Ko Aotearoa Tēnei (report) 83
Koh, Harold 138–39

lakes and rivers, ownership of 110–12
Lamer, Chief Justice 53
land rights
　Australian 24
　Māori Land Act 72, 106–7
　natural resources, and 116, 117, 121, 124, 125, 127, 128
　North American 31–32
　Treaty of Waitangi, and 70, 73, 74, 101, 105–8, 117, 168
　Universal Periodic Review (UPR) 203
　UN special procedures 169–70
Latin America 34, 37, 185
　see also specific countries
legal cases
　Amaltal Fishing Co Ltd v Nelson Polytechnic 54–55, 57
　Attorney-General v Ngati Apa 66
　Barton-Prescott v Director-General of Social Welfare 64, 73, 84
　Cropp v A Judicial Committee 81
　Hemmes v Young 73–74
　Huakina Development Trust v Waikato Valley Authority 64
　Maloney v The Queen 60
　New Zealand Māori Council v Attorney-General 70, 100–1, 146
　R v Hansen 46–47
　R v Kapp 47, 59, 60
　Saramaka People v Suriname 120
　Sefic v Denmark 59
　Takamore v Clarke 68–70, 73, 84, 146, 148
　Wi Parata v The Bishop of Wellington 116–17
　see also Court of Appeal; High Court of Australia; High Court of New Zealand; Supreme Court of New Zealand
liberalism 53–54, 61
Littlechild, Wilton 182
lobbying 171, 177, 178, 179–80, 182, 185–86, 189
Lord Cooke of Thorndon *see* Cooke, Robin

Mahuta, Nanaia 109
Maloney v The Queen (legal case) 60
mana motuhake 141, 170
　see also Whaia te Mana Motuhake

(Waitangi Tribunal inquiry)
Māori 15–17 (gen)
  children, rights of 86, 89, 90–98
  collective rights 44, 47, 60, 68–69, 84, 146
  criminal justice system, and the 167, 168, 169, 201, 203
  customary rights 74
  lakes and rivers, ownership of 110–12
  land rights and claims 72, 73, 74, 85, 125, 169–70, 203
  mountain ownership 108–12
  natural resources, rights to 19, 71, 101–2, 103, 112, 115–16, 116–34
  New Zealand Bill of Rights Act (BORA), and 41–42
  New Zealand law, and 41–42
  political authority, rights to 40, 41
  tikanga 67–75, 146
  whakapapa 72, 73–74, 75
  World Conference on Indigenous Peoples 2014, and 187–88, 189–90
  see also Office of Treaty Settlements; Treaty of Waitangi; Waitangi Tribunal
Māori Community Development Act 1962 84, 137, 141, 142, 149
Māori Land Court 74
Maungatautari 108–11
Mazower, Mark 27–28
McMahon, Edward 207–8
Mexico 163, 195, 197, 208
mining 116, 117
  business and human rights, and 122–23
  corporate responsibility 133
  environmental regulation in New Zealand 125–27
  international law 117–21
  Māori co-management model 131–33
  Māori effective participation 129–30
  New Zealand legislating relating to 123–27
  ownership of natural resources model 127–29
Ministry of Business, Innovation and Employment (MBIE) 133
modalities resolution, World Conference 178–80, 183
mountain ownership 108–12
Moyn, Samuel 26

National Freshwater and Geothermal Resources Claim 101–2, 112
Native Land Court 101, 117
Nehru, Jawaharlal 28

New Zealand Bill of Rights Act (BORA) 41–42
  common law, and 42–50, 54, 55, 62, 63, 68–69
  Māori, and 41–42, 43–44, 45, 46–47
  Treaty of Waitangi, and 43, 44–45, 48–51, 55–56, 60–63, 66–71, 148–49
New Zealand Human Rights Commission (NZHRC) 123, 143, 153, 172, 200, 204, 206, 209
New Zealand Human Rights National Plan of Action 2015–2019 (NPA) 204–9
New Zealand Māori Council 82–83, 141
New Zealand Māori Council v Attorney-General (legal case) 70, 100–1, 146
New Zealand Medical Association (NZMA) 93, 94
Ngāi Tahu 72, 105, 129, 132
  Ngāti Koroki Kahukura Claims Settlement Bill 103, 106
Ngāti Koroki Kahukura settlement 108–11
Ngāti Ruanui 133
Ngāti Whātua o Ōrākei settlement 107–8
non-government organisations, use of UN Declaration by 200–202
non-Māori, rights of 44, 45, 56, 71
North American Indigenous Peoples' Caucus 179–80, 183, 184
Norway 163, 178, 180, 197, 203

Office of Treaty Settlements 15, 104–5

Palmer, Geoffrey 65
Palmer, Matthew 16, 19, 62, 65, 81, 82–83
Peace Movement Aotearoa 196, 200
Petroleum Report (Waitangi Tribunal) 83, 128, 130
President of the General Assembly (PGA) 177–78, 179, 182–83, 184, 185
Protection and Integration of Indigenous and Other Tribal and Semi-Tribal Populations in Independent Countries (ILO Convention 105) 26–27, 87

R v Hansen (legal case) 46–47
R v Kapp (legal case) 47, 59, 60
racial discrimination 25, 32, 54–55, 56–60, 120, 206
Racial Discrimination Act (Australia) 57
Resource Management Act 1991 (RMA) 103–4, 111, 113, 115, 123, 125–27, 128, 129–30, 131–32
Rishworth, Paul 49, 50, 60, 68, 148

Risse, Thomas 140
Roche, Denise 106
Ruggie, John 122, 165–66

Saramaka People v Suriname (legal case) 120
Sefic v Denmark (legal case) 59
self-determination 13–14, 24–25
  denial of right to 99
  education, rights to 94, 96
  Friendly Relations Declaration, and 30
  health, rights to 92
  human rights model, and 35, 37
  ILO Conventions, and 27
  indigenous peoples, rights of 13, 30–31, 115–16, 117, 121, 129–32, 149
  International Covenants, and 28–29
  UN Charter, and 27–28
  UN Convention on the Rights of the Child (CRC) 89
  UN Declaration, and 23, 32–33, 36–41
  UN special procedures, and 170–71
self-government 13, 17, 23, 32–33, 89, 121, 141–42, 150–51
shaming states, as a tool for indigenous people's rights 20, 158–61, 166, 174
Sharples, Pita 147
Sikkink, Kathryn 140
Smith, Matthew 19, 62, 83
social movement theory 138, 139–40
South Africa 28
Soviet bloc countries 28–29, 30, 37
Stamatopoulou, Elsa 147
State-Owned Enterprises Act 68, 70
Stavenhagen, Rodolfo 156, 157, 158, 163, 164, 168, 169, 170, 172–73
Supreme Court of Belize 80
Supreme Court of Canada 47, 53, 59, 127
Supreme Court of New Zealand 55, 68–69, 70, 81, 84–85, 138, 143, 146

Taiwan 178
Takamore v Clarke (legal case) 68–70, 73, 84, 146, 148
Takamore, James 69–70, 146
Tauli-Corpuz, Victoria 156, 157
Te Aho, Fleur 20
Te Aho, Linda 15, 19, 131
Te Arawa Lakes Settlement Act 2006 110, 113, 114
Te Awa Tupua (Whanganui River Claims Settlement) Act 2017 114
Te Ture Whenua Māori (Māori Land Act) 1993 72, 106–7
territorial integrity, right to 13–14, 30, 32–33, 36, 37–38, 40, 52, 121
tino rangatiratanga 44, 70, 73, 100, 115–16, 117, 170
transnational legal process theory 138
Treaty of Waitangi, 100–3
  Article 1 44, 100
  Article 2 44, 100
  breaches 16, 48, 73, 83, 85, 102, 106–7, 117, 128, 141
  history 100–1
  Māori versus English interpretations 100
  Ministry of Business, Innovation and Enterprise, and 133
  natural resources, and 19, 101–2, 117, 121, 123–24, 126, 128, 131
  negotiations 103–5, 140
  New Zealand Bil of Rights Act (BORA), and 43, 44–45, 48–51, 55–56, 60–63, 66–71, 148–49
  rights reforms 17, 18, 65
  settlements 15–17, 55–56, 68, 71, 73, 74–75, 99–115, 117, 121, 131, 169, 201
  Treaty presumptions 42–47, 62, 63–67, 73, 75
  Universal Periodic Review (UPR) 201, 202, 203
  UN special procedures, and 168, 169, 170
  see also Waitangi Tribunal; *specific legal cases and settlements*

UN Charter *see* Charter of the United Nations
UN Commission on Human Rights (CHR) 25, 33, 143, 152, 154–55, 174
  see also UN Human Rights Council (HRC)
UN Committee on the Elimination of Racial Discrimination (CERD Committee) 58–59, 60, 120, 206
UN Convention on the Rights of the Child (CRC) 19, 86, 87–91, 94–97, 98, 206–7
UN Declaration on the Rights of Indigenous People 13–15
  adoption of by UN General Assembly 13, 37, 38, 59, 116, 143, 175
  children's rights 19; *see also* children, indigenous
  development of 24–25, 30–33, 35–36, 51–52
  implementation of 20
  legal status in New Zealand 79–85
  Māori, relevance to 15, 17, 19

mixed-model interpretative approach to 23, 38, 39, 40
negotiations 14–15, 23, 31–32, 36–37
New Zealand compliance with 20
New Zealand government, and 40, 82
New Zealand, relevance to 15, 17–18, 19
New Zealand, use of 202–4
non-government organisations, use of 200–202
Universal Periodic Review (UPR) 20, 191–209
UN special procedures 20, 152–74, 192–93, 206
Working Group on the Draft Declaration (WGDD) 33, 37, 51–52
UN Guiding Principles on Business and Human Rights 19, 116, 117, 122–23, 133
UN Human Rights Committee 46, 59, 68, 87, 120, 149, 206
UN Human Rights Council (HRC) 20, 51–52, 122, 140, 143–44, 145, 152, 153, 165, 168, 182, 191, 207
see also UN Commission on Human Rights (CHR); Universal Perdiodic Review
UN Office of the High Commissioner for Human Rights (OHCHR) 153, 154, 160, 193, 196
UN Permanent Forum on Indigenous Issues 144, 184, 206
UN special procedures 20, 152–74, 192–93, 206
see also UN Human Rights Council (HRC); UN Special Rapporteur on the Rights of Indigenous Peoples
UN Special Rapporteur on the Rights of Indigenous Peoples 20, 120, 145, 152, 153, 155–59, 161–67, 169–70, 171, 172, 173, 175, 192–93, 205
United States of America
indigenous peoples' advocacy 24–25
racial discrimination 54
Universal Periodic Review 191, 196, 197, 198, 199, 208
UN special procedures 155
World Conference on Indigenous Peoples 2014 178, 184–85
Universal Declaration of Human Rights (1948) (UDHR) 26, 27–28, 65–66, 142, 193
Universal Perdiodic Review (UPR) 20, 140, 145, 153, 191–209

Waikato-Tainui River settlement 104, 105, 107, 111–12, 113, 131–32
Waitangi Tribunal 15, 101, 103, 117, 168
National Freshwater and Geothermal Resources Claim 101–2, 112
Ngāti Whātua o Ōrākei settlement 108
Resource Management Act 1991 (RMA) 126, 128 130, 132
Waikato-Tainui River settlement 104, 105, 107, 111–12, 113, 131–32
Whaia te Mana Motuhake inquiry 20, 82–84, 137–38, 141, 142
Whanganui River settlement 104, 112–15, 131–32
UN Declaration, findings on 149–51
UN Declaration, use of in hearings 142–49
see also Treaty of Waitangi
Waters, Melissa 79–80
Whaia te Mana Motuhake (Waitangi Tribunal inquiry) 20, 82, 83, 137–38, 141–42
Whanganui River settlement 104, 112–15, 131–32
Whare, Tracey 20
Wi Parata v The Bishop of Wellington (legal case) 116–17
Wilberg, Hannah 67
Williams, Joe 103
women's rights 58, 89, 180
see also indigenous women, rights of
Working Group on Arbitary Detention 167, 168
Working Group on Indigenous Populations (WGIP) 24, 25, 31, 33
Working Group on the Draft Declaration (WGDD) 33, 37, 51–52
World Bank 145
World Conference on Indigenous Peoples 2014 176–82, 186–89

Young, William 73–74